San Francisco Giants: An Interactive Guide to the World of Sports

Tucker Elliot & Zac Robinson

Printed in the United States of America.
Copyright © 2011 by Tucker Elliot & Zac Robinson.

All rights reserved. No part of this publication may be reproduced, stored in a retrieval system, or transmitted in any form or by any means, electronic, mechanical, recording, or otherwise, without the prior written permission of the author.

This title is part of the Sports by the Numbers series, which is a trademark owned by Daniel J. Brush, Marc CB Maxwell, and David Horne.

Cataloging-in-Publication Data is available from the Library of Congress.

ISBN: 978-0-9826759-9-1
First edition, first printing.

Cover photo courtesy of Jill Clardy.

Black Mesa Publishing, LLC
Black.Mesa.Publishing@gmail.com

www.blackmesabooks.com

Contents

Introduction	1
The Legends	5
Courage	25
The Rookies	43
1951	63
The Batting Champions	81
The Bay Bridge Series	101
Cy Young Worthy	119
Dominican Dandy	139
Splash Hits	159
The Rivalry	179
2010 World Champions	199
About the Authors	207
References	209
About Black Mesa	211

For Jace and Xin Ai

"It's great to be young and a Giant."

— Larry Doyle

Introduction

ON MAY 1, 1883, a newly formed National League baseball team known as the New York Gothams played its first game on a field located at 110th street and Sixth Avenue in New York, a field where previously polo matches had been held—and with that game, the Polo Grounds and the franchise soon to be known as the Giants came into existence.

There were several different ballparks used in those first years, four of which were known by the iconic name Polo Grounds. It was at the third Polo Grounds where the franchise claimed its first modern World Series title in 1905, but during the 1954 World Series it was at the fourth Polo Grounds where Willie Mays made "The Catch."

There is a lot of history in the Giants franchise.

The title won by the 1905 club was the first for any National League team in baseball's modern era—and overall, the Giants claimed five world championship titles during the New York era of franchise history. In a half-century of play after moving to San Francisco in 1958, the Giants made it to the postseason eight times and won three additional pennants ... and then the 2010 ballclub claimed the fourth pennant and the first world championship during the San Francisco era of franchise history.

Ask any fan to name "great" baseball franchises and you will surely hear the Chicago Cubs, Los Angeles Dodgers, Boston Red Sox, and New York Yankees, but *none* of those teams have won as many regular season games as the Giants.

In fact, the Giants have the most regular season wins of any team in the history of organized sports—*period*. Now that makes for a very impressive franchise history.

And it only gets better.

The Giants can "drop" names with the best of them. As spring training got underway in February, 2009, Giants MLB.com beat writer Chris Haft perfectly illustrated this very point with a blog titled, "Now we know its baseball season: Mays is here." He went on to write: "The Giants were graced Monday by the arrival of Willie Howard Mays, who needs no introduction." *No kidding*. You might hear about the Yankees having a player at every position in the Hall of Fame, but more Hall of Fame players suited up for the Giants than any other franchise in baseball history—including the Yankees—and a quick glimpse at just a *partial* list of those players is awe-inspiring: Orlando Cepeda, Monte Irvin, Willie Mays, Willie McCovey, Mel Ott, Bill Terry, Monte Ward, Carl Hubbell, Juan Marichal, Christy Mathewson, and John McGraw, and these are but a few of the iconic figures who stand out among baseball's elite, and who called the Giants their "Home Team."

And every Hall of Famer from Giants history is in this book. As is every award winner, the greatest performances in franchise history, the postseason triumphs, the fan-favorite players who never became stars, all the glory, all the passion, and all the emotion that the greatest moments in franchise history evoke are all here in this Sports by the Numbers title. A thousand numbers await you, and they all tell the story of the New York and San Francisco Giants. The format is unique, intriguing, and compelling, because as baseball fans we all love the numbers, and in these pages the numbers celebrate records, lore, trivia, personalities, anomalies, championships won, championships lost, the good and the bad, and all that is great about baseball and the Giants.

Sit back, reminisce, and enjoy.

Tucker Elliot
Tampa, FL
March 2011

Willie Mays—greatest legend in franchise history.
(Courtesy National Baseball Hall of Fame Library, Cooperstown, NY)

"Willie Mays, the 'Say Hey Kid,' played with enthusiasm and exuberance while excelling in all phases of the game—hitting for average and power, fielding, throwing, and base running."

— *National Baseball Hall of Fame*

Chapter One

The Legends

THE LIST OF truly great players is relatively short, considering the long history of our National Pastime. And shorter still is the list of players who surpassed greatness and entered the realm of "heroic," or "legendary," or "iconic." The ones who gave us goose bumps just swinging the stick, or hurling that pearl, because we knew it wasn't a matter of *if*, but *when* our eyes would feel deceived by the sheer magnitude of their skill, at how they made the impossible seem routine.

It is always special to see a legend on the diamond.

As Giants fans we have seen more than most. And for good reason, the history of our franchise comprises some of the greatest names to ever play this glorious game. This game does end though for every player—even the legends—and perhaps we appreciate their talents even more when it is clear the end is close at hand, when despite being a legend a player's best days are behind him, and all that remains are a few precious games.

On August 25, 1979, one such legend strode to the plate in the bottom of the fourth with his team trailing the Cubs 1-0. His name was Willie McCovey, and a lucky 17,584 fans in attendance that day collectively scooted to the edge of their seats.

Lynn McGlothen delivered.

Big Mac waited.

And then he launched his 520th career home run, his last ever at The Stick.

Somewhere John McGraw was smiling. And who knows, maybe Christy Mathewson leaned over to his old skipper and said, "Boy, I'm glad I never had to face that big bat of his."

McGraw and Mathewson are, of course, legends in their own right—two of the biggest from the early 20th century. McGraw for his incredible leadership as manger (he was a good player as well) and Mathewson for his uncanny ability to sit down opposing hitters and rack up wins at an alarming rate. Mathewson was a member of the Hall of Fame's inaugural class in 1936. McGraw became a member a year later in 1937.

A trio of legends followed in the footsteps of McGraw and Mathewson.

Bill Terry, Mel Ott, and Carl Hubbell.

Terry was one of the league's premier hitters, who after nearly a decade playing first base with the club took over managerial duties as well—and in 1933 he was an All-Star and a world champion as player-manager. Ott and Hubbell were on that world championship team as well. Ott was an outfielder who hit 511 home runs in 22 seasons, and in 1942 he took over managerial duties from Terry, becoming a player-manager in his own right. Hubbell, a lefty screwballer, spent 16 seasons in a Giants uniform and was every bit as dominant as Mathewson.

Hubbell was inducted into the Hall of Fame in 1947. Ott got his turn in 1951, and then Terry was inducted in 1954. Of course 1954 is remembered fondly, not just because the Giants won the World Series, but because another legend, Willie Mays, made "The Catch." And you know your team is great when no further explanation is needed.

The club packed up and moved west along with the Dodgers, beginning play in San Francisco in 1958.

It was one year later that McCovey made his big league debut—and what a debut it was. The big first baseman batted behind Willie Mays and in front of Orlando Cepeda on July 30, 1959, and all he did was go 4 for 4 with two triples and two RBI (scoring Mays each time).

His fast start was a sign of things to come. McCovey blasted balls out of Seals Stadium and Candlestick Park for 15 seasons until he was traded to the Padres in 1973. He made his way back to San Francisco for a second tour of duty from 1977-80, launching the final 56 homers of his career. A true legend, it was a no-brainer that McCovey was on his way to the Hall of Fame. He was inducted in 1986.

Of course Mays was in the Hall of Fame already, having been inducted in 1979. It took Cepeda a bit longer, but he was inducted in 1999.

The same year McCovey joined the Hall, another legend debuted in Pittsburgh. After seven seasons he made the move west and became a Giant in 1993. Barry Bonds hit a dinger or two out of The Stick. Then in 2000 he started hitting them into China Basin, of course we Giants fans know it as McCovey Cove.

The Giants franchise boasts a lot of legends, on both coasts, from every era of baseball history, guys who have impacted the game, who have been there for so many of the greatest moments in the game, and the stories of every one of those legends begins here, in Chapter One.

1 Hall of Fame pitcher Carl Hubbell made (1) start in the mid-Summer Classic—and it was one of the most historic on record. On July 10, 1934, at the Polo Grounds in New York, Hubbell struck out five consecutive future Hall of Fame players to start the All-Star Game. Bob Ryan of the *Boston Globe* wrote in 2002, "Any self-respecting historian knows the names by heart, and almost invariably rattles them off so quickly it's as if the five men had one name: Ruthgehrigfoxxsimmonscronin." That translates to: Babe Ruth, Lou Gehrig, Jimmie Foxx, Al Simmons, and Joe Cronin.

2 Only once in baseball history has there been (2) teammates to surpass 230 hits during the same season. Bill Terry (254) and Fred Lindstrom (231) did it for the Giants in 1930, leading an offense that hit safely a franchise record 1,769 times.

3 The jersey number (3) retired in honor of Hall of Fame legend Bill Terry. He won four pennants with the Giants—one as a player, two as a player-manager, and one as strictly the manager. He won his only World Series title in 1933 during a season he was a player-manager.

4 The jersey number (4) retired in honor of Hall of Fame legend Mel Ott. He spent his entire career with the Giants, 22 seasons in all, and was on the 1933 club that won the World Series. In 1945 he became the first player in National League history to surpass 500 career home runs.

5 The Baseball Hall of Fame elected (5) players to be the first class of inductees at Cooperstown in 1936: Babe Ruth, Ty Cobb, Walter Johnson, Honus Wagner, and New York Giants legend Christy Mathewson. The Giants did not wear uniform numbers back then, but a jersey is retired in Mathewson's honor by the club—it hangs in the left field corner of AT&T Park and is denoted with an "NY."

6 The Pittsburgh Pirates selected Barry Bonds with the overall number (6) pick in the first round of the 1985 amateur draft. The five players chosen ahead of Bonds: B.J. Surhoff, Will Clark, Bobby Witt, Barry Larkin, and Kurt Brown.

7 Barry Bonds won a record (7) Most Valuable Player Awards. He won two in Pittsburgh, and then he became the first player in baseball history to win three MVP Awards when he took home the hardware in 1993—his first year in San Francisco. Bonds won the award five times as a member of the Giants: 1993, 2001, 2002, 2003, and 2004.

8 The franchise record for home runs (8) in a single game. On April 30, 1961, the Giants got 14 hits on its way to a 14-8 victory over the Braves—and eight left the ballpark. Willie Mays tied a major league record by going yard four times, but it was just that kind of day, as light-hitting shortstop Jose Pagan hit the first two home runs of his major league career (in 15 seasons he hit only 52 total), and Orlando Cepeda and Felipe Alou each went yard once. It was a good day to be in the bleachers—Hank Aaron hit two home runs for the Braves, bringing the total to ten bombs on the day, seven of which were hit by a future Hall of Famer.

9 On August 28, 1884, Hall of Famer Mickey Welch struck out the first (9) batters he faced—a record that has yet to be duplicated. He also was a nine-time 20-game winner who once notched 17 straight victories in a single season. Welch was the third pitcher in history to reach the 300 victory milestone.

10 Hall of Fame manager John McGraw led the New York Giants to (10) pennants during 31 years at the helm. He also won three World Series titles for the club, and a jersey is retired in his honor by the Giants organization. Like Christy Mathewson, it is denoted with an "NY" and is on display at AT&T Park.

11 The jersey number (11) retired in honor of Hall of Fame legend Carl Hubbell. The lefty spent his entire career as a member of the New York Giants, 16 seasons in all, and his screwball and gutsy performances led the Giants to three pennants in a span of five seasons from 1933-37.

12 Matt Cain struck out (12) batters in a 6-2 victory vs. Colorado on August 6, 2006. Cain became the first Giants rookie since John Montefusco in 1975 to notch at least 12 Ks in one game. He said afterwards, "I'm definitely going to savor this one."

13 The franchise record for runs (13) in a single inning. It has been done five times through 2008, most recently in a 16-2 thrashing of the Padres on July 15, 1997. Barry Bonds hit two home runs in that game—but neither came in the record tying outburst. The Giants sent 19 batters to the plate against pitchers Andy Ashby, Pete Smith, Rich Batchelor, and Sean Bergman in the top of the seventh, scoring 13 runs on nine hits, five walks, two errors, a wild pitch, and a hit batter. Outfielder Stan Javier was 2 for 3 with a stolen base, two runs, and an RBI—just in the seventh inning.

14 Christy Mathewson gave up (14) hits during the 1905 World Series. The legendary hurler was on the mound for 27 innings vs. the Philadelphia Athletics—and he tossed three consecutive shutouts. Mathewson struck out 18 batters but gave up only one walk as he won Games 1, 3, and 5 to lead New York to victory in the series.

15 Barry Bonds hit at least 25 home runs in (15) consecutive seasons. The streak ran from 1990-2004, tying him with Babe Ruth (1919-33) for the longest such streak in baseball history.

16 Mike McCormick faced (16) batters vs. Philadelphia on June 12, 1959. In five innings, he gave up one walk, but no hits. In the sixth inning the Phillies finally got a hit against McCormick—but then a heavy rain began to fall, the game was delayed, and eventually it was called. The official game was reverted back to a five inning affair, which gave the Giants a 3-0 victory and McCormick a no-hitter.

17 The number of seasons (17) Willie Mays hit at least 20 home runs. Only Barry Bonds (19) and Hank Aaron (20) posted more 20-homer seasons. Other extraordinary feats for Mays that involve the long ball include: he hit at least one home run in four consecutive games a record 13 times, and he hit at least one home run in five consecutive games four times.

18 Don Robinson gave up (18) home runs in 1990—but he hit two of his own. He was respected on the mound where his towering frame was an imposing figure, but he was *feared* at the plate. Yes, he was a pitcher, but he could flat hit. Robinson launched 13 homers in his career, and incredibly, one of his 1990 blasts came as a pinch-hitter. The fans saw something special that day. The next pitcher to hit a pinch-hit home run was Micah Owings, who did it for the Arizona Diamondbacks on April 30, 2008.

19 Chili Davis hit (19) home runs as a 22-year-old rookie in 1982. Davis set a rookie record by hitting five lead off home runs, and he placed fourth in Rookie of the Year balloting behind Steve Sax, Johnny Ray, and Willie McGee. Hanley Ramirez of the Florida Marlins broke Davis' record in 2006.

20 Willie Mays hit (20) home runs as a 20-year-old rookie in 1951. He hit .477 in 35 minor league games that season before he got the call and made his big league debut on May 25, 1951. The club issued a press release stating, "No minor league player in a generation has created so great a stir as has Mays." Then, of course, he went hitless in his first 12 at bats. His first hit was a big fly against future Hall of Fame pitcher Warren Spahn—and despite starting his rookie season 1 for 26, he went on to earn Rookie of the Year honors.

21 The Giants placed first or second (21) times under the leadership John McGraw. Little Napoleon, as he was sometimes called, placed second 11 times—in addition to the ten pennants he won.

22 Mike McCormick won (22) games in 1967. He won only 30 games the previous five seasons for the Giants, Orioles, and Senators. It was the only 20-win season of his career, earning him N.L. Comeback Player of the Year honors. That was also the first season that separate Cy Young Awards were given for each league—and McCormick won that as well. Giants sluggers have dominated the MVP Award, but McCormick was the only Cy Young recipient in franchise history until Tim Lincecum won the award in 2008.

23 Hall of Famer George Kelly hit (23) home runs in 1921. Kelly led the league with the first 20-homer season in franchise history.

24 The jersey number (24) retired in honor of Hall of Fame legend Willie Mays. He is an American icon, the "Say Hey Kid," and one of the greatest names in the history of sports.

25 Larry Doyle hit (25) triples in 1911. George Davis hit a franchise record 27 triples in 1893, but Doyle's total is a franchise record for baseball's modern era.

26 The New York Giants won (26) consecutive games in 1916. New York was in fourth place, 13.5 games behind Brooklyn on September 7. New York beat Brooklyn that day to begin the streak. After the longest winning streak in baseball history and a 29-5 record during September, the season ended with the Giants seven games back and still in fourth place.

27 The jersey number (27) retired in honor of Hall of Fame legend Juan Marichal. Hank Aaron described Marichal better than anyone, saying, "The foot's up in your face, and that's bad. Then he comes through like a fullback charging. He lunges off the hill. Sometimes he even stumbles from the force of his delivery. With all that confusion of motion it's a problem seeing the ball. But his control is a bigger thing. He can throw all day within a two-inch space, in, out, up or down. I've never seen anyone as good as that."

28 George Burns stole home (28) times during 15 major league seasons. Burns stole home five times in 1918 alone, and his 62 steals in 1915 set a franchise record for baseball's modern era.

29 The franchise record for runs (29) in a single game. On June 15, 1887, the New York Giants beat the Philadelphia Quakers 29-1. That same team scored 26 runs vs. the Indianapolis Hoosiers on May 17, and then lit up the original Washington Nationals for 26 runs on June 11. On the season, however, the Giants were the fifth lowest scoring team in the league—and placed fourth out of eight teams in the pennant race.

30 The jersey number (30) retired in honor of Hall of Fame legend Orlando Cepeda. The "Baby Bull," he struck fear into the hearts of opposing pitchers from the time he made his big league debut as a 20-year-old kid on April 15, 1958. He hit a home run against the Dodgers that day—always a good thing from the Giants perspective—and he never let up until he got the call from Cooperstown.

31 John McGraw managed the Giants for (31) seasons from 1902-32. He led the club to three World Series titles, and won four consecutive pennants from 1921-24. McGraw, who was known as a taskmaster, once observed, "One percent of ballplayers are leaders of men. The other ninety-nine percent are followers of women."

32 On August 9, 2008, Dodgers second baseman Jeff Kent raised his season extra-base hits total to (32) in spectacular fashion—he hit a tenth inning home run against his former club. Kent's 11th home run of the season gave the Dodgers a 2-1 lead, but Aaron Rowand singled home Randy Winn as the Giants rallied for a 3-2 walk-off win in the tenth. The next day, it was Rowand who scored the winning run ahead of a Eugenio Velez single as the club again rallied, this time for a 5-4 walk-off win in the ninth. It was the first time since April 1998 that San Francisco won back-to-back games despite trailing in their last at bat.

33 George Davis posted a (33)-game hitting streak in 1893. The Giants traded popular catcher Buck Ewing to get Davis from Cleveland just prior to the season—and Davis batted .355 with a franchise record hitting streak.

34 Juan Marichal gave up (34) home runs in 1962. The second highest total in franchise history (Larry Jansen gave up 36 in 1962), Marichal also won 18 games and made his first All-Star appearance.

35 Harvey Watkins managed the New York Giants for (35) games in 1895. He won 18 games, but he is the reason many people refer to Andrew Freedman as possibly the worst owner in franchise history. Watkins was a circus performer with no baseball experience, and yet Freedman gave him the job. In eight seasons, Freedman ran through 12 different managers—but to his credit, his last hiring was Hall of Fame skipper John McGraw.

36 The jersey number (36) retired in honor of Hall of Fame legend Gaylord Perry. He spent his first decade playing for San Francisco, tossing a no-hitter and fostering his image as a "spit-baller." There is a story that a reporter once asked Perry's five-year-old daughter if her dad threw spit-balls. It is said that she replied immediately, "No, it's a hard slider."

37 Christy Mathewson won (37) games in 1908—best in the league, and a career high. He also tossed a franchise record 11 shutouts that season. Mathewson holds the franchise record for career shutouts as well: 79.

38 The number of games (38) started by Johnny Antonelli in 1959. The lefty was 19-10, completing 17 starts with four shutouts. Antonelli was also selected to his fourth consecutive All-Star team.

39 The San Francisco Giants selected Barry Bonds with the overall number (39) pick in the second round of the 1982 amateur draft. He came out of Junipero Serra High School in San Mateo, California, the same school as future Mets star Gregg Jefferies. Bonds elected to attend college at Arizona State instead of signing with the Giants, and he and Jefferies went on to become first round picks in the 1985 draft. Bonds finally became a member of the Giants when he signed as a free agent prior to the 1993 season.

40 The number of saves (40) for Robb Nen in 1998—fourth best in the league. In five seasons with the Giants, Nen was among the league's top five leaders for saves every year—including a league best 45 in 2001.

41 Alvin Dark hit a career high (41) doubles in 1951. The former Rookie of the Year made his first All-Star team and led the Giants in runs, hits, total bases, and doubles—plus, he batted .417 during the 1951 World Series. Dark also hit 41 doubles in 1953.

42 The jersey number (42) retired in honor of Hall of Fame legend Jackie Robinson. He did not play for the Giants, but he did play in New York. The Brooklyn Dodgers star became the first African American to break baseball's color barrier in 1947. Robinson also became the first African American inducted into the Hall of Fame in 1962. On the 50th anniversary of his major league debut, in 1997, every major league franchise retired his jersey number to honor his legacy.

43 Brian Dallimore batted (43) times in 2004. He was a 30-year-old rookie who made his debut on April 29 as a pinch-hitter. He got out, but the next day he got the start and was 3 for 3 vs. the Florida Marlins—including a grand slam. Dallimore played ten seasons of minor league ball, chasing the dream. He hit a grand slam in The Show, but played only 27 career games and never hit another home run.

44 The jersey number (44) retired in honor of Hall of Fame legend Willie McCovey. He was such a force at the plate that Hall of Fame manager Sparky Anderson once said of him, "If you pitch to him he'll ruin baseball. He'd hit 80 home runs. There's no comparison between McCovey and anybody else in the league."

45 Willie McCovey hit (45) home runs in 1969. One through five in MVP balloting that season: McCovey, Tom Seaver, Hank Aaron, Pete Rose, and Ron Santo. McCovey kept some pretty impressive company—and beat them all, setting career highs in homers, average (.320), RBI (126), and slugging (.656).

46 The New York Gothams won (46) games during its inaugural season in 1883. John Clapp was the first manager in franchise history, and on May 1, 1883, in front of 15,000 fans that included former president Ulysses S. Grant, New York beat the Boston Beaneaters 7-5 in the team's inaugural game. The Gothams were 46-50 on the season.

47 Hall of Famer Tim Keefe won games in (47) different ballparks—a major league record. Randy Johnson is second on that list, having won games in 41 different ballparks.

48 Tim Lincecum was drafted out of high school during round (48) of the 2003 amateur draft by the Chicago Cubs. He chose to attend the University of Washington instead of signing. It was a good choice—he became the first player to earn Pac-10 Freshman of the Year and Pitcher of the Year honors in the same season, but it gets even better. He was drafted in round 42 of the 2005 amateur draft by the Cleveland Indians. He did not sign then, either. The next season he was first team All-American and won the Golden Spikes Award as the best player in the collegiate ranks. The Giants took him with the tenth overall pick in the first round of the 2006 amateur draft—and when he finally signed it was for a cool $2,025,000.

49 Jeff Kent hit (49) doubles in 2001. He was slightly overshadowed by Bonds, but the reigning MVP posted impressive numbers: a .298 average, 22 home runs, 106 RBI, and a franchise record for doubles.

50 Carl Hubbell returned to the All-Star game (50) years after his historic 1934 performance. Hubbell, who struck out five future Hall of Fame players to start the 1934 All-Star Game, tossed out the ceremonial first pitch for the 1984 All-Star Game at San Francisco's Candlestick Park. He threw a screwball, of course, his signature pitch—and then it felt like a Hollywood screenwriter took over. Hubbell and an electrified crowd of 57,756 fans watched N.L. aces Fernando Valenzuela and Dwight Gooden combine to strikeout six consecutive A.L. batters (though it was in the fourth and fifth innings), breaking the record of five consecutive that was held by Hubbell for 50 years. Only three of those batters, however, turned out to be Hall of Famers: Dave Winfield, Reggie Jackson, and George Brett.

51 Johnny Mize hit (51) home runs in 1947. The Hall of Fame first baseman set career highs for homers and RBI (138) as he led the league in two of the three Triple Crown categories.

52 Willie McCovey played (52) games in 1959. That's all it took to convince the sportswriters that he was the best rookie in the league. He received all 24 first place votes in the balloting, despite the fact he did not make his debut until July 30, with 100 games already in the books. The 21-year-old slugger hit .354 with 13 home runs as the club battled the Dodgers and Braves down the stretch, though it was the Dodgers that made the postseason.

53 The number of RBI (53) for J.T. Snow in 2002. His numbers were way down, he batted just .246 with six homers—after batting .284

with 19 homers and 96 RBI only two seasons earlier. The 34-year-old first baseman was slowing down, but maybe he was just saving it all for October. He belted two homers with nine RBI in the playoffs. He batted .407 and hit one of those bombs in the World Series vs. Anaheim, the only Fall Classic of his career. And he got three of the Giants six hits in Game 7, but lost, of course.

54 Al Worthington pitched in (54) games in 1958. All but 12 were out of the bullpen, and he posted a career best 11-7 record. It was as a reliever that Worthington had the most success during 14 big league seasons, but as a starter he garnered a lot of attention when he notched back-to-back shutouts in his first two starts as a rookie in 1953. Worthington became a born again Christian at a Billy Graham crusade in 1957, and he later served terms as head coach, pitching coach, and athletic director at Liberty University. The baseball facility at the Christian college now bears his name.

55 The number of saves (55) for Dodgers reliever Eric Gagne in 2003. He earned the Cy Young Award for piling up the saves in LA that season—while up the coast Barry Bonds won his third consecutive Most Valuable Player Award for the prodigious home runs he kept piling up. The next season, 2004, Gagne gave up just five home runs all year, but Bonds hit one of them. It was the seventh time that Bonds hit a home run against a reigning Cy Young recipient while he was also the reigning MVP. The list of victims: Greg Maddux (1993, twice), Randy Johnson (2002, twice), Barry Zito (2003), Randy Johnson (2003), and Eric Gagne (2004). Notice that in 2003 he got the reigning Cy Young recipient from both leagues—Zito and Johnson.

56 The number of games (56) for pitcher Mickey Welch in 1885. The Hall of Famer made 55 starts and completed them all—plus he tossed a game in relief. He logged 492 innings, but that was his lowest total during a three-year stretch from 1884-86. Welch also posted a 1.66 earned run average while facing a seemingly impossible number of batters: 1,963. The crazy part is his ERA was only second best on the club behind Tim Keefe—but it still ranks among the ten best in franchise history.

57 Carl Hubbell gave up (57) earned runs in 1933. There is a good reason he won the Most Valuable Player Award that season—he was nearly unhittable. He faced 1,206 batters and was on the mound for 308-plus innings, yet he gave up only 57 earned runs. Hubbell's remarkable run included an 18-inning shutout vs. St. Louis and a franchise record 46 1/3 consecutive scoreless innings.

58 The Giants lost (58) regular season games in 1951. Bobby Thomson's pennant-winning blast, though magical, and certainly historic, was not the most miraculous feat for the 1951 club. New York lost its 51st game of the season on August 11. It was the fourth straight loss for the Giants, and the club fell 13 games out of first with only 44 left on the schedule. Then the miraculous occurred. A 16-game winning streak beginning August 12, a torrid 37-7 finish that forced a three-game playoff, and then the magical blast, seemingly penned by a Hollywood screenwriter, for everything that fell into place after August 11 defies explanation.

59 Dusty Baker made (59) starts in 1984—his lone season playing for the Giants. The 35-year-old veteran outfielder was a two-time Silver Slugger recipient, a two-time All-Star, and a world champion prior to his stop in San Francisco. He played in 111 games total before moving across the Bay to Oakland for his final two seasons as a player, but in the next phase of his career Baker was a three-time Manager of the Year recipient in San Francisco.

60 Keiichi Yabu pitched (60) games for the Giants in 2008. A veteran player in Japan, Yabu made his big league debut for Oakland in 2005 at the age of 36, but did not surface again at the big league level until making the Giants staff in 2008 at the age of 39. He was 3-6 out of the bullpen with a respectable 3.57 earned run average, but missed two games in April when he was injured by an elastic exercise band. The band is supposed to slip over a hook on his locker, but it came off the hook and snapped him in the eye, causing blurry vision for a couple of days. Yabu reportedly found the elastic band tied up in his locker the next day with a note that said, "No!"

61 San Francisco scored only (61) runs in 18 games vs. Los Angeles in 1979—but gave up 110 runs to the Dodgers. The result, an embarrassing 4-14 record against its biggest rival.

62 The ratio (.62) of walks per nine innings for Christy Mathewson in 1913. This is an astounding stat: 21 walks in 306 innings, including 68 consecutive innings without a single walk. Mathewson led the league in this category seven times, including every season from 1911-15. His ratio in 1913 is the franchise record, but he also owns all of the top five spots for this category, and six of the top ten.

63 Terry Adams gave up (63) home runs during an 11-year career with the Cubs, Dodgers, Phillies, Blue Jays, and Red Sox. He gave up as many as ten just once, and in 2001 he gave up only nine homers despite pitching a career high 166-plus innings for the Dodgers. He was, however, just one of many victims for Barry Bonds that season. Adams was on the mound when Bonds launched his 500th career home run on April 17, 2001.

64 The number of RBI (64) for Randy Winn in 2008. Winn spent a lot of time early in the year batting third, but by season's end was back in his more familiar role of batting leadoff. After batting leadoff seven times in eight games, Winn batted third again on August 10, 2008, vs. Los Angeles. He was 3 for 4, with three RBI and a run. And for the next week he was an RBI machine, batting leadoff or third, didn't matter—Winn had multi-RBI games four times in six days, including batting 4 for 4 with a homer and two RBI to beat Atlanta 5-1. The homer was the 100th of his career. He said after the game, "It was good, but it wasn't something I really focused on. When I retire, I may look back on it."

65 The number of games (65) started by Mickey Welch in 1884—a franchise record. Welch completed 62 of those starts to set another franchise record (tied in 1886 by Tim Keefe), and his 557-plus innings set yet another franchise record.

66 The number of pitches (66) for Dave Dravecky vs. Montreal on August 15, 1989. Dravecky carried a three-hit shutout into the sixth inning in only his second start after recovering from cancer surgery on his pitching arm. Three batters into the sixth, Dravecky threw a wild pitch and then collapsed to the ground in sheer agony with a broken arm. It was the final pitch of his career, but he has since used his story to impact the lives of thousands of people as an inspirational speaker.

67 George Kelly got (67) extra-base hits in 1924. Kelly led the club with the second best total in the league. It was the third time in four seasons that he was among the league's top ten leaders for extra-base hits, and in those same four seasons he ranked first, third, sixth, and fourth in home runs.

68 Keiichi Yabu pitched (68) innings out of the Giants bullpen in 2008. On May 30, he actually pitched an entire inning with only one pitch. Yabu entered in the eighth inning of a 3-3 game vs. San Diego with runners on first and second and no outs. His first pitch fastball was hit sharply to third by Kevin Kouzmanoff. Jose Castillo fielded it cleanly, stepped on the bag for the first out, threw to second baseman Ray Durham for the second out, and Durham threw on to John Bowker at first for the triple play. "It doesn't get any bigger than that," said manager Bruce Bochy. Bowker gave the ball to Yabu's translator, Teira Uematsu, to keep for Yabu—but the translator lost track of which ball it was.

69 Mel Ott struck out (69) times in 1937. He hit 31 home runs and walked 102 times. Ott struck out 896 times during his career—2,730 games—but drew 1,708 walks. The man hit 511 career home runs but showed incredible discipline at the plate, numbers that today's power hitters rarely prove themselves capable of for a season, let alone an extended career. Incidentally, the 69 strikeouts set a career high. And Ott never struck out more times than he walked in any full season.

70 Barry Bonds batted (70) times in August, 2004. He did slightly better than your average N.L. player. Bonds hit .414 with 11 homers and 27 RBI that month. He was 29 for 70, adding six doubles and a triple, and he scored 27 runs. And the craziest numbers of them all: *38 walks, only seven strikeouts.* Bonds was named National League Player of the Month for the 13th time.

71 The Giants won (71) games in 2007. San Francisco was the only team in the West with a losing record, 19 games out of first, and 11 games behind LA—the team with the second worst record in the division. It was definitely not what new manager Bruce Bochy envisioned when he took over the club.

72 The Giants won (72) games in 2008. Bruce Bochy improved by one game, though his team climbed from the cellar to fourth place (which is only one spot out West). And there were plenty of reasons to be optimistic looking ahead: Tim Lincecum, Fred Lewis, and Brian Wilson to name a few.

73 Barry Bonds hit (73) home runs in 2001. His longest drought without a homer was 13 games. Bonds went deep against San Diego on opening day, and from there the chase was on. He hit 17 home runs in May, his biggest month, but only six in July, by far his slowest month. Bonds tied Mark McGwire at 70 on October 4 vs. Houston, and he broke the record twice on October 5, hitting home runs 71 and 72 vs. LA. Bonds closed out the season just how he opened it—home run 73 came against the Dodgers on the season's final day.

74 Bill Voiselle won (74) career games. His nickname was Ninety-Six, because that was the name of his hometown in rural South Carolina, population a few hundred. He made a big splash as a rookie with the

Giants, however, when in 1944 he was 21-16 and led the league with 161 strikeouts. He also logged more than 300 innings, making him the only rookie in baseball history to record 20 wins, 300 innings, and lead the league in strikeouts. Nearly a third of his career wins came as a rookie, unfortunately, and by 1950 he was back in South Carolina playing for the local mill club.

75 On September 29, 1976, John Montefusco pitched a no-hitter vs. the Atlanta Braves in his (75th) career start. The Count struck out four and walked one in the 9-0 victory during his final start of 1976.

76 The number of games (76) for Rod Beck in 1993. That was his highest total while pitching for the Giants and he used them to record a franchise record 48 saves.

77 The number of RBI (77) for Phil Weintraub in 1944. His total was a career high, and he drove home just 207 runs during a career that spanned seven seasons and 444 games—but on April 30, 1944, he set a franchise record by driving home 11 runs in one game, a 26-8 drubbing of the Dodgers. In that game he hit two doubles, a triple, and a home run, but was a single short of the cycle.

78 Jamie Easterly pitched (78) innings for the Atlanta Braves in 1978. He was 3-6, with a 5.65 earned run average, mainly because he allowed so many base runners. Easterly gave up 91 hits and walked 45 batters (1.74 WHIP). He did, however, become an asterisk in the record books. Easterly was on the mound when Willie McCovey launched his 500th career home run on June 30, 1978.

79 The number of pitches (79) for Kevin Correia vs. the Chicago Cubs on July 12, 2008. He got shelled—nine hits and seven earned in three-plus innings as Chicago took a 7-0 lead. Correia did not get the loss, however, because the Giants rallied for two in the eighth and five in the ninth to tie the game 7-7. That rally denied newly acquired Rich Harden his first win with the Cubs, but it unwittingly set the stage for the Cubs to do something they had not done in over 30 years. Mark DeRosa scored ahead of a Reed Johnson single in the 11th inning to give the Cubs an 8-7 victory—and according to the Elias Sports Bureau, it was the first time since July 25, 1977, that Chicago blew a seven-run lead after the seventh inning, but won anyway.

80 Joel Youngblood hit (80) career home runs during 14 major league seasons—a career high 17 of which came in 1983, his first year with the Giants. He also set a career high when he batted .292 that season, though he hit only 22 homers total his next five years with the club.

81 Mike Jackson pitched (81) games out of the pen in 1993—the highest total in the league. Jackson, Dave Burba, and Bill Swift came over from Seattle after 1991 and provided an enormous boost to the pitching staff. San Francisco won seven of the last eight games in which he appeared during the final days of 1993, as the club battled Atlanta for the division title.

82 The New York Giants won (82) games in 1907. After losing 71, however, the Giants placed only fourth among eight teams in the pennant race. Outfielder George Browne led the club with a career best five homers. As a team the Giants hit 23 home runs, which was the highest total in the league. This was definitely the dead ball era at its finest. The Giants pitching staff posted a 2.45 earned run average—but that was only sixth best in the league.

83 The New York Gothams won (83) games in 1889. The club was 83-43 for a .659 winning percentage—good enough to claim the league title by a single game over the Boston Beaneaters. Hall of Famers Tim Keefe and Mickey Welch combined to win 55 of those games for New York.

84 The number of games (84) at shortstop for Omar Vizquel in 2008. After playing both ends of a doubleheader vs. Florida on May 25, Vizquel became the major league record holder for most career games at shortstop with 2,584. The record was previously held by Luis Aparicio, and despite playing on the road in front of a partisan Marlins crowd, Vizquel received a loud ovation when the game became official after the fifth inning. He later said, "I appreciate them doing that. I have a lot of friends here in Miami and it made it very special."

85 The New York Gothams won (85) games in 1885. In only its third season of play, the franchise was led by Jim Mutrie to a remarkable 85-27 record. Despite a .759 winning percentage the club placed second in the league, two games back of the Chicago White Stockings. The other six teams in the league were all at least 30 games out of first.

86 The number of games (86) for pitcher Scott Eyre in 2005—third highest in franchise history. The lefty was phenomenal in situational pitching out of the pen. Lefty batters were just 18 for 99 against him—with 30 Ks and no homers.

87 The number of games (87) Roger Bresnahan caught in 1905. The Hall of Fame catcher previously played center field and he was a great base stealer, so when he became a fulltime catcher in 1905 he continued to hit from the leadoff spot. Bresnahan stole 25 bases in 1906 while catching fulltime. The next season he became the first catcher in history to wear shin guards—gear he is credited with inventing because he wanted to protect his legs and base stealing ability.

88 The career batting average (.088) for pitcher Hoyt Wilhelm. He was just 38 for 432 throughout 21 big league seasons—and never got more than six hits in any one year—but the Hall of Famer began his career with a bomb, going yard in his first major league at bat. As it happens, he was also the winning pitcher that day, and he never hit another big league homer.

89 The number of games (89) for journeyman pitcher Jim Brower in 2004. San Francisco was the fourth stop for the right handed reliever—but Brower pitched for another four teams from 2005-07. Brower's most effective season was 2004, however, and the Giants used him so much that his games total led the league and tied the franchise record first set by Julian Tavarez in 1997.

90 Willie Mays got (90) extra-base hits in 1962—a career high, but only second best in the league. Mays got 13 fewer extra-base hits the following season, but *led* the league. He got 1,289 extra-base hits throughout his career with the Giants—and that total is second to no one.

91 Hall of Fame legend Bill Terry led the club to (91) victories as player-manager in 1933. That gave the Giants the pennant, and in his first full season as skipper Terry claimed the fourth World Series title in franchise history, disposing the Washington Senators in five games.

92 The number of innings (92) for Noah Lowry in 2004. The rookie lefty made 14 starts and posted a perfect 6-0 record that included a dominating performance vs. the New York Mets on August 20. With only 12 major league starts under his belt, Lowry held the Mets in check on six hits over six-plus innings—and he struck out ten batters without allowing a walk. No major league rookie was able to match that feat of ten-plus strikeouts and no walks until Washington's John Lannan did it vs. the New York Mets on April 17, 2008. Lowry won his game 7-3, while Lannan got a no-decision as the Mets beat the Nats 3-2 in 14 innings.

93 Hall of Fame second baseman Joe Morgan walked (93) times for the Houston Astros in 1980. It was the fourth and final time he led the league in walks. Morgan, who joined the Giants for two seasons beginning in 1981, is fifth all-time with 1,865 career walks. Barry Bonds, of course, holds the major league record with 2,558 walks—and Bonds also led the league in walks a record 12 times. A little known and perhaps surprising tidbit, however, is that Morgan placed among the league's top ten leaders for walks a record 18 times. Bonds is second on that list, having placed in the top ten 17 times.

94 Willie Mays hit (94) career home runs during one-run victories—fourth highest in history behind Hank Aaron, Babe Ruth, and Barry Bonds.

95 The number of games (95) for Ross Youngs in 1926. He was only 29, but the career for the hard-nosed competitor once described by John McGraw as "the greatest outfielder I ever saw" came to an abrupt halt in August, 1926, when Youngs was diagnosed with a kidney disorder known as Bright's disease. He was the youngest starter on the club that won the 1921 pennant, and his Hall of Fame play contributed to the four consecutive pennants won by the Giants from 1921-24, but by the end of the decade, both his career and his life were cut tragically short. Youngs died on October 22, 1927.

96 The number of RBI (96) for Orlando Cepeda in 1958. His total tied him with Willie Mays for the club lead, which was no small feat, considering Cepeda was a 20-year-old rookie. He also hit 25 home runs and was the overwhelming choice for N.L. Rookie of the Year.

97 The number of RBI (97) for Orlando Cepeda in 1964. In his last full season with the Giants, Cepeda once again was among the league's top ten leaders for RBI. His totals from 1958-64 were all among the league's best: 96, 105, 96, 142, 114, 97, and 97.

98 George Davis hit (98) triples for the Giants during parts of ten seasons from 1893-1903. Davis is among the top 40 in baseball history with 163 career triples, and the 98 he hit for the Giants is one of the top ten totals in franchise history.

99 Fred Lindstrom scored (99) runs in 1928. He led the league with 231 hits and reached base a total of 258 times, but he did not hit the century mark in runs. Lindstrom was the first player in baseball history to get 230 or more hits and *not* score at least 100 runs—the second was Joe Torre, who got 230 hits while scoring 97 runs for the Cardinals in 1971.

100 Willie Mays surpassed (100) runs 12 consecutive seasons from 1954-65. He led the league twice (1958, 1961) and is among baseball's all-time top ten for career runs. In franchise history no one scored more often than the Say Hey Kid: 2,011 times with the Giants.

Major League Baseball Hutch Award Recipients

Year	Player	Team	Year	Player	Team
1965	Mickey Mantle	Yankees	1988	Ron Oester	Reds
1966	Sandy Koufax	Dodgers	1989	Dave Dravecky	Giants
1967	Carl Yastrzemski	Red Sox	1990	Sid Bream	Pirates
1968	Pete Rose	Reds	1991	Bill Wegman	Brewers
1969	Al Kaline	Tigers	1992	Carney Lansford	Athletics
1970	Tony Conigliaro	Red Sox	1993	John Olerud	Blue Jays
1971	Joe Torre	Cardinals	1994	Andre Dawson	Red Sox
1972	Bobby Tolan	Reds	1995	Jim Abbott	Angels
1973	John Hiller	Tigers	1996	Omar Vizquel	Indians
1974	Danny Thompson	Twins	1997	Eric Davis	Orioles
1975	Gary Nolan	Reds	1998	David Cone	Yankees
1976	Tommy John	Dodgers	1999	Sean Casey	Reds
1977	Willie McCovey	Giants	2000	Jason Giambi	Athletics
1978	Willie Stargell	Pirates	2001	Curt Schilling	Diamondbacks
1979	Lou Brock	Cardinals	2002	Tim Salmon	Angels
1980	George Brett	Royals	2003	Jamie Moyer	Mariners
1981	Johnny Bench	Reds	2004	Trevor Hoffman	Padres
1982	Andre Thornton	Indians	2005	Craig Biggio	Astros
1983	Ray Knight	Astros	2006	Mark Loretta	Red Sox
1984	Don Robinson	Pirates	2007	Mike Sweeney	Royals
1985	Rick Reuschel	Cubs	2008	Jon Lester	Red Sox
1986	Dennis Leonard	Royals	2009	Mark Teahen	Royals
1987	Paul Molitor	Brewers	2010	Tim Hudson	Braves

"Growing up I had two heroes, Sandy Koufax and Vida Blue... All I cared about as a little kid was that I wanted to throw a baseball like they did."

— Dave Dravecky

Chapter Two

Courage

THE HUTCH AWARD is given to an active major league baseball player who exemplifies the fighting spirit and competitive desire to win. It was created in honor of Fred Hutchinson in 1965. Hutchinson put up solid numbers in ten seasons on the mound for the Tigers from 1939-53, with a break to serve in the Navy during World War II.

Hutchinson went on to manage the Tigers, Cardinals, and finally the Reds from 1959-64. It was prior to the 1964 campaign when he asked his brother, who was a surgeon, to check out a lump on his neck. The lump was a cancerous tumor. Hutchinson wanted to continue to manage the club despite the chemotherapy, and he did so all the way through July 27, 1964, when he was hospitalized.

He returned a week later, but managed only nine more games. Just three months after leaving the Reds, Fred Hutchinson passed away.

So you see the Hutch award is one of the most important of them all. It isn't about on-field performance. It's about character, about the desire to go on no matter how difficult the road. We can't help but be inspired by this courage, and that is why the winner of the 1989 Hutch Award made perfect sense. Dave Dravecky inspired each and every one of us.

The Giants, in the thick of a pennant race, traded for the lefty Dravecky on July 5, 1987. He went 7-5 the rest of the way and helped the club win the N.L. West. He then went on to blank the Cardinals in Game 2 of the League Championship Series, and gave up only one run in six innings in Game 6, but the Giants lost 1-0.

Still, he was a young, talented, major league ball player with seemingly unlimited potential, and the future was something to be looked forward to.

At least until a cancerous tumor was found on the deltoid of his left arm, and then it became a living nightmare. On October 7, 1988, exactly one year after he shutout the Cards in Game 2, Dravecky underwent surgery to remove the tumor and half his deltoid muscle. The doctor told him, "Outside of a miracle you will never pitch again."

And yet... sometimes miracles happen.

He was back out on the mound just a few months later, on August 10, 1989, against the Cincinnati Reds, pitching with only half his deltoid muscle. He threw eight innings, giving up three runs on four hits while fanning five. The Giants won 4-3, and it seemed the Dave Dravecky comeback story was as complete and as inspirational as they come.

Five days later it came to a crashing end.

With a 3-0 lead at Montreal, Dave headed out for the sixth inning. He gave up a home run to Damaso Garcia, hit Andres Galarraga, and then on his first pitch to Tim Raines, his left arm snapped in half.

He rolled on the ground in agony, and then was wheeled off on a stretcher. A second comeback seemed unlikely.

On October 9, 1989, the Giants clinched the N.L. pennant with a 3-2 victory over the Cubs in Game Five of the League Championship Series. During the celebration Dave's arm was broken again. It was soon discovered that the tumor had returned.

On July 18, 1991, his left arm and shoulder was amputated.

San Francisco manager Roger Craig had watched in awe as Dravecky took the mound back on August 10, 1989, and he'd said, "You don't ever use the word finished when you're talking about Dave Dravecky because he's never finished."

Craig couldn't have grasped the depth of that statement. Although times were obviously tough, Dave and his wife Jan were not finished by a long shot. Since his cancer, comeback, and eventual amputation, he has become a motivational speaker, written motivational books, and founded Dave Dravecky's Outreach of Hope.

He only pitched 162 1/3 innings as a Giant. His record was just 11-7. But sometimes it isn't about how many games are won or lost. Sometimes it's about so much more. Giant fans young and old are proud that Dave Dravecky wore the Orange and Black. And Fred Hutchinson would surely be proud to know that the award named in his honor was given to the lefty who made a comeback that none of us will ever forget.

101 The number of RBI (101) for Barry Bonds in 2004. It was the 12th and final time he surpassed the century mark in a season, and for his efforts he won his third career Hank Aaron Award.

102 Barry Zito walked (102) batters in 2008. It was a frustrating year for the lefty with the big contract—and no one was more down on Zito than he was on himself. Only two guys issued more walks, and his 17 losses tied Cincinnati's Aaron Harang for most in the league.

103 The Giants won (103) games in 1993. The club spent 133 days in first but was tied with Atlanta for the division lead on the final day of the season. LA thumped San Francisco 12-1, and after a red hot Atlanta club beat Colorado 5-3 to complete a 22-8 run in the season's final month, it was the Braves celebrating a division title by a single game.

104 The number of RBI (104) for Babe Young in 1941. A career high, it was the second year in a row that Young led the Giants in RBI. Young, a left-handed outfielder out of Fordham University, also hit a career high 25 homers that season. He missed three of his prime years serving in the Coast Guard during World War II, and not long after returning to baseball he suffered an injury that cut the rest of his career short.

105 Frankie Frisch hit (105) career home runs. His season high 12 came for the Giants in 1923, and he hit ten or more five times. Frisch, however, has the distinction of owning the fourth highest number of career at bats without hitting a grand slam: 9,112. Only Ozzie Smith, Sam Rice, and Nellie Fox batted more times and never went deep with the bases full—but if it's any consolation, all four of those players are in the Hall of Fame.

106 The number of games (106) for Josh Devore in 1912. He was a fulltime outfielder the previous two seasons, but by 1912 his playing time was declining, and after 1914, despite being just 26 years old, he was out of the game. Devore does own a piece of history, however, because on June 20, 1912, during a game in which the Giants beat the Boston Beaneaters 21-12, Devore stole four bases in one inning, and five total for the game. Devore batted twice in the ninth, singled twice, and stole second and third twice, becoming the first player in baseball history with four steals in one inning, and the only player to do so during the 20th century.

107 Barry Bonds got (107) extra-base hits in 2001. He broke the franchise record 90 set by his godfather Willie Mays in 1962. It was the third time Bonds led the league in extra-base hits and the second time he did so as a Giant.

108 Red Ames was nearly perfect on opening day, 1909—but the Giants pitcher settled for being consistent, notching (108) victories for the club over the course of 11 seasons, while posting a 2.45 earned run average that remains one of the ten best in franchise history.

109 The number of RBI (109) for Will Clark in 1988. Clark was fifth in Most Valuable Player balloting for the second year in a row, after having placed fifth in Rookie of the Year balloting in 1986. He trailed no one in RBI, however, leading the league for the only time in his career.

110 Carl Hubbell gave up (110) earned runs in 1929. In 268 innings that computes to a 3.69 earned run average for the 26-year-old lefty in his sophomore season. Hubbell was 18-11, however, and he completed 19 of 35 starts, including one very impressive shutout vs. Pittsburgh. On May 8, 1929, Hubbell pitched a no-hitter in an 11-0 victory against the Pirates.

111 The number of steals (111) for John Ward in 1887—in only 129 games. The Hall of Fame shortstop led the league and set a franchise record. Ward stole 540 bases while playing for several different teams over the course of 17 seasons.

112 Chris Speier hit (112) major league home runs. He played parts of 19 seasons and hit a career high 15 homers in 1972, his sophomore season in the league with the Giants. Speier followed that with season totals of 11, nine, and ten from 1973-75, but then he suffered a serious power outage. He spent several years in Montreal, then made stops in St. Louis, Minnesota, and Chicago where he played at hitter-friendly Wrigley Field, but he never came close to double digits in homers again until 1987—when as a 37-year-old veteran he returned to San Francisco and hit 11 homers in only 111 games.

113 It took Aaron Rowand (113) games to hit ten home runs in 2008. Rowand homered against Chuck James on August 6, leading the Giants to a 3-2 victory over the Braves. The absence of Barry Bonds was noted by the Elias Sports Bureau—because as it turns out, the Giants were the last team in baseball without a ten-homer guy. Rowand was the first to get there for San Francisco. The last time the Giants went so far into a season before a player hit his tenth home run was 1986, when it took Candy Maldonado 114 games.

114 The earned run average (1.14) for Christy Mathewson in 1909. He was 25-6, and led the league in ERA for the third time. Mathewson gave up just 35 earned runs in 275-plus innings—producing an ERA that is a franchise record and one of the ten best in baseball history.

115 Luther Taylor won (115) games from 1900-08. Taylor, who was a deaf-mute, won a career high 21 games for the pennant-winning Giants in 1904.

116 The number of RBI (116) for Will Clark in 1991. He led the club with a career high total, earning his second Silver Slugger Award. It was also the third time in four seasons that Clark was among the top three RBI leaders in the N.L.

117 Dave Bancroft scored (117) runs in 1922. He scored a career high 121 the previous season, tying Frankie Frisch for the team lead, and he backed that total up by leading the team in 1922. It was the third consecutive season that Bancroft was among the league's top three scorers.

118 Mel Ott scored (118) runs in 1942. Ott led the league for the second time in his career. It was also the ninth and final time in his career that he surpassed the century mark.

119 Willie Mays scored (119) runs in 1954. Mays was third in the league in scoring during his first MVP season. Mays was among the top three scorers in the league 11 times in 12 seasons from 1954-65.

120 The number of pitches (120) for Matt Cain vs. the Oakland Athletics on May 21, 2006. The 21-year-old rookie tossed a one-hit shutout as the Giants won 6-0. He struck out five, threw 80 pitches for strikes, and the only hit was a third inning double by Jay Payton. Cain offered this assessment of his performance, "It's exciting." He went on to post a 13-12 record and was fifth in Rookie of the Year balloting.

121 Tim Lincecum made (121) pitches in a 1-0 shutout vs. San Diego on April 24, 2008. The young phenom improved to 4-0 to start the season, striking out nine in six-plus innings before letting the bullpen close out the Padres at Petco Park. Two weeks earlier, Tyler Walker got a win in relief as starter Jonathan Sanchez and the bullpen teamed for a 1-0 shutout of the Padres at AT&T Park. The Elias Sports Bureau reported that it was the first time San Francisco notched a pair of 1-0 victories against a team in the same month since August, 1968, when the Giants did it to the Mets.

122 Mel Ott scored (122) runs in 1930. He led the league in on-base percentage, which allowed him to score a lot of runs. Ott was only eighth in the league in scoring, however, and just third on the team.

Three of the top 30 runs totals in franchise history were posted that season.

123 Willie Mays scored (123) runs in 1955—second best in the league. Duke Snider led the league with 126 runs for Brooklyn. Mays led the league in slugging, OPS, home runs, and total bases, and was among the top five leaders for average, OBP, runs, hits, triples, RBI, steals, extra-base hits, and times on base. He was fourth in MVP balloting.

124 Bill O'Hara played just two seasons and (124) games of major league baseball. The outfielder played 115 games for the Giants in 1909, and the most memorable game of his career came that same season on August 8, during a 3-0 Giants victory vs. the St. Louis Cardinals, when O'Hara stole second, third, and home—in the same inning.

125 The number of RBI (125) for Irish Meusel in 1923. His numbers were actually down from the previous season, but he still led the league in RBI and helped the Giants to a third consecutive pennant.

126 Alvin Dark scored (126) runs in 1953. He led the club and was third in the league. Dark's total also set a career high, and ranks among the top 25 season efforts in franchise history.

127 Fred Lindstrom scored (127) runs in 1930. He got on base 279 times, which led to a career high runs total. His total, however, was only second highest on the club and seventh highest in the league.

128 The earned run average (1.28) for Christy Mathewson in 1905. It was the first time he led the league in ERA, and it remains the second lowest in franchise history. Later, after his career ended, Mathewson was asked what he thought his best pitch had been. He replied, "Anybody's best pitch is the one the batters ain't hitting that day." The numbers say Mathewson had a lot of "best pitches."

129 Barry Bonds scored a career high (129) runs four times: 1993, 2000, 2001, and 2004. The only time Bonds led the league in scoring was 1992, when he touched the plate 109 times during his final season in Pittsburgh.

130 Willie Mays scored (130) runs in 1962. He scored at least 100 runs during 12 consecutive seasons from 1954-65, twice leading the league (1958, 1961), and his 130 runs in 1962 set a career high.

131 Bobby Bonds scored (131) runs in 1973. It was the second time in five seasons that he led the league, and no one in baseball scored more runs than Bonds from 1969-73.

132 The number of RBI (132) for Irish Meusel in 1922. In his first full season with the club, Meusel led the team and set a career high for RBI. His total was also second best in the league, one of seven seasons in his career that he cracked the league's top ten leader board for RBI.

133 Barry Bonds got (133) hits in 2003. He hit 45 big flies, and 68 of his base knocks went for extra bases. He batted .341 and posted a .749 slugging percentage, and he easily won his sixth MVP Award. Bonds' former skipper, Felipe Alou, once said, "Barry is the reincarnation of Ted Williams—with more power."

134 Bobby Bonds scored (134) runs in 1970—a career high, and one of the top ten seasons in franchise history. It was also the first of three consecutive seasons that he was second in the league in runs.

135 Tim Lincecum struck out (135) batters during the first half of 2008. The 24-year-old ace became the first Giants pitcher since Juan Marichal to carry a league best total into the mid-Summer Classic. Marichal led the league at the break in 1967 and 1968, but he never led the league in strikeouts for an entire season. Lincecum closed out 2008 with a 13 K performance vs. LA on the season's final day—giving him 265 and the highest total in baseball. When told that he was the first player in franchise history to lead the majors in strikeouts, Lincecum replied, "Really? That's cool."

136 The number of RBI (136) for George Kelly in 1924. A career high total, it was the second time he led the league and it was the fourth consecutive season he surpassed the century mark—coinciding nicely with the Giants fourth consecutive pennant.

137 Tim Lincecum received (137) points in the 2008 Cy Young Award balloting. His name was on 23 of 32 first place ballots, making Lincecum the second pitcher to win the award for the Giants. Arizona's Brandon Webb was considered the frontrunner by many, but he was a distant second with just four first place votes and 73 total points.

138 Tim Lincecum made (138) pitches vs. the San Diego Padres on September 13, 2008. He threw 86 for strikes as he fanned 12 while giving up just four hits. The Giants won 7-0, giving Lincecum his first career shutout and improving his record to 17-3. He said afterwards, "The adrenaline kind of takes over a little bit. I kind of got a little extra energy with the last couple of batters. It was nice to finish up the game."

139 Bill Terry scored (139) runs in 1930. He got on base 312 times, which gave him a lot of opportunities to score. And score he did. Terry's total not only was a career high, it was also the highest total of the 20th century for any Giants player.

140 Bill Madlock played (140) games for the Giants in 1977. The two-time defending N.L. batting champion, Madlock came over in a deal with the Cubs and batted .302 in 533 at bats. He hit .309 in 1978, but after beginning the 1979 season with a .261 average through 69 games the Giants traded him to Pittsburgh. Madlock hit .328 the rest of the season for the Pirates—and won the 1979 World Series.

141 Rich Aurilia played (141) games in 2000. The Giants shortstop experienced a power surge the previous season, hitting 22 homers after connecting for a total of only 17 in three seasons from 1996-98, and in 2000 he proved that surge was not a fluke. Aurilia hit 20 homers with 79 RBI and a .444 slugging percentage for the second year in a row.

142 Roger Bresnahan got (142) hits in 1903. That set a career high for the Giants catcher, who hit .350 that year to lead the club. Bresnahan also led the club with a .443 on-base percentage and a .493 slugging percentage, establishing career highs with every one of those numbers.

143 The earned run average (1.43) for Christy Mathewson in 1908. It was the second time he led the league and he did so with an ERA that remains the third best in franchise history—Mathewson owns each of the top three. Connie Mack, the legendary manager of the Philadelphia Athletics, said of Mathewson, "He was the greatest pitcher who ever lived. He had knowledge, judgment, perfect control and form. It was wonderful to watch him pitch when he wasn't pitching against you."

144 The earned run average (1.44) for Fred Anderson in 1917. Only 18 of his 38 games that season were starts, and his record was just 8-8, but he led the league with the fourth best ERA in franchise history. His success, unfortunately, did not carry over into the postseason—

he was 0-1 with an 18.00 ERA as the Giants lost the 1917 World Series to the Chicago White Sox.

145 The New York Giants hit (145) homers in 1956. Led by Willie Mays (36) and Bill White (22), five members of the club hit double digits in homers—the only problem, no one was on base ahead of the sluggers. The Giants were dead last in the league, scoring a paltry 540 runs, which led to a disastrous sixth place finish.

146 Pedro Feliz batted (146) times in 2002. Feliz was primarily a third baseman who hit .253 with two home runs in limited duty. The Giants won the pennant, however, and Feliz was on the World Series roster. His only start was the deciding Game 7, when he was the DH for Dusty Baker's club. The Elias Sports Bureau reports that Feliz, who was 0 for 3 with two strikeouts, was just the fourth player in baseball history to start Game 7 of a World Series after having started no games at all during the rest of the postseason. The others: Dave Duncan (1972, Oakland), Bernie Carbo (1975, Boston), and Steve Lake (1987, St. Louis).

147 Mike Tiernan scored (147) runs in 1889—*in only 122 games*! His total led the league and set a franchise record.

148 The number of steals (148) for the Giants in 1986. That total, despite being only the eighth best among 12 teams in the league that season, is the highest on record during 50 seasons since the club relocated to the Bay area in 1958. Seven players were in double digits, led by 27 for outfielder Dan Gladden. The Giants were caught stealing 93 times, however, which unfortunately was the second highest number in the league.

149 The World Series batting average (.149) for Travis Jackson. The Hall of Fame infielder hit .291 during 15 seasons with the Giants, but he struggled in the postseason. Jackson played in four World Series: 1923, 1924, 1933, and 1936. The Giants lost three of those, winning only the 1933 World Series. Jackson's final season was 1936, and his last big league game was in the World Series—but he hit just .190 in that series as the Giants fell to the Yankees in six games.

150 Jumbo Brown pitched (150) games during five seasons with the Giants. He was 13-12 as a reliever from 1937-41, posting a very respectable 2.93 earned run average. As for his name, well, Jumbo weighed in at nearly 300 pounds! He is considered by many to be the heftiest player of his era . . . not to mention one of baseball's all-time heftiest.

151 The number of RBI (151) for Mel Ott in 1929. He was a 20-year-old outfielder playing in his fourth season when he set a career high and a franchise record for RBI. His total was only the second highest in the league behind Hack Wilson of the Chicago Cubs, but Ott did lead the league in RBI once, with 135 in 1934, and his 1,860 career RBI are also a franchise record.

152 Johnny Antonelli struck out (152) batters in 1954. He pitched five no-hitters as a senior in high school and was a highly touted prospect for the Braves. The Giants got him in a trade that sent Bobby Thomson to Milwaukee—and Antonelli delivered during his first season with the club. He led the team in strikeouts and wins (21), and was 1-0 with a save during the 1954 World Series.

153 Bill Terry got (153) hits in 1933. He hit just .322 during 123 games that season. I say *just* .322 because that was his lowest average during a nine-year stretch from 1927-35. In that same stretch he collected 200 or more hits six times.

154 Bill Terry hit (154) career home runs. Terry hit a career high 28 homers in 1932, placing third in the league. His career total is among the top 15 in franchise history.

155 Byung-Hyun Kim pitched (155) innings for the Colorado Rockies in 2006. He struggled to an 8-12 record with a 5.57 earned run average. Kim actually beat the Giants on May 28, 2006, but in that same game he inadvertently became an historical footnote. Barry Bonds took him yard to surpass Babe Ruth with 715 career home runs.

156 Alex Rodriguez led baseball with (156) RBI in 2007. One of the biggest stars in the game, he hit five home runs with 13 RBI during the Yankees first six games that season—but the best players of today are still measured against the legends of the past, and A-Rod is no different. In the previous 50 years, only one player posted more home runs during the first six games of a season: Willie Mays. The Giants Hall of Fame legend hit *six* home runs with 13 RBI during the first six games of 1964.

157 Bill Swift struck out (157) batters in 1993. The former Olympian led the club in Ks, but it was also the only time in his career that he cracked the league's top ten leader board.

158 The earned run average (1.58) for Tim Keefe in 1885. He pitched 400 innings and won 32 games—but gave up just 70 earned runs. The Hall of Fame hurler led the league with the fifth best ERA in franchise history. Mickey Welch, a Hall of Fame pitcher from that same era, said of Keefe, "I never saw a better pitcher."

159 The ratio (1.59) of walks per nine innings for Christy Mathewson during 634 career games with the Giants. That ratio is one of the top 30 in baseball history, and it is the third best in franchise history.

160 The number of singles (160) for Brett Butler in 1990—the highest total in the league. The Giants leadoff man led the league in hits and times on base as well, but no one ever mistook the speedster for being a power guy. He got 32 extra-base hits that year—only three of which left the yard. Butler did steal 51 bases, however, so he wound up in scoring position a lot more often than most.

161 The earned run average (1.61) for Joe McGinnity in 1904. The Hall of Famer led the league with a 35-8 record—the fourth time in five seasons that he led the league in wins—and he also led the league with the sixth best ERA in franchise history. He was so good that baseball icon Connie Mack once said, "McGinnity was a magician in the box."

162 Mike Tiernan hit (162) career triples. The outfielder, often referred to as Silent Mike because of his soft-spoken demeanor, is the franchise leader for both triples and steals. He hit a career high 21 triples twice (1890, 1895) and was among the league's top ten leaders for triples five times.

163 The number of times (163) Johnny Mize struck out during five seasons with the Giants. The powerful first baseman walked more than twice that number—340 times, in fact—and he nearly hit as many homers as times he struck out: 157. Mize batted .299 for the Giants with 505 RBI in 655 games.

164 John Ward won (164) games during his Hall of Fame career. He pitched from 1878-82 for the Providence Grays, winning a career high 47 games in 1879. Ward pitched two seasons for New York from

1883-84, after which he made a highly successful transition to shortstop. Monte, as he was called, hit a career high .338 in 1887.

165 Al Cuccinello batted (165) times in 1935. That was all he got for his career, just the one season. He hit four homers, including one vs. Brooklyn on July 5. His brother Tony Cuccinello also hit a home run in that game—for Brooklyn—marking the first time in baseball history that two brothers hit home runs in the same game for opposing teams.

166 Carl Hubbell posted a (1.66) earned run average in 1933. That number led the league, the first of three such titles he won with the club, and it remains among the top ten on record in franchise history. He also led the league with 23 wins and became the first pitcher in franchise history to win the league MVP Award.

167 Alvin Dark batted (.167) for the Boston Braves during the 1948 World Series. The rookie shortstop and his club lost to Cleveland in six games. Dark and Eddie Stanky were traded to the Giants in 1949. He was a more seasoned player when he batted .417 during the 1951 World Series. It took three trips, however, to win a title, which he did in 1954. He batted .412 in that series.

168 The Giants launched (168) homers in 1993—the second highest total among 14 teams in the league. Not bad, considering San Francisco hit only 105 homers in 1992. The difference, of course, was Barry Bonds, who hit 46 bombs to win his first home run title during his first season by the Bay.

169 Three different players have hit (169) singles in a season for the Giants: Frankie Frisch (1923), Fred Lindstrom (1928), and Bill Terry (1934)—all Hall of Famers. It is the third highest season singles total in franchise history.

170 The Giants blasted (170) homers in 1958. The third highest total among eight teams in the league, it included five rookies who hit at least a dozen each: Orlando Cepeda (25), Willie Kirkland (14), Bob Schmidt (14), Leon Wagner (13), and Jim Davenport (12). It was the first time in baseball history that one team boasted that many rookies with at least 12 home runs.

171 Casey Stengel got (171) hits during three seasons playing with the Giants. He batted .349 in limited action, 490 at bats total. The legendary manager was actually a good player for a lot of years, batting .284 overall in parts of 14 big league seasons.

172 Mickey Witek got (172) singles in 1943—the second highest season total in franchise history. He batted .314 with six homers on the strength of 195 hits, all career highs. After the season he entered the Coast Guard and he missed all of 1944 and 1945 serving during World War II. Witek returned to the diamond in 1946, but he never regained the form that got him to the brink of stardom in 1943.

173 Jake Peavy struck out (173) batters for the San Diego Padres in 2004. He was 15-6 with an impressive 2.27 earned run average that led the league. Peavy gave up only 13 homers in 166-plus innings as well. Of course, Barry Bonds didn't care. Peavy will forever be an historic footnote because he delivered the pitch on September 17, 2004, that Bonds deposited over the wall for his 700th career home run.

174 The earned run average (1.74) for Tim Keefe in 1888. It was the third and final time he led the league, and he did so with an ERA that remains among the ten best in franchise history. Keefe also led the league with 35 wins, and he gave up just 84 earned runs in 434-plus innings.

175 Jeff Kent hit (175) home runs for the Giants. He hit a career high 37 in 2002, and his total with the club is among the top 15 in franchise history.

176 Jim Barr walked (1.76) batters per nine innings in 1974—the best ratio in the league. He was a true workhorse that season, completing 11 of 27 starts, and throwing another 17 games out of the bullpen. He logged nearly 240 innings and faced 959 batters, but issued only 47 walks. Barr posted one of the ten best ratios in the league for walks per nine innings seven consecutive seasons from 1972-78, and he was the Giants team leader in six of those seasons.

177 Bill Terry hit a franchise record (177) singles in 1930. And the truly crazy part is . . . not only did he lead the league in singles, but because he got so many hits (254) he was also seventh in the league in extra-base hits: 77.

178 It took (178) walk-off hits by major league clubs in 2008 before a game ended on a triple. On September 9, 2008, Eugenio Velez beat the Arizona Diamondbacks with a ninth inning walk-off single that gave the Giants a 5-4 victory. The very next day, Arizona led the Giants in the ninth when Velez hit a two-out, two-run triple that gave the Giants a 4-3 victory. It actually goes a little deeper, too. Giants closer Brian Wilson gave up a two-run triple in the top of the ninth inning to Chris Young, which gave Arizona a one-run lead going into the bottom of the ninth and set the stage for Velez and his heroics. On Velez winning two straight games for his club, Bruce Bochy said, "Same guy, same hero—he's a battler, I'll say that."

179 The earned run average (1.79) for Carl Hubbell during six starts in the World Series. He posted a career 4-2 record during three trips to the Fall Classic and he tossed a pair of complete game victories vs. Washington as the Giants claimed a world championship in 1933. Hubbell's second complete game effort in that series went 11 innings.

180 Juan Marichal gave up (1.80) walks per nine innings during 14 seasons pitching for the Giants—the fourth best ratio in franchise history. Marichal logged 3,444 innings and struck out 2,281 batters, but gave up only 690 free passes. He led the league in this category four times and owns one of the top 75 ratios in baseball history.

181 Shawn Estes struck out (181) batters in 1997. The 24-year-old lefty led the club and made his only career All-Star appearance. He pitched one inning in the 1997 All-Star Game at Jacobs Field and struck out Milwaukee third baseman Jeff Cirillo—but he also gave up a two-run homer to Sandy Alomar and was the losing pitcher.

182 The batting average (.182) for Fred Snodgrass during three trips to the World Series. On the one hand, he did play for three pennant-winning New York clubs. On the other, Snodgrass not only struggled at the plate in the postseason, but he dropped a routine fly ball in the tenth inning of the final game of the 1912 World Series that allowed Boston to rally from a 2-1 deficit and snatch a championship away from the Giants.

183 Randy Winn got (183) hits in 2008—fifth best in the league. He batted .306, and scored a team high 84 runs. Winn also hit his 100th career home run in 2008.

184 The earned run average (1.84) for Fred Toney in 1919. He pitched in just 24 games but posted a 13-6 record and notched four complete game shutouts. Toney led the club and was fourth in the league with an ERA that ranks among the top ten in franchise history. The next season he won 21 games, and he won 18 more in 1921 when the Giants won the pennant. Toney made two starts vs. the Yankees in the 1921 World Series—but he got shelled. Seven earned in two-plus innings for a 23.62 ERA, though luckily the club bailed him out and still won the series.

185 Don Robinson batted (.185) in 1989. The veteran pitcher was 12-11 on the mound, and at the plate he got 15 hits, including a double, three homers, and seven RBI. And because he swung the bat better than any other pitcher in the league, Robinson won his second career Silver Slugger Award. He hit two more homers the next season, and won the award for a third time.

186 Joe McGinnity pitched (186) complete games for the Giants—one of the ten highest totals in franchise history. In seven seasons he completed 78.5% of his 237 starts, which means his nickname (though earned for other reasons—see #434) was entirely appropriate: Iron Man.

187 Bill Carrick gave up (187) earned runs in 1899—a franchise record, though not one worth writing home about. In all fairness, he completed 40 of 43 starts (pitched once more from the bullpen) and logged more than 360 innings. His earned run average was 4.65, a high number for that era and well above the league average. Carrick gave up 250 runs total and was 16-27. After making his debut with a 3-1 record in 1898, Carrick lost 27, 22, 22, and 17 games in four complete seasons—and then, shockingly, his career was over.

188 The earned run average (1.88) for Pol Perritt in 1917. Third best in the league, it ranks among the 15 best in franchise history. He was 17-7 in the second of a three-year stretch in which he won 18, 17, and 18 games.

189 The earned run average (1.89) for Christy Mathewson in 1910. Third best in the league that season, it ranks among the top 15 in franchise history. Actually, Mathewson owns ten of the top 30 earned run averages in franchise history—including the three best.

190 Ernie Bowman batted (.190) during three big league seasons. He played 165 games from 1961-63, batted only 205 times, hit one big league homer, and scored 29 runs. Bowman was never a star to be sure, but in 1962 he scored one of the most important runs in franchise history. He pinch-ran for Willie McCovey in the top of the ninth, with the Giants trailing the Dodgers 4-2 in the third game of a best-of-three playoff with the pennant hanging in the balance. After an RBI single by Willie Mays made it a 4-3 game, Orlando Cepeda lifted a fly ball to right field, allowing Bowman to tag from third and score the tying run. The Giants scored twice more for an improbable 6-4 come-from-behind win to steal the pennant from the Dodgers.

191 The number of hits (191) for Orlando Cepeda in 1962. His total was good for sixth highest in the league, but it led the club and an offensive unit that hit safely 1,552 times on the season—which is a record that still stands through 2008 for the San Francisco era of franchise history.

192 Orlando Cepeda got a career high (192) hits in 1959. No sophomore slump for the reigning Rookie of the Year—Cepeda batted .317 and blasted 27 homers with 105 RBI, and he made the first of six consecutive All-Star teams.

193 Dave Bancroft got (193) hits in 1921—his first full season playing shortstop with the Giants. Bancroft batted .318, was eighth among league leaders in hits, and was second in the league with 121 runs.

194 Alvin Dark led the Giants with (194) hits in 1953. He batted .300, and set career highs with 126 runs, 23 homers, 88 RBI, and a .488 slugging percentage.

195 Willie Mays got (195) hits in 1954. In his first MVP season Mays led the league with a .345 average, a .667 slugging percentage, and 13 triples. He was third in the league in hits, second in total bases, and third in home runs. Years later, Mays offered some great advice for today's stars when he was asked to comment on some of his finest seasons: "I didn't think like that, about best seasons. What if you thought '97 was your best year, what would you do now? I never looked back. I couldn't dwell on last year's season. I always looked forward. I never worried about what other people were doing, except the guy I was playing against."

196 Jeff Kent got (196) hits in 2000. In arguably one of the greatest offensive seasons for a second baseman in baseball history, Kent led the club and set a career high for base hits—but he also placed among the top ten league leaders in average, on-base percentage, slugging, OPS, runs, hits, total bases, doubles, triples, RBI, extra-base hits, and times on base. His numbers were worthy of the MVP—and the writers agreed, placing him first in the balloting ahead of teammate Barry Bonds and Mets catcher Mike Piazza.

197 George Van Haltren got (197) hits in 1896—*in only 133 games!* He batted .351, led the club in hits, and tied a career high with 136 runs.

198 Bobby Thomson got a career high (198) hits in 1949. He belted 27 homers, made his second consecutive All-Star team, and he also set career highs with a .309 average and 109 RBI.

199 Rod Beck saved (199) games from 1991-97. He was a three-time All-Star for the Giants and six times he was among the league's top ten leaders in saves. He left San Francisco as the Giants all-time saves leader, a title that now belongs to Robb Nen.

200 Bobby Bonds got (200) hits in 1970. Sixth best in the league, it was the only season in his career he reached that plateau. Fewer than 25 players have posted a 200-hit season for the Giants.

New York / San Francisco Giants Rookie Award Winners

Rookie of the Year

Player	Year
Buster Posey	2010
John Montefusco	1975
Gary Matthews	1973
Willie McCovey	1959
Orlando Cepeda	1958
Willie Mays	1951

The Sporting News Rookie of the Year

Player	Year
Robby Thompson	1986
Larry Herndon	1976
Gary Matthews	1973
Dave Rader	1972
Willie McCovey	1959
Orlando Cepeda	1958

The Sporting News Rookie Pitcher of the Year

Player	Year
John Montefusco	1975
John D'Acquisto	1974
Frank Linzy	1965

"McCovey didn't hit any cheap ones. When he belts a home run, he does it with such authority it seems like an act of God. You can't cry about it."

— *Walter Alston*

Chapter Three

The Rookies

THERE'S SOMETHING SPECIAL about walking through the turnstile for your first big league game. The anticipation builds as you cross the concourse, all the while in danger of breaking into a run. In an instant it's in front of you. For the first time ever your eyes fall upon the smooth dirt and perfectly manicured grass. It is a moment when everything else just slips away, and the game is all that matters.

Now consider how it must feel to walk out of a different tunnel, with spikes on and glove in hand. Consider what it must be like to traverse the dugout steps and feel the spikes dig into the plush grass—to gaze upon the fast-filling seats. Surely, a rookie's first game is much like that of a fan's, but amplified to near immeasurable proportions.

No matter how confident, the nerves have to be turning. This is it! A day when odds are defied and dreams are realized. Some players shine in their debuts, others struggle, either way it is still a day to remember. And then there are those debuts that are the beginnings of remarkable careers, and they should be celebrated.

It was May 25, 1951, when 20-year-old rookie Willie Mays, who had created quite a stir in 35 games with the Triple-A Minneapolis Millers, made his debut in center field for the New York Giants against the Philadelphia Phillies at Shibe Park. He struggled at the plate, going 0 for 5 and taking a called third strike against Bubba Church in his first at bat. Mays actually went 0 for 12 before finally getting a hit. It came at the Polo Grounds off one of the greatest left-handers of all time, Warren Spahn, and it actually sailed over the left field roof. Mays batted .274 with 20 home runs and 68 RBI that season, and was named the franchise's first Rookie of the Year.

It was April 15, 1958, when 20-year-old rookie Orlando Cepeda debuted in the first ever major league baseball game on the West Coast. It was only minutes prior to the first pitch when the native Puerto Rican signed his first big league contract. He went 1 for 5 in the game and blasted his first homer in the fifth, against Dodgers reliever Don Bessent. Cepeda went on to have a tremendous rookie season, batting .312 with 25 home runs. He also had a 17-game hitting streak in July and a 12-game streak in August. He ran away with the N.L. Rookie of the Year.

It was July 30, 1959, when 21-year-old rookie Willie McCovey debuted at first base for the Giants against the Phillies. If he was nervous, his performance didn't show it. The big lefty went 4 for 4 with two triples, and even though he played in only 52 games he was still named Rookie of the Year, giving the franchise back-to-back winners. Much like Cepeda, McCovey was an obvious choice with a .354 batting average and 13 home runs.

It was September 6, 1972, when 21-year-old rookie Gary Matthews debuted in right field for the Giants at San Diego. He went 1 for 5 on the night with a single and an RBI in the top of the second. He only played in 20 games in 1972, but in 1973 he was with the club the entire year. He made the most of it too, batting .300 with 12 homers and ten triples, and he was named Rookie of the Year.

It was September 3, 1974, when 24-year-old rookie John Montefusco made his debut against LA at Dodger Stadium. He entered the game in the bottom of the first for Ron Bryant. The bases were loaded with no outs and he got a ground ball and two strikeouts to keep the game close at 4-2. He then walked and scored in the top of the second and hit a home run in the top of the third! On the mound he baffled the Dodgers and gave up only one earned run in nine innings. The righty only saw action in seven games in 1974, but went 15-9 with a 2.88 ERA in 1975 and became the fifth Giant and first Giant pitcher to be named Rookie of the Year.

Five debuts and five Giants who went on to earn ROY honors—that in and of itself is worth celebrating, but how about this. All of them went on to earn at least one trip to an All-Star game. Three of them: Willie Mays, Orlando Cepeda, and Willie McCovey, are now in the Hall of Fame. The quintet accounted for 1,399 Giants home runs (Montefusco hit four). And finally the final scores of each of these debuts:

- May 25, 1951   Giants beat the Phillies 8-5
- April 15, 1958   Giants beat the Dodgers 8-0
- July 30, 1959   Giants beat the Phillies 7-2
- September 6, 1972   Giants beat the Padres 6-0
- September 3, 1974   Giants beat the Dodgers 9-5

It's rather appropriate that the orange and black would win each of these games in convincing fashion. Each was the beginning of something special ... just like seeing your first major league game.

201 Rube Marquard won (201) career games. The Hall of Famer won the first 103 with the Giants. After winning 19 straight in 1912, plus two more in the World Series, his celebrity status was so high that he made a movie titled "19 Straight." He also starred in a stage show with Blossom Seeley titled "Breaking the Record," and the two later married. In the show, Marquard and Seeley did a dance called the "Marquard Glide."

202 Matt Cain struck out (2.02) batters per walk during four seasons from 2005-08. The talented righty struggled to a 30-43 record in that time, but no one questions his stuff. Cain struck out 558 batters in 654-plus innings, issuing just 276 free passes. Though still early in his career that gives him a ratio that ranks among the 25 best in franchise history.

203 Hank Leiber and Bill Terry tied for third in the league with (203) hits in 1935. For Leiber it was a career high total. For Terry, it was the sixth and final time he surpassed 200 hits in a season. They share one of the top 25 efforts in franchise history.

204 Ross Youngs got a career high (204) hits in 1920. He batted .351, placing second in the league for hits and average. Youngs did lead the league in times on base, 281, and his hits total is one of the top 25 in franchise history.

205 Rogers Hornsby got (205) hits in 1927. Fourth best in the league, Hornsby, in his only season with the Giants, carved out one of the top 20 efforts in franchise history.

206 Robb Nen saved (206) games from 1998-2002. That total is a franchise record. In all five seasons he closed for the Giants, Nen recorded a saves total that ranks among the top ten in franchise history: 40, 37, 41, 45, and 43.

207 Phil Douglas gave up (2.07) walks per nine innings during parts of four seasons with the Giants from 1919-22. He was 42-28 with a respectable 3.15 earned run average during that time, and his walks ratio ranks among the top 15 in franchise history. His problem, however, was apparently alcohol. In the midst of the 1922 season, with a record of 11-4 and the best ERA in the league, Douglas argued with manager John McGraw, with alcohol the suspected topic of discussion, and the end result was he never pitched in the majors again.

208 Willie Mays got (208) hits in 1958—a career high and second highest in the league. Mays led the league only once, when he got 190 hits in 1960, but he was among the league's top ten leaders in hits ten times on his way to compiling a franchise record 3,187 career hits.

209 Dave Bancroft got (209) hits in 1922. The Hall of Fame shortstop set a career high and led the club with the third highest total in the league.

210 The earned run average (2.10) for Juan Marichal in 1969. He was 21-11, good for his sixth 20-win campaign. It was also the only season of his career that the Hall of Famer led the league in ERA.

211 Hall of Famer Frankie Frisch led the club with (211) hits and a .341 average in 1921. New York also won the first of four consecutive pennants, and the second baseman went on to collect nine hits and score five runs as the Giants beat the Yankees in the 1921 World Series.

212 The earned run average (2.12) for Christy Mathewson during 17 seasons pitching for the Giants. Mathewson led the league five times while accumulating the lowest ERA in franchise history—and one of the ten best in baseball history as well. He was so good that writer Damon Runyon once observed, "Mathewson pitched against Cincinnati yesterday. Another way of putting it is that Cincinnati lost a game of baseball. The first statement means the same as the second."

213 Bill Terry got (213) hits in 1931—and again in 1934. He was second in the league both times, but his total remains one of the ten best in franchise history.

214 Deion Sanders batted (214) times in 52 games with the Giants in 1995. He played really well after coming over in a trade with the Cincinnati Reds. Sanders batted .285 with a .444 slugging percentage, hitting nine doubles, five triples, and five homers, while picking up 18 RBI, eight steals, and scoring 29 runs. He became a free agent after the season and did not return to the Giants, opting to focus on the NFL instead—though he did play for Cincinnati again in 1997, and briefly in 2001.

215 Hooks Wiltse gave up (2.15) walks per nine innings during 11 seasons pitching for the Giants—one of the top 20 ratios in franchise history. Five times he posted one of the ten best ratios in the league, and if not for his teammates Christy Mathewson and Joe McGinnity (both of whom dominated this category) he would have led the Giants in this stat a few times.

216 Mike Donlin got (216) hits in 1905—one of the ten best seasons in franchise history. Donlin batted .356 and played a key role for the club that defeated Philadelphia to win the World Series. In addition to a very successful career in baseball, Donlin took his talents to Hollywood, where he enjoyed a second career as an actor in movies and on the stage.

217 Frank Linzy finished (217) games during seven seasons with the Giants. He saved 78 games and was a premier reliever during his time. His games finished total is among the ten highest in franchise history.

218 Ron Kline gave up (218) career homers—including a memorable bomb for Willie McCovey on August 2, 1959. It was McCovey's first career home run.

219 Johnny Antonelli started (219) games during seven seasons with the Giants. He was 108-84 and six times he was among the league's top ten leaders in strikeouts. Twice he led the league in shutouts, once in winning percentage, and once in earned run average.

220 The at bats (22.0) per strikeout ratio for Jo-Jo Moore during parts of 12 seasons with the Giants—one of the top 100 ratios in baseball history, and one of the 15 best in franchise history. Moore batted .298 with 79 homers and 809 runs during 1,335 career games, and was a perennial All-Star. He struck out only 247 times in 5,427 career at bats.

221 Christy Mathewson struck out (221) batters in 1901. He was a 20-year-old kid in his first full season with the club. Mathewson led the Giants and was fourth in the league in strikeouts.

222 Shawon Dunston batted (.222) vs. Anaheim during the 2002 World Series. The 18-year veteran was just 2 for 9, but he launched a Game 6 home run—his only career blast during eight postseason series. Dunston was a career .275 hitter in the postseason, but he never won a ring.

223 Frankie Frisch got (223) hits in 1923. He was only fifth in the batting title race, but he led the league in hits with a career high total.

Frisch never led the league in hits again, but his career total of 2,880 ranks among the top 50 in baseball history.

224 The earned run average (2.24) for Hooks Wiltse in 1908. He was 23-14, and gave up only 82 earned runs in 330 innings. The most dominating performance of his career was on July 4 that season vs. the Philadelphia Phillies. Wiltse retired the first 26 batters he faced, but with two outs in the ninth he hit Phillies pitcher George McQuillan and lost his bid for a perfect game. The game was scoreless, and Wiltse went on to retire the next four batters he faced before the Giants won it in the bottom of the tenth—giving Wiltse a ten-inning no-hitter that was a darn-near perfect game.

225 The length in hours and minutes (2:25) of the Giants vs. Phillies matchup during game one of a doubleheader on August 12, 1951. Philly had beaten the Giants the day before to extend New York's losing streak to four games and its deficit in the pennant race to 13 games behind Brooklyn. After Sal Maglie earned a 3-2 victory to stop the skid, something quite magical began to take place. The Giants won 16 straight and rocketed to within five games of first. New York later won 12 of 13 to close out the season dead-even with the Dodgers. A three-game playoff ensued, setting the stage for Bobby Thomson and "The shot heard 'round the world."

226 Frankie Frisch batted (.226) during 54 games as a 20-year-old rookie in 1919. He batted .280 his sophomore season and .341 the year after that. The Hall of Fame second baseman played eight seasons with the Giants and led the club in batting four times. New York won four pennants and two world championships with Frisch, who hit .363 during 26 career World Series games.

227 Tim Lincecum pitched (227) innings in 2008. He gave up only 182 hits and 66 earned runs—and led the majors with 265 strikeouts.

228 The earned run average (2.28) for Scott Garrelts in 1989—a career best, and the best in the league as well. Garrelts was 14-5 in 29 starts. A first round draft pick a decade earlier, Garrelts was, unfortunately, 0-2 with a 9.82 ERA vs. Oakland in the 1989 World Series—the only one he ever played in.

229 Bill Swift struck out (2.29) batters per walk during three seasons pitching for the Giants. He was 39-19 with an impressive 2.70 earned run average. Swift struck out 296 batters, but gave up only 129 walks during 506-plus innings—which, oddly enough, means his ratio of walks per nine innings was also 2.29.

230 The length in hours and minutes (2:30) of the Giants vs. Astros matchup at AT&T Park on May 13, 2008. Matt Cain hit his second homer and earned his second victory of the season, tossing eight solid innings in a 4-2 decision. Cain was very impressive, but five of the 30,858 fans on hand to witness the game can boast an even more stellar performance: Malik Coleman, Brianna Doherty, Jeffrey W. Doong, Toby Hammett, and Casey McNamara were at the game as guests of the Giants because they earned perfect scores of 36 on the ACT. All five students came from high schools in northern California—and they each received an award on the field prior to the start of the game (a sixth student, Archit Sheth-Shah, also earned a perfect score on the ACT but was unable to attend the game).

231 Fred Lindstrom got (231) hits in 1928. That total led the league and set a franchise record. Lindstrom got 231 hits again in 1930, but the second time he was only fourth in the league and just second on the team—as Bill Terry eclipsed Lindstrom's record that season.

232 Barry Bonds walked (232) times in 2004. Bonds walked more times than anyone in baseball history. He led the league in walks 12 times, but his 2004 total is almost incomprehensible. He broke the major league record for walks for the third time in four seasons—and 120 of them were intentional.

233 John Montefusco and Vida Blue both gave up (233) hits in 1978. Both were 28-year-old starters. Montefusco made 36 starts, Blue made 35. Montefusco gave up 68 walks, Blue gave up 70. Montefusco struck out 177, Blue struck out 171. Montefusco pitched 238-plus innings, Blue pitched 258 innings. The real contrast, however: Blue was 18-10 with a 2.79 earned run average; Montefusco was 11-9 with a 3.81 earned run average. How do you explain that disparity when the other numbers are so close? Well, Blue tossed nine complete games compared to only three for Montefusco, Blue tossed four shutouts compared to none for Montefusco, and Blue gave up only 12 home runs compared to 25 for Montefusco.

234 The earned run average (2.34) for Jason Schmidt in 2003. He was 9-4 with a 2.37 ERA in the first half of the season, and for his effort he was selected to his first All-Star team. Schmidt tossed two scoreless innings and struck out three batters vs. the A.L. in the mid-Summer Classic. In the second half of the season he was even better, posting an 8-1 record with a 2.29 ERA. Schmidt won the ERA title, but lost the Cy Young to Eric Gagne.

235 The Giants launched (235) homers in 2001. Barry Bonds, of course, hit a major league record 73 big flies, which contributed to a team total that led the league and set a franchise record. The Giants also set a franchise record with 14 pinch-hit home runs in 2001.

236 Ross Youngs hit (236) career doubles. The Hall of Famer led the league with 31 doubles in 1919 and he hit a career high 34 doubles in 1922. Youngs was among the league's top seven leaders for doubles four times from 1919-24.

237 Jose Uribe batted (.237) in 1985. The 26-year-old rookie shortstop got 113 hits and scored 46 runs while playing solid baseball on defense. He became a fixture in the middle of the Giants infield for the next few years, and hit a career high .291 in 1987.

238 The career earned run average (2.38) for Joe McGinnity during seven seasons with the Giants from 1902-08. McGinnity posted totals of 31, 35, 21, and 27 wins from 1903-06. Three times in that stretch he was among the league's top ten leaders in ERA, and his career mark with the club is the third best in franchise history.

239 Rich Aurilia batted (.239) as a 24-year-old rookie shortstop in 1996. In 105 games he hit just three homers with 26 RBI, but within three years he was one of the premier offensive shortstops in the league. Aurilia hit three, five, and nine homers from 1996-98, but from 1999-2001 he hit 22, 20, and 37. He also batted .324 with 97 RBI in 2001, made the All-Star team, and won the Silver Slugger Award.

240 Bill Terry batted (.240) during the 1936 World Series. Terry, Sandy Koufax, Willie Mays, Eddie Mathews, Jackie Robinson, Johnny Mize, Frank Baker, Travis Jackson, and Joe DiMaggio are all Hall of Fame legends who got to play their final big league game during the World Series—which is a pretty cool way to go out. Terry and Jackson did so as teammates for the Giants in 1936. It is, of course, cooler still to go out having won that last game in the World Series. Unfortunately, both Terry and Jackson had poor numbers and they lost to the Yankees and DiMaggio, who was a rookie playing in his first World Series. DiMaggio, Mathews, and Mize all won that last game—the others all lost.

241 Mike Ivie batted (.241) in 1980. He struggled, hitting just four homers in 79 games after setting career highs in 1979 with 27 homers and 89 RBI. San Francisco traded him to the Houston Astros the following spring for Dave Bergman and Jeffrey Leonard, which turned out to be an excellent trade indeed.

242 Steve Holm batted (.242) in the minors from 2001-08. He made the big club for the first time in 2008, and on May 11, he came off the bench in the top of the seventh to replace catcher Bengie Molina, who was hit by a pitch in the sixth. Holm hit only 39 minor league homers, so when he went yard in the bottom of the seventh, after only 36 big league at bats, the Giants and the Phillies were equally shocked. The two-run shot proved to be the game winner in a 4-3 decision. "I didn't know it was out until I hit second," Holm said later. It turns out both teams, and Holm, had good reason to be surprised—the Elias Sports Bureau reported that it was only the second time since 1996 that a player entered the game as a defensive replacement, and then hit a go-ahead home run for his first big league bomb.

243 The career earned run average (2.43) for Jeff Tesreau. His entire career lasted just seven seasons, but every one of them was with the Giants. Tesreau never posted anything higher than a 3.09 ERA. He led the league once, in 1912, and was among the league's top ten leaders four times—and his career mark is the fourth best in franchise history.

244 Juan Marichal tossed (244) complete games during 14 seasons pitching for the Giants. He made 446 starts and tossed 52 shutouts. He is sixth in franchise history for complete games and second in shutouts—and his career numbers for both categories are among the top 100 in baseball history.

245 Hall of Famer Amos Rusie won (245) career games. Known as The Hoosier Thunderbolt, Rusie, from a small town in Indiana, led the league with 341 strikeouts as a 19-year-old kid in 1890. The next season he tossed a no-hitter vs. Brooklyn on his way to winning 33 games—the first of four consecutive seasons he topped 30 victories.

246 Charlie Hayes batted (.246) during 216 career games with the Giants. He was 1 for 5 during three games in 1989, his rookie season, and then he was traded to the Phillies along with Dennis Cook and Terry Mulholland for Steve Bedrosian and a player to be named later. Hayes then hit eight homers in 87 games for the Phillies and placed fifth in Rookie of the Year balloting. He came back to the Giants in

1998 and hit .286 with 12 homers, but in 1999 (his last year with the club) he hit only .205 with six homers.

247 Jeff Tesreau pitched (247) career games. He played from 1912-18, and was very effective, posting a 115-72 record with a 2.43 earned run average. Tesreau, who later became the head coach at Dartmouth, was, unfortunately, somewhat less effective in the postseason. He was only 1-3 with a 3.62 ERA in the World Series, and the Giants lost all three series he played in: 1912, 1913, and 1917.

248 The earned run average (2.48) for Hooks Wiltse during 11 seasons with the Giants—one of the ten best in franchise history. His brother Snake was also a lefty and pitched briefly in the majors, but it was Hooks who enjoyed the most success in baseball.

249 Royce Clayton batted (.249) during parts of five seasons playing shortstop for the Giants from 1991-95. The Giants drafted him #15 overall in the first round of the 1988 amateur draft, and Clayton was only 23 when he batted .282 with five homers and 70 RBI in 1993. After 1995, however, the club gave up on his potential and traded him to St. Louis—and Clayton, though he enjoyed a long career, was on the job carousel from then on: St. Louis, Texas, Chicago (White Sox), Milwaukee, Colorado, Arizona, Washington, Cincinnati, Toronto, and Boston.

250 Pedro Feliz batted (.250) in 2005. The third baseman led the team with 20 homers, 54 extra-base hits, 81 RBI, and 240 total bases. It was the first time since Matt Williams led the team in homers in 1994 that Barry Bonds was not the Giants leading home run hitter. Bonds was limited to just 42 at bats in 14 games due to injuries—and he hit five home runs.

251 Jason Schmidt struck out (251) batters in 2004—a career high, and third best in the league. Schmidt could be found on many leader boards that season: earned run average, winning percentage, wins, and shutouts. He was fourth in Cy Young balloting.

252 The career batting average (.252) for Jim Thorpe. He is widely considered to be the greatest athlete of the 20th century and is a member of the United States Olympic Hall of Fame, the Pro Football Hall of Fame, and the College Football Hall of Fame—and he also played baseball for the Giants. His baseball career was less than stellar compared to his other exploits (he couldn't hit curveballs for anything), though he did make one appearance for the Giants in the

1917 World Series (which unfortunately was won in six games by the White Sox).

253 Carl Hubbell won (253) career games. He won them all for the Giants, giving him the second highest total in franchise history behind Christy Mathewson. Hubbell led the league in wins three times, including 26 in 1936 for a career high.

254 Bill Terry got (254) hits in 1930. In his .401 season he set franchise records for both hits and average. The Hall of Famer tied Lefty O'Doul for what at the time was the second highest hits total in baseball history, behind the 257 for George Sisler in 1920. Ichiro Suzuki broke that record with 262 hits in 2004, which moved O'Doul and Terry down a spot to the third highest total in history.

255 Darrell Evans batted (.255) during eight seasons with the Giants. He hit ten homers in 92 games after joining the club in a trade with Atlanta in 1976. A true slugger with 414 career bombs, Evans launched season totals of 17, 20, 17, 20, 12, 16, and 30 during his next seven seasons in San Francisco.

256 Candy Maldonado batted (.256) during four seasons with the Giants from 1986-89. After hitting only 11 homers in 296 games with the Dodgers, Maldonado launched 18 bombs during his first season with the Giants in 1986. He did even better in 1987, batting a career high .292 with 20 homers, and driving home 85 runs for the second consecutive season. Unfortunately, he hit only 21 homers total the next two seasons, and after he hit .091 during the 1989 World Series the club did not resign him.

257 Robby Thompson batted (.257) during his career. He played all 11 seasons with the Giants, was a two-time All-Star, and batted a career high .312 in 1993—the same season he won his only Silver Slugger Award.

258 The earned run average (2.58) for Pol Perritt during parts of seven seasons pitching for the Giants—one of the ten best in franchise history. Perritt was the winning pitcher in a 1-0 contest that took just 57 minutes in 1918, one of the shortest games in baseball history.

259 Juan Marichal gave up (259) hits in 1963—*in 321-plus innings*. Marichal was especially stingy vs. Houston on June 15. Nearly three years after he tossed a one-hitter vs. Philadelphia in his big league debut, Marichal tossed a no-no against the Astros.

260 Carl Hubbell pitched (260) complete games—the fourth highest total in franchise history, and one of the top 75 in baseball history. Hubbell led the league once, with a career high 25 in 1934, a total he matched in 1936 when he was second in the league. Hubbell was among the league's top four leaders in complete games eight times.

261 The earned run average (2.61) for Gaylord Perry in 1967. He was only 15-17 because he was on the wrong end of one-run losses *nine times*. Perry's stuff was so good—and his luck so bad—that on September 1, he tossed 16 shutout innings vs. Cincinnati, but the Giants couldn't score either. Frank Linzy got the W after tossing five scoreless innings in relief. San Francisco won 1-0 after Dick Groat walked with the bases loaded—in the 21st inning.

262 The earned run average (2.62) for young ace Tim Lincecum in 2008. That number led the team and was second best in the league. Only 24, Lincecum became the youngest Cy Young recipient since Roger Clemens won his first Cy Young in 1986, also at the age of 24.

263 The earned run average (2.63) for Ferdie Schupp during parts of seven seasons pitching for the Giants—one of the 15 best in franchise history. Schupp gave up just 14 earned runs in 140-plus innings in 1916, primarily as a reliever, going 9-3 with a 0.90 ERA.

264 Bobby Thomson hit (264) career home runs. If ever there was a player defined by one swing of the bat, it was Bobby Thomson. His pennant-winning blast, in his own words, ". . . raised me to a high level, with the top guys in the game."

265 Willie McCovey received (265) points in the 1969 MVP balloting. He tied pitcher Tom Seaver, who won 25 games that season for the New York Mets, with 11 first place votes. McCovey batted .320 and led the league with 45 home runs, and he also edged out Seaver for the MVP by garnishing more second place votes in the balloting. Hank Aaron, Pete Rose, and Ron Santo rounded out the top five—and eight of the top 13 vote getters that season are members of the Hall of Fame.

266 Joel Youngblood batted (.266) during six seasons with the Giants. Youngblood signed with the Giants as a free agent prior to the 1983 season but he is remembered primarily for a feat he accomplished in 1982 while playing for the Mets *and* the Expos. On August 4, 1982, he was 1 for 2 vs. the Cubs in an afternoon game at Wrigley Field. He found out after the game that he had been traded to the Expos, so he got on a plane and flew to Philadelphia where Montreal was playing that night. He was 1 for 1 in that game as a pinch-hitter, making him the first player in baseball history to get a hit for two different teams in one day. Coincidentally, both of the pitchers he got hits against that day are in the Hall of Fame: Ferguson Jenkins and Steve Carlton.

267 Christy Mathewson struck out (267) batters in 1903—a career high, it was also the first time he led the league. Mathewson led the league in Ks a total of five times, and his career total of 2,499 with the Giants is a franchise record.

268 Fred Merkle was a 19-year-old kid when he batted (.268) in 41 at bats for the Giants in 1908. The Giants and Cubs were battling down the stretch for the pennant, and as it happens, one of Merkle's 11 hits that season came on September 23, with two outs in the ninth inning of a tie game vs. Chicago. His single put runners on the corners, and after Al Bridwell followed with another single it appeared that New York had won the game—but Merkle, in all the excitement that ensued with fans rushing the field, never ran to second base. After the Cubs brought this to the attention of the umpires, Merkle was called out and the game ended in a 1-1 tie. The two teams finished the season with identical records, forcing the tied game to be replayed. The Cubs won 4-2, claiming the pennant, and they went on to win the World Series as well.

269 The earned run average (2.69) for Red Ames in 1909. He was a veteran righty in his seventh season when he posted a 15-10 record, but those numbers don't even come close to the level of play with which he began the season. On opening day, 1909, Ames held Brooklyn hitless until one out in the ninth. Ames gave up a hit but no runs, and the scoreless game moved on into extra-innings. It stayed scoreless until the 13th, but then Ames lost a heartbreaker, surrendering three runs, while his opponent, Brooklyn's Kaiser Wilhelm, held the Giants to only three hits for the contest.

270 The earned run average (2.70) for Bill Swift during three seasons pitching for the Giants—one of the top 15 in franchise history. The Giants included 1989 MVP Kevin Mitchell as part of a package to get Swift from the Mariners after the 1991 season, and Swift paid immediate dividends. He posted back-to-back campaigns where his ERA was 2.08 and 2.82, first and fourth in the league respectively.

271 The earned run average (2.71) for Frank Linzy during parts of seven seasons pitching for the Giants. Linzy was a sinkerball specialist who was 9-3 with 21 saves and a 1.43 ERA as a rookie in 1965, and later, in 1969, he led the league with 14 wins in relief.

272 Matty Alou got (272) hits during parts of six seasons with the Giants. He got only 11 hits in 1963, but that same season, on September 15, Alou and brothers Felipe and Jesus got to play a game in which the three brothers were the Giants starting outfield. It was the first "all-brothers" outfield in major league history. In terms of Alou family members that played for the Giants, Matty ranks third in hits behind Felipe (655) and Jesus (626) but ahead of his nephew Moises (241).

273 Fred Merkle batted (.273) vs. Boston during the 1912 World Series. He earned the moniker "Bonehead" for his base running mistake that cost the Giants the pennant in 1908 (he was the youngest player in baseball that season—*for the second year in a row*). Merkle was, unfortunately, involved in another play that is a painful part of Giants history. In the final game of the 1912 World Series the Giants took a 2-1 lead in the top of the tenth inning. Merkle was playing first base when Tris Speaker hit a foul pop his direction. It should have been caught, but Merkle and catcher Chief Meyers let the ball fall between them. With new life, Speaker singled in the tying run and Boston rallied to win the game and the series. Merkle was called "Bonehead" for his base running mistake, and the fielding mishap has forever been called "Merkle's Muff."

274 Jim O'Rourke batted (.274) in 1888. That was the lowest average during eight seasons in New York for the Hall of Famer, who hit .300 or better five times during his tenure with the club. He could definitely hit, but O'Rourke was also considered to be one of the finest outfielders of his era. In 1878 *The Sporting Life* reported: "O'Rourke has made a brilliant record for himself as an outfielder, being an excellent judge of a ball, a swift runner, and making the most difficult running catches with the utmost ease and certainty. As a thrower, too, he stands pre-eminent, being credited with a throw of 365 feet, the next to the longest yet accomplished by any player."

275 Randy Winn batted (.275) for Seattle in 2005. The switch-hitting outfielder hit .359 after joining the Giants at the trade deadline—but that was nothing compared to what he did in the season's final week.

He batted .556 with a pair of 4 for 4 performances, and had seven consecutive hits during two games vs. San Diego. Winn got 15 hits and 29 total bases for the week and earned Bank of America National League Player of the Week honors. On his behalf, Bank of America donated $1,000 to the Little League Urban Initiative.

276 Bengie Molina batted (.276) in 2007. The veteran catcher hit 19 home runs and led the club with 81 RBI during his first season in the N.L. He hit two of those homers in one inning of a game vs. the Mets on May 7, becoming the first Giant to accomplish that feat since Willie McCovey did it in 1977. Molina was also just the third catcher in baseball history to hit two homers in one inning.

277 The earned run average (2.77) for Luther Taylor during nine seasons pitching for the Giants—one of the top 20 in franchise history. Taylor was known by the name Dummy because he was a deaf-mute. Skipper John McGraw learned basic signing to communicate with Taylor, and there is a story that the two were once thrown out of a game for signing back and forth about an umpire—not realizing the umpire was proficient in signing as well.

278 The batting average (.278) for the Giants in 2000. It was the second best team effort in the league, led by Jeff Kent, who hit .334 and placed sixth in the batting title race—but it was also the highest team average on record since the club relocated to the Bay area from New York in 1958.

279 The earned run average (2.79) for Rube Benton during seven seasons pitching for the Giants—and only once in that time did he post an ERA above 3.00. Benton won 16 games in 1916 and 15 games in 1917, and after missing almost all of 1918 serving in the military, he returned to win 17 games in 1919.

280 Duane Kuiper batted (.280) in 1982—his first season with the Giants. The second baseman was 61 for 218, with nine doubles and a triple, but no home runs. In fact, Kuiper, who along with Mike Krukow became a popular broadcaster for the Giants after his playing days, was a notoriously light-hitting infielder. In 12 seasons and 1,057 major league games, Kuiper hit just one major league homer. It came on August 29, 1977, against another player known for his broadcasting career: Steve Stone.

281 The earned run average (2.81) for Fred Toney during five seasons pitching for the Giants. Toney was involved in some pretty spectacular moments before coming to New York. While pitching in the Blue Grass League in 1909, he tossed a 17-inning no-hitter with 19 strikeouts. He also tossed a ten-inning no-hitter for Cincinnati on May 2, 1917, and in the same game Hippo Vaughn pitched nine no-hit innings for the Reds—the only time in history two opposing pitchers have thrown no-hit ball for nine innings. And two months later, Toney pitched both ends of a doubleheader vs. Pittsburgh, winning 4-1 and 5-1. All of that was before he came to New York. With the Giants, however, Toney became a world champion in 1921—and his ERA with the club is one of the top 20 in franchise history.

282 Fred Lewis batted (.282) in 2008. A second round pick in 2002 out of Southern University, Lewis put together solid numbers in his first full season of play—but he definitely enjoyed AT&T Park more than he did the road. Lewis batted only .233 on the road (232 at bats), but he batted .331 at home (236 at bats).

283 The earned run average (2.83) for Carl Hubbell in 1928. He was a 25-year-old rookie who went 10-6. The next season Hubbell was among the league's top ten leaders for ERA, a feat he accomplished ten times from 1929-39, including eight consecutive seasons, three of which he was the league leader.

284 Will Clark hit (284) career home runs. He hit 176 as a member of the Giants, which places him among the top ten in franchise history, but he is best remembered for his first career home run. He went yard against Hall of Fame legend Nolan Ryan in his first big league at bat, on his very first swing.

285 The earned run average (2.85) for Rube Marquard during parts of eight seasons with the Giants. After winning 20 games and pitching a perfect game for Indianapolis in the American Association, New York purchased his contract for a record $11,000 in 1908, as the Giants and Cubs were in the midst of an historic pennant race. His first start was September 25, shortly after Fred Merkle's bonehead base running incident, and it was not good. Marquard hit Miller Huggins, the first man he faced, and walked the next two. He gave up five runs in five innings and took the loss, prompting fans to call him the "$11,000 lemon." The label fit from 1908-10, when Marquard was just 9-18, but he quickly earned a new reputation after winning 24, 26, and 23 games from 1911-13.

286 The batting average (.286) for the Giants in 1912. Led by Chief Meyers (.358), Fred Merkle (11 homers), and Larry Doyle (98 runs) the Giants led the league in average, homers, runs, and, most importantly, victories. New York scored 823 runs en route to winning 103 games and the pennant.

287 Hank Leiber batted (.287) during seven seasons with the Giants. By far his best year was 1935, when he batted .331 with 203 hits, 110 runs, 22 homers, 107 RBI, and a .512 slugging percentage. Leiber walked 48 times but struck out only 29 times, and placed 11th in league MVP balloting. He was also with the club for back-to-back pennants in 1936 and 1937, but he was hitless in losing the 1936 World Series to the Yankees. He hit .364 in the 1937 World Series, but the Giants again lost to the Yankees.

288 The earned run average (2.88) for John Montefusco in 1975. The Count beat out Hall of Fame catcher Gary Carter for Rookie of the Year honors after posting a 15-9 record with 215 strikeouts.

289 The earned run average (2.89) for Doc Crandall during six seasons pitching for the Giants—one of the top 25 in franchise history. Crandall was 45-16 from 1910-12, and was one of the first pitchers in history to be used almost exclusively as a reliever.

290 Larry Doyle batted (.290) during 14 major league seasons—including 13 with the Giants. Doyle, who won the 1912 Most Valuable Player Award, is famous for declaring shortly thereafter, "It's great to be young and a Giant." He had good reason to voice such sentiment, as he also won three pennants and a batting title with the Giants.

291 Chief Meyers batted (.291) for his career. Meyers, a catcher who was a native Cahuilla Indian, batted .301 during seven season with the Giants, and was a key contributor on the clubs that won three consecutive pennants from 1911-13.

292 Bengie Molina batted (.292) in 2008. He also led the club with 95 RBI, including a league best 11 sacrifice flies (tied with the Mets David Wright). Randy Winn hit nine sacrifice flies, sixth best in the league—making that the only offensive leader board in 2008 with two players from San Francisco.

293 Bobby Thomson batted (.293) in 1951. He hit 32 homers with 101 RBI—including one of the most dramatic bombs in baseball history. Thomson hit a three-run ninth inning homer against Ralph Branca that won a three-game playoff vs. Brooklyn and sent the Giants to the World Series, prompting Russ Hodges' famous call: "The

Giants win the pennant! The Giants win the pennant! The Giants win the pennant!"

294 The at bats (29.4) per strikeout ratio for Freddy Leach in 1929. He batted .290 during his first season with the Giants, scoring 74 runs in 113 games, but striking out only 14 times in 411 at bats. He led the club with the eighth best ratio in the league, one that remains among the top 40 in franchise history.

295 Omar Vizquel batted (.295) in 2006. The 39-year-old veteran shortstop led the club in batting, runs (88), hits (171), steals (24), and times on base (233) during his second season by the Bay. Not bad, seeing as it was his defense the club was after when it signed him to a free agent contract prior to 2005. Vizquel won nine consecutive Gold Gloves in the A.L. from 1993-2001, and he brought his slick-fielding with him to San Francisco where he won Gold Gloves in 2005 and again in 2006.

296 The earned run average (2.96) for Gaylord Perry during ten seasons pitching for the Giants—one of the top 30 in franchise history. Perry won just 24 games during his first four seasons from 1962-65, which makes his 314 career victories an impressive feat. He found his stride in 1966, and won 21, 15, 16, 19, 23, and 16 games during his last six seasons with San Francisco. Perry was the first player in baseball history to win the Cy Young in both leagues. His N.L. award, however, was with the Padres, not the Giants.

297 Jeff Kent batted (.297) during six seasons with the Giants. Kent batted only .250 in 1997, his first year with the club, but never batted below .290 for five consecutive years thereafter. He batted .334 in 2000 and .313 in 2002, which were the only two seasons in his career that he placed among the league's top ten leaders for average.

298 Mel Ott got on base (298) times in 1929. That total was third in the league, but it set a career high for the Hall of Famer who got on base more often than anyone else in franchise history: 4,648 times over the course of his career.

299 Andres Galarraga batted (.299) during parts of two seasons wearing a Giants uniform. The Big Cat is one of only two players to finish his career with exactly 399 home runs—the other is Hall of Famer Al Kaline. Galarraga hit 19 big flies during 159 games for the Giants.

300 Gary Matthews batted (.300) in 1973. He also hit 12 home runs and scored 74 runs, and his numbers were good enough that he beat out some pretty stiff competition to earn N.L. Rookie of the Year honors: Steve Rogers, Bob Boone, Dan Driessen, Ron Cey, and Davey Lopes all got first place votes in the balloting.

Bobby Thomson—after one of history's greatest moments.
(Courtesy National Baseball Hall of Fame Library, Cooperstown, NY)

"The Giants win the pennant! The Giants win the pennant! The Giants win the pennant! The Giants win the pennant!"

— *Russ Hodges, calling "The shot heard 'round the world"*

Chapter Four

1951

HISTORY IS REMEMBERED in moments. Some are heartbreaking, others are joyful, and often they can be both at the same time ... depending on your perspective. The reason these moments become a part of history is because they have meaning, they become personal. They are not something that must be remembered, but rather something we can't forget. Baseball is no different. It is a sport so driven by numbers that sometimes it seems they constitute the game of both today and yesteryear. But then there are *those* moments. The ones we can never forget...

In such a superstitious game it would seem the number 13 should be avoided at all costs. Oddly enough though, Giants fans can't look upon this number with derision because it represents troubling times that eventually led to one of the greatest moments in baseball history.

When the 1951 campaign began the Giants were in the midst of a 13-season drought—having last won a pennant in 1937, the second longest drought since a 14-year stretch after 1889, when the Giants beat the Brooklyn Bridegrooms to win a second straight pre-modern era World Series, to 1904 when John McGraw led the club to his first pennant as manager.

During the aforementioned 13 seasons leading up to 1951, the Giants best finish was third (1938, 1942, and 1950). The 1940s were rough on the franchise and it appeared 1951 would end in disappointment as well. The Giants began play on May 15, at 13-15, and after a loss at Pittsburgh the club fell to 13-16 and into last place. Ten days later, Willie Mays made his debut and the club slowly began to climb into contention. Still, after a loss on August 11, the club was 59-51 and 13 games behind the hated Brooklyn Dodgers (those same Bridegrooms we beat in 1904).

Then a miraculous thing occurred. The Giants caught fire and reeled off 16 straight victories to pull within five games of the Dodgers. The lead was down to three games on September 22, and the boys could taste it. They won the final seven games of the season to tie Brooklyn.

From August 11 to September 30 the club went 37-7! The miraculous run forced a three-game tiebreaker and it seemed there was no stopping the Giants as the club nipped the Dodgers on October 1 by the score of 3-1. It was the first lead for the G-men all year. It didn't last, as Brooklyn claimed the second game, 10-0.

It all came down to October 3, 1951. Both clubs were 97-59.

Nine innings left, the pennant on the line.

Sal Maglie took the hill for the Giants and Don Newcombe for the Dodgers. Maglie walked Pee Wee Reese and Duke Snider in the first and Jackie Robinson knocked Reese in. The Dodgers led 1-0.

In the second the Giants threatened. With Whitey Lockman on first Bobby Thomson singled to left. He rounded first heading for second and realized Lockman still stood on the bag. He was caught in a rundown and tagged out.

In the fifth Thomson redeemed himself at least in some fashion when he doubled against Newcombe, but the Dodgers fireballer left him stranded.

Thomson came up again in the seventh with Monte Irvin on third. With two strikes he lofted a fly ball into center field, deep enough for Irvin to score easily. The game was tied, 1-1.

The eighth inning was all Brooklyn as Reese and Snider singled. Then Maglie uncorked a curve that got away from Wes Westrum and Reese scored. The Dodgers went on to score a couple more runs in the inning when Thomson failed to make two tough plays at third. The score was 4-1, and it seemed New York's miracle season was about to end.

In the ninth Don Newcombe got ahead of Alvin Dark with two strikes, and hopes of a comeback were slim. Then Dark slapped a single through the right side. Irvin popped out, but Dark eventually scored when Lockman doubled to left. The score was 4-2 with two runners on.

Newcombe was exhausted and Charlie Dressen decided to go with Ralph Branca, who had been warming up off and on since the fifth. Branca was stiff after pitching in the last game of the regular season and then in the 3-1 loss only a couple days before, but he loosened up and was ready to go.

Bobby Thomson stepped to the plate and Branca threw a fastball on the inside corner for strike one. He came back with a fastball up and in, thinking he'd set up a curveball low and away. But Thomson swung and the ball sailed toward the left field seats. The nation listened as broadcaster Russ Hodges made his famous call: "There's a long drive ... It's gonna be ... I believe ... The Giants win the pennant! The Giants win the pennant! The Giants win the pennant! The Giants win the pennant! Bobby Thomson hits it into the lower deck of the left field stands! The Giants win the pennant and they're going crazy!"

The Giants won 5-4.

In a single pitch Ralph Branca and Bobby Thomson attained baseball immortality. That joyful and heartbreaking moment that can never be forgotten.

Thomson and the Giants celebrated. There was a time when the club had only 13 wins and was in last place. There was a time when the club was 13 games behind the Dodgers, and was suffering through 13 consecutive seasons without a pennant, but on October 3, 1951, there was nothing but joy for the New York Giants.

Branca and the Dodgers were heartbroken.

He made his way to his car where Father Frank Rowley waited. Branca said, "I don't smoke. I don't drink. I don't run around. Baseball is my whole life. Why me?"

Father Rowley had an answer, although years later these moments don't necessarily need explanation. They happened, they have meaning for everyone involved, and they are a part of history.

301 Terry Kennedy played (301) games during three seasons with the Giants. A catcher out of FSU selected by the Cardinals in the first round of the 1977 amateur draft, Kennedy was a four-time All-Star who enjoyed a productive 14-year major league career. His final three seasons were spent in San Francisco, where he batted .252 with ten homers in 829 at bats.

302 Willie Mays batted (.302) for his career. Speed, power, average—he had the whole package. Bill Rigney, who played with Mays, said of his teammate, "As a batter, his only weakness is a wild pitch."

303 The number of total bases (303) for Barry Bonds in 2004. Bonds got off to a quick start. In the season's second week he batted .733 with six homers, 13 RBI, and 31 total bases. He hit a three-run blast in San Francisco's home opener on April 12, tying Willie Mays for third on the all-time home run list. The next day he surpassed his godfather with career home run number 661. He homered again two days later, once more the day after that, and then closed out the week going 4 for 4 with two more homers—his 65th career multi-home run game. Bonds was named the Bank of America National League Player of the Week. It was the 12th time he won Player of the Week honors, an accomplishment he did once more later that season.

304 Carl Hubbell pitched (304) innings in 1936. He faced 1,202 batters but gave up only 78 earned runs. That led to a 26-6 record and a 2.31 earned run average—both numbers were the best in the league, and as a result Hubbell became the first player in franchise history to win multiple MVP Awards.

305 Barry Bonds got on base (305) times in 1998. He was second in the league behind fellow slugger Mark McGwire. Bonds led the league with 29 intentional walks, and McGwire (in his 70 homer season) was second with 28 intentional walks. McGwire led the league with 162 walks total, Bonds was second with 130.

306 Randy Winn batted (.306) in 2008. He led the club in batting and placed seventh in the league overall, but he was hitting only .277 as late as August 2. Well, he got hot. On August 15, Winn was 4 for 4 against Atlanta and his average climbed above .300 for the first time since late June—and he never looked back.

307 The earned run average (3.07) for Hall of Famer Rube Marquard during 11 World Series games. Marquard won five pennants—three with New York and two with Brooklyn—but despite pitching well, he only posted a 2-5 career record in the World Series. Worse, despite five pennants, he never won a World Series title.

308 The on-base percentage (.308) for Kirt Manwaring during ten seasons catching for the Giants from 1987-96. ESPN broadcaster Chris Berman, known for giving players creative nicknames on SportsCenter, used to call him Kirt "What's That" Manwaring. The Giants backstop was never known for his offensive prowess. His best campaign at the plate was 1993 when he batted .275 with five homers, 49 RBI, 48 runs, a .345 OBP, and a .350 slugging percentage—all career highs.

309 Fred Merkle batted (.309) in 1912. His career wasn't completely defined by his "bonehead" base running or "Merkle's Muff," because the truth is he could flat play some ball. His average in 1912 was a career high and in his prime Merkle could be found among the league's top ten leaders in a number of offensive categories. Merkle went on to play for five pennant-winning teams—three in New York, one in Brooklyn, and one in Chicago. Some things, however, aren't meant to be. Merkle lost all five World Series he played in.

310 The earned run average (3.10) for Jesse Barnes in 1921. He made 42 appearances, 31 starts, tossed 15 complete games, and led the team in ERA—but when the Giants won the pennant, Barnes was relegated to the bullpen against the Yankees in the World Series. If you think he was disappointed, think again—Barnes tossed 16-plus innings of relief during the series and posted a 2-0 record as the Giants beat New York in eight games.

311 Mike Tiernan batted (.311) for the Giants from 1887-99. He got a career high 192 hits in 1896, seven times he batted above .300 for a season, and his average ranks among the top 15 in franchise history.

312 Barry Bonds batted (.312) during 15 seasons with the Giants. Nine times he batted above .300, five times he ranked among the league's top ten leaders, twice he won the league batting title, and his career average with the club is among the top ten in franchise history.

313 Roger Bresnahan batted (.313) during the 1905 World Series. The Hall of Fame catcher was 5 for 16 and scored three runs in the series. He also hit an eighth inning double in Game 5 to set up the second run in the 2-0 victory that clinched the series.

314 The Giants hit (314) doubles in 2004. Ten different players hit at least 20 doubles, led by Pedro Feliz, who hit 33. The team total was third highest in the league, but it represents the highest total in franchise history. San Francisco nearly set a new team record in 2008, hitting 311 doubles, led by 38 from Randy Winn.

315 Juan Marichal gave up a franchise record (315) home runs. Well, someone has to hold the record. And Marichal is in good company. Quite a few Hall of Fame pitchers, especially those with serious heat, were known for giving up the long ball—13, in fact, gave up more career gophers than Marichal. Not to mention future Hall of Fame pitchers Randy Johnson, Greg Maddux, and Tom Glavine—oh, and Roger Clemens, too.

316 Felipe Alou batted (.316) in 1962—seventh best in the league. He made his first All-Star team after belting 25 homers with 98 RBI, and scoring 96 runs. The Giants future manager was signed by the club in 1955. His long career in baseball enabled him to play with brothers Matty and Jesus in 1963, manage his son Moises both with the Expos and Giants, and manage his nephew Mel Rojas for the Expos.

317 Roger Connor batted (.317) during 18 major league seasons. He did slightly better than that during his tenure in New York, posting a .319 career average for the Giants. Connor's overall average is among the top 75 in baseball history, and his average with the Giants is among the top ten in franchise history.

318 Fred Lindstrom batted (.318) during nine seasons with the Giants. He never won a batting title, but his career average with the club is among the top ten in franchise history.

319 The batting average (.319) for the Giants in 1930. Bill Terry won the batting title with a .401 average, and a total of nine players batted .300 or better for the Giants. The team average was the best in the league that season, and it remains the highest in franchise history.

320 The earned run average (3.20) for Jason Schmidt in 2004. Schmidt gave up just 165 hits and 80 earned runs in 225 innings for the best ERA on the team, and one of the ten best in the league. He was 18-7, and placed fourth in Cy Young balloting.

321 Frankie Frisch batted (.321) during eight seasons with the Giants. The Hall of Fame infielder was referred to as the "Fordham Flash" because of his Alma Mater and the quickness he displayed both in the field and on the bases. His attitude and hustle earned him the title of team captain for the Giants, and his ability at the plate left him with the fourth highest career average in franchise history.

322 Ross Youngs batted (.322) during his Hall of Fame career with the Giants. The right fielder played ten seasons from 1917-26 and six times he was among the league's top ten hitters. His career average is the third highest in franchise history—and it is also among the top 75 in major league history.

323 The earned run average (3.23) for Kirk Rueter in 2002. He led the club with one of the ten best numbers in the league. Rueter also led the club in winning percentage and he tied Russ Ortiz for the team lead in victories after posting a 14-8 record.

324 George Kelly batted (.324) in 1924. That was only third best on the club, and nowhere near the league's top ten leaders—but the heavy hitting by the Hall of Fame first baseman led New York to a fourth consecutive pennant. And he did place among the league's top ten leaders in runs, hits, total bases, doubles, home runs, RBI, extra-base hits, and times on base.

325 The number of RBI (325) for Felipe Alou during six seasons with the Giants. His best year was 1962 when he batted .316 with 25 homers and 98 RBI—and made his first All-Star team.

326 The earned run average (3.26) for Brooklyn's Kaiser Wilhelm in 1909. After tossing a three-hit 13-inning shutout vs. the Giants on opening day (see #269), Wilhelm was much more human—giving up 176 hits in 163 innings of work, while posting an embarrassing 3-13 record. The embarrassment cuts two ways, of course, one for him, because it's a lousy record, but one for the Giants as well—because New York was the first of Wilhelm's three victories.

327 Buck Ewing batted (.327) in 1889. Ewing and the Giants won a second consecutive pre-modern era World Series, defeating the Brooklyn Bridegrooms in nine games. Considered by many to be among the greatest players of the 19th century, Ewing became the first Hall of Fame catcher in baseball history when he was enshrined in 1939.

328 George Kelly batted (.328) in 1922. The Hall of Famer was called "Highpockets" because he stood 6' 4" without his spikes, which made him an intimidating presence at the plate—never mind he could flat hit anyway. John McGraw said Kelly got "more important hits for me than any player I ever had." Kelly's average in 1922 was a career high, but it was only the second of six consecutive seasons he hit .300 or better.

329 Irish Meusel batted (.329) during 62 games with the Giants in 1921. New York trailed Pittsburgh by four games on July 25 when it traded Curt Walker, Butch Henline, and $30,000 to the Phillies in exchange for Meusel—and by season's end two months later, the Giants were on top of the Pirates by four games.

330 Larry Doyle batted (.330) in 1912. It was a career high for the second baseman and as a result he became the first player in franchise history to win league MVP honors. His strong play also contributed to the Giants claiming the pennant—but he hit only .242 in the World Series as the Giants lost to the Red Sox. Doyle won three pennants, but never won a world championship.

331 The ratio (3.31) of strikeouts per walk for Juan Marichal from 1960-73. He led the league three consecutive seasons from 1966-68, and was among the league's top ten leaders 11 times. His career ratio is among the top 25 in baseball history, and it is the absolute best in Giants history.

332 George Davis batted (.332) during nine-plus seasons with the Giants. He hit a career high .355 in 1893, his first year with the club, and the Hall of Fame shortstop ranks second in franchise history for career average.

333 Kirt Manwaring batted (.333) during the 1989 postseason. Okay, he was only 1 for 3 . . . but after going 0 for 2 vs. Chicago in the League Championship Series, the backup catcher got just one at bat vs. Oakland in the World Series and he made the most of it. Manwaring replaced Terry Kennedy behind the plate in the ninth inning of Game 3 after Oakland took a 13-3 lead. He came to bat with one on and one out in the ninth—the only time in his life that he batted in the World Series—and he dropped a double down the right field line. He later came around and scored, though of course the Giants lost the game, and the series.

334 Jeff Kent batted (.334) in 2000. A career high, it came during his monstrous MVP campaign: 114 runs, 196 hits, 41 doubles, 33 homers, and 125 RBI.

335 The number of total bases (335) for Willie Mays in 1959. Mays led the club and was fourth in the league in total bases on the strength of 82 extra-base hits, 34 of which left the yard.

336 Barry Bonds batted (.336) in 1993. He also led the league with 46 home runs and 123 RBI. It was his first season with the Giants, and it was also the first HR and RBI titles for Bonds—but he came up short of the Triple Crown by placing fourth in the batting title race behind Gregg Jefferies, Tony Gwynn, and Andres Galarraga, who hit .370 to win the title. Bonds did win his third MVP Award.

337 The postseason slugging percentage (.337) for Willie Mays. In 89 postseason at bats, Mays hit only one home run—and that blast came in 1971, after Mays already had hit 646 regular season homers. That is by far the most regular season home runs in history for a player at the time of their first postseason home run. The next four on that list: Sammy Sosa (539), Jeff Bagwell (446), Dave Winfield (432), and Carlos Delgado (407).

338 Willie Mays stole (338) career bases. He stole a career high 40 bases in 1956, was twice a member of the 30/30 club, and in 1969 he became the first player with 300-plus career homers to also steal 300 career bases.

339 Shanty Hogan and Travis Jackson each batted (.339) in 1930. It was a career high for both players. Logan got 132 hits in 122 games.

Jackson got 146 hits in 116 games, but came to bat 42 more times than Logan. Neither led the team, however, and in fact, Hogan and Jackson only shared the fourth best average on the club behind Bill Terry, Fred Lindstrom, and Mel Ott.

340 The number of total bases (340) for Mel Ott in 1932. One of the top 25 totals in franchise history, Ott was third in the league, but only second on the club behind the 373 total bases for Bill Terry. Chuck Klein led the league with 420 total bases for Philly.

341 Bill Terry batted (.341) during 14 seasons with the Giants—a franchise record. The Hall of Famer hit only .239 during 77 games in 1924, his first full season, but he hit .319 the next year and never looked back. He won one batting title, and eight times he was among the league's top ten leaders.

342 Tim Keefe won (342) career games. The Hall of Famer, known as Sir Timothy, won 174 of those games for the Giants, including 19 straight in 1888.

343 Frank Snyder batted (.343) in 1922. A career high, Snyder led the club and was sixth in the league. Even better, he was coming off a .364 performance with one homer during the 1921 World Series vs. the Yankees, and he kept it up, batting .333 during the 1922 World Series vs. the Yankees as the Giants won a second straight championship.

344 The earned run average (3.44) for all N.L. pitchers in 1978. Bob Knepper was fourth in the league with a much healthier 2.63 ERA for the Giants, thanks to a league high six shutouts. He was 17-11, and completed 16 of 35 starts.

345 Mickey Welch struck out (345) batters in 1884. Only fourth in the league, it remains a franchise record. The Hall of Famer was 39-21 that year—imagine a pitcher taking the hill for 60 decisions (and 65 starts) nowadays.

346 Buck Ewing batted (.346) during the 1888 World Series. Ewing led the Giants with a .306 average during the regular season and was a major reason the club won its first of two pre-modern era world championships, defeating the St. Louis Browns in seven games during the 1888 World Series.

347 The Giants stole (347) bases in 1911. Seven players posted 20 or more steals, led by 61 for outfielder Josh Devore, who was second in the league. The club total, however, was easily the highest in the league—and it remains a franchise record.

348 Frankie Frisch batted (.348) in 1923. He placed fifth in the batting title race, but he led the club with a career high mark. The Hall of Famer also led the Giants to a third consecutive pennant that same season.

349 Bill Terry, Hughie Critz, Fred Lindstrom, and Travis Jackson combined for a (.349) average in 1930—the highest in history for a starting infield. Terry batted .401 at first, Lindstrom batted .379 at third, Jackson batted .339 at short, and all three are members of the Hall of Fame. Critz, on the other hand, he batted .265 at second—but hey, it's a *team* effort.

350 Jim O'Rourke batted (.350) for the Boston Red Stockings in 1873. Boston was 43-16 and won the National Association pennant, thanks to O'Rourke, the 22-year-old first baseman with a big bat who later starred for the New York Giants. The Hall of Famer is truly an old-timer, seeing as he is credited for having recorded the first base hit in N.L. history way back in 1876.

351 George Van Haltren batted (.351) in 1896. It was a career high average for the outfielder, but it was only the second best on the club behind Mike Tiernan, and it was nowhere near the league's top hitters that season. Still, he hit .300 or better eight consecutive seasons from 1894-1901, and his .321 career average for New York is tied with Frankie Frisch for the fourth highest in franchise history.

352 The number of total bases (352) for Jeff Kent in 2002. He was second in the league behind the 364 total bases for Montreal's Vladimir Guerrero. Kent did set a career high, however, on the strength of a league best 81 extra-base hits—and his 352 total bases is among the top 15 season efforts in franchise history.

353 Dan Gladden got (353) hits during 348 games with the Giants. He actually got 120 hits in only 86 games as a rookie in 1984, setting a career high with a .351 batting average and placing fourth in Rookie of the Year balloting. He hit only .243 in his sophomore season.

354 Bill Terry batted (.354) in 1934. One of the top 20 season efforts in franchise history, Terry nearly won his second career batting title that season. He placed second behind Paul Waner, the Hall of Fame outfielder who batted .362 for the Pirates.

355 The earned run average (3.55) for the Giants pitching staff in 1921. The club won the pennant and squared off against the Yankees in the World Series—the team that scored the most runs in baseball that season. The Giants used only four pitchers in the eight-game series, and all they did was post an impressive 2.54 ERA against the vaunted Yankees lineup. Art Nehf was only 1-2 in the series, but he had an impressive 1.38 ERA and he tossed a complete game four-hit shutout to win the title in the deciding eighth game.

356 Ross Youngs batted (.356) in 1924. A career high, he led the club and was third in the league. Youngs also hit a career high ten homers, surpassed the century mark in runs for a third consecutive year, and placed fifth in league MVP balloting.

357 Mike McCormick pitched (357) games for the Giants. The first Cy Young winner in franchise history made his big league debut as a 17-year-old lefty who was 49-4 playing American Legion ball in 1956. McCormick, who pitched four no-hitters and struck out 26 batters in one game while playing Legion ball, signed for a reported $60,000 and made his big league debut when he was still 17. In 1957, an 18-year-old McCormick became the youngest player in baseball's modern era to win three games.

358 Fred Lindstrom batted (.358) in 1928. Lindstrom led the league in hits but his team leading average was only third best in the league—although he did place second in league MVP balloting. Jim Bottomley, one of the more obscure members of the Hall of Fame, hit 31 home runs for St. Louis and won the MVP.

359 Randy Winn batted (.359) during 58 games with the Giants in 2005. He hit only .275 in 102 games with the Mariners, but after coming over to the Giants in a July 30 trade he caught fire. Just two weeks later, on August 15, Winn singled to lead off the game, homered to lead off the third, doubled in the fourth, and tripled to lead off the sixth—giving him the cycle in his first four at bats of the Giants 7-3 victory vs. Cincinnati.

360 The earned run average (3.60) for Noah Lowry during five consecutive starts beginning July 26, 2006. He pitched at least six innings four times, gave up two runs or less three times, and tossed nine innings of four-hit ball in one of his starts—but he was 0-1 with four no-decisions. On August 21, after a five-game drought, Lowry finally broke through for a W. He pitched a complete game shutout vs. Arizona, and then five days later he won again, pitching eight innings and giving up just one run vs. Cincinnati. His efforts earned him Bank of America co-National League Player of the Week honors, along with Miguel Cabrera of the Florida Marlins.

361 Rogers Hornsby batted (.361) in 1927. Frankie Frisch once said of Hornsby, "He's the only guy I know who could hit .350 in the dark." Hornsby only played one season for the Giants, but he was second in the league in hitting and he was third in MVP balloting.

362 Barry Bonds batted (.362) in 2004. Bonds won his second batting title and earned yet another spot in the franchise record. Bonds owns two of the top ten averages in franchise history (2002, 2004).

363 Warren Spahn won (363) career games. The lefty won his final three games with the San Francisco Giants. It was against Spahn that Willie Mays hit his first career home run. Spahn later said, "He was something like zero for twenty-one the first time I saw him. His first major league hit was a home run off me and I'll never forgive myself. We might have gotten rid of Willie forever if I'd only struck him out." The Hall of Fame legends were teammates on September 13, 1965, when Mays hit the 500th home run of his career.

364 The on-base percentage (.364) for Mike Tiernan in 1888. It was the first of five seasons with the club that Tiernan was among the league's top ten leaders for OBP, but he only got better from there. Tiernan posted a .452 OBP in 1896, setting a career high, and his .392 career OBP is among the top 100 in baseball history, and one of the top ten in franchise history.

365 The earned run average (3.65) for Matt Cain in 2007. That number was the best on the club and tenth best in the league, but unfortunately for Cain the Giants offensive struggles led him to a dismal 7-16 record in his sophomore campaign. He did lead the league with 12 wild pitches though ... okay, in all fairness, throw out the won-loss record and he really did have a great year. He led the club and was fifth in the league after giving up just 7.79 hits per nine innings, and he was also the team leader with 7.33 strikeouts per nine innings.

366 The number of total bases (366) for Willie Mays in 1957. He was second in the league with 82 extra-base hits, and he was second as well in total bases. Ernie Banks got a league best 83 extra-base hits, and Hank Aaron led the league with 369 total bases. It was Aaron who won league MVP honors.

367 Jack Doyle batted (.367) in 1894. The Irish-born first baseman was sometimes referred to as "Dirty Jack" because of the fights he frequently started, but he was a good player and an especially good hitter. Doyle led the club and set a career high with his 1894 average, one that remains among the top ten in franchise history. He was nowhere near a batting title however, as the league's top five hitters all batted .400 or better.

368 The slugging percentage (.368) for Red Murray in 1909. His first year with the Giants, it was the third consecutive season he hit seven home runs . . . and that was enough to give Murray (who hit 37 career homers) the league home run title.

369 Mike Tiernan batted (.369) in 1896. All 13 of his major league seasons were with the Giants, but 1896 was his best. The outfielder led the team with a career high average that was also the fifth best in the league, and that remains among the top ten in franchise history.

370 Barry Bonds batted (.370) in 2002. A career high, he won his first batting title and fifth MVP Award. That stretch of his career was so prolific that former teammate Matt Williams reportedly said, "He's the one guy in our league I would pay to watch."

371 Roger Connor batted (.371) in 1885. That was the first season that New York played as the Giants—the previous two seasons they were the Gothams. Connor's average in 1885 set a franchise record that lasted until 1929.

372 Bill Terry batted (.372) in 1929. It was good enough to set a new benchmark for the franchise, but it was only fourth best in the league. Terry got 226 hits, but that total was also fourth in the league.

373 Christy Mathewson won (373) career games—tied for third most in baseball history. He won a franchise record 372 games for the Giants. Mathewson became the manager of the Cincinnati Reds in 1916, and later that year he decided to pitch one final game. He won, giving him 373 for his career.

374 The slugging percentage (.374) for long-time manager Dusty Baker in 1984—his only season playing for the Giants. Baker batted .292 with three homers in limited play. He batted just 243 times in 100 games. Less than a decade later he returned as manager, guiding the club to 103 wins in 1993 during one of the most exciting division races in history.

375 The earned run average (3.75) for Livan Hernandez in 2000. That number led the club, as did his 17 wins, 240 innings, and 1.363 WHIP.

376 Barry Bonds got on base (376) times in 2004. It was the fifth time Bonds led the league in times on base, but his 2004 total also set a career high and a franchise record. Bonds came up three short of Babe Ruth's major league record 379 times on base, set in 1923.

377 The on-base percentage (.377) for Willie McCovey during 19 seasons with the Giants—one of the top 20 in franchise history. McCovey reached base at a .453 clip during his 1969 MVP campaign. A career high, it was the only time he led the league in OBP.

378 The on-base percentage (.378) for Darrell Evans in 1983. In his final of six seasons with the Giants, Evans led the club with the eighth highest OBP in the league. Since he also led the club in slugging, his .894 OPS was the best on the club as well. In fact, Evans was the offensive leader in runs, hits, total bases, doubles, homers, walks, and extra-base hits—all of which explains why he was able to sign a big free agent contract with Detroit in the offseason.

379 Fred Lindstrom batted (.379) in 1930. The Hall of Famer never won a batting title, despite posting terrific numbers, because of bad timing more than anything else. His career high mark in 1930 was only fifth in the league, but it was only the second best on the club behind teammate Bill Terry.

380 The ratio (3.80) of strikeouts per walk for Juan Marichal in 1969. One of the top 20 ratios in franchise history, Marichal led the league in this stat three consecutive seasons from 1966-68, and he was second in the league in 1969 when he struck out 205 batters, but walked only 54.

381 The on-base percentage (.381) for Brett Butler during three seasons batting leadoff for the Giants from 1988-90. He batted .293 and scored 317 runs in 471 games—hitting the century mark in runs all three years. He led the league with 109 runs in 1988, was fourth with 100 in 1989, and third with 108 in 1990.

382 The number of total bases (382) for Willie Mays in 1955. A career high total thanks to 51 homers, Mays reached that mark again in 1962 when he hit 49 homers. He led the league in home runs and total bases both seasons. Mays is the franchise leader for career total bases: 5,907.

383 George Burns stole (383) bases during 15 major league seasons. He spent 11 years in New York, stealing 334 bases for the Giants. His career total is among the top 100 in baseball history, and his total for the Giants is among the top ten in franchise history. John McGraw once called him "one of the most valuable players" to suit up for the franchise.

384 The earned run average (3.84) for Mike Krukow during seven seasons pitching for the Giants. He was 66-56, and was known primarily for a very effective 12-6 curveball that he used to strike out 802 batters in 1,154 innings before developing arm trouble.

385 Will Clark batted (.385) during six All-Star appearances. Clark was a five-time All-Star for the Giants and he was the starting first baseman for the N.L. from 1988-91. He also made one appearance as a member of the Texas Rangers. He batted 5 for 13 overall with one home run. His home run was a three-run blast that came in his final All-Star at bat as a member of the Giants.

386 The number (386) of the 1974 Topps Gary Matthews baseball card. The picture on the card shows Matthews, the reigning Rookie of the Year, sliding safely as third base coach John McNamara applauds.

387 The Giants scored (3.87) runs per game in 1918—not bad, considering the pitching staff gave up only 3.35 runs per game. The only problem was the Chicago Cubs. In 20 meetings the Giants scored only 2.95 runs per game vs. Chicago, but gave up 5.00 runs per game. New York was only 6-14 vs. Chicago and placed second in the pennant race, 10.5 games back of the Cubs.

388 Rich Aurilia got (388) extra-base hits for the Giants from 1995-2008. Aurilia batted .283 with 32 extra-base hits in 2008 (21 doubles, a triple, and ten homers), which moved him past an impressive list of names and into the top 20 in the franchise record book: Fred

Lindstrom, J.T. Snow, Ross Youngs, Whitey Lockman, George Davis, and George Burns.

389 The on-base percentage (.389) for Monte Irvin from 1949-55. He was the first African-American player for the New York Giants, and was once described by fellow Hall of Fame great Roy Campanella as, "The best all-around player I have ever seen." Irvin might have spent his best playing days in the Negro Leagues, but he still had plenty of game left when he joined the Giants. His OBP is among the top ten in franchise history.

390 Jack Clark got (390) extra-base hits during parts of ten seasons with the Giants. He led the league as a 22-year-old kid in his second full season with 79 extra-base hits in 1978, a career high. Clark made his first All-Star team and placed fifth in MVP balloting that season as well, and over the next six seasons he slugged his way to one of the top 25 totals in franchise history.

391 The slugging percentage (.391) for Randy Winn during 102 games with Seattle in 2005. Winn hit six homers for Seattle, but after being traded to San Francisco on July 30, Winn hit 14 homers in 58 games for a .680 slugging percentage with the Giants. Winn hit .447 in September on the strength of 51 hits (including 11 homers). No surprise, he earned National League Player of the Month honors. "I haven't thought about it," Winn said. "That's a lot of hits."

392 Jeff Kent received (392) points in the 2000 MVP balloting. That total easily gave Kent his only career MVP, but it also set the stage for Barry Bonds—who placed second behind Kent that year—to put the Giants in the record book as the only franchise in history that can boast five consecutive league MVP winners. Bonds followed Kent's 2000 campaign by winning the award from 2001-04.

393 The on-base percentage (.393) for George Davis during parts of ten seasons with the Giants. The Hall of Fame shortstop reached base at a .435 clip in 1894, a career high, and his career OBP with the Giants is among the top ten in franchise history.

394 Bud Black faced (394) batters in 1993. San Francisco was 11-5 during his 16 starts, and the resurgent 36-year-old veteran was 8-1 after beating Philadelphia on July 9. Unfortunately, after being sidelined for three weeks he lost to the Dodgers and then struggled against the Padres—and then he was lost for the rest of the season. Obviously that hurt the club, which held a ten-game lead in July but wound up losing the division by a single game (after losing eight straight in September).

395 The ratio (3.95) of strikeouts per walk for Juan Marichal in 1967. One of the top 15 ratios in franchise history, Marichal fanned 166 batters but gave up only 42 walks for the best ratio in the league that season.

396 Robby Thompson got (396) extra-base hits. The first round pick out of the University of Florida never made the league's top ten for extra-base hits (he made it for sacrifices, though—three times), but over the course of a steady 11-year career he banged out one of the top 20 totals in franchise history.

397 The on-base percentage (.397) for Brett Butler in 1990. The Giants leadoff man led the league with 192 hits during his final year with the club, and he was sixth in the league in OBP. Butler batted .309, scored 108 runs, and led the league in reaching base 288 times.

398 Ernie Lombardi got (398) hits during five seasons with the Giants. The Hall of Fame catcher was a world champion and MVP during his playing days with the Cincinnati Reds. Lombardi was still a fine player, however, in the final years of his career when he played with the Giants. He batted .307 with 19 homers in only 368 at bats in 1945, and was an All-Star for the second time since coming to New York. Lombardi was notoriously slow, but he could flat hit. Hall of Fame infielder Billy Herman once said of Lombardi, "He could hit a ball as hard as anybody I ever saw—and that includes Ruth and Foxx."

399 The career on-base percentage (.399) for Ross Youngs. The Hall of Fame outfielder was among the league's top ten leaders seven times. His career OBP is among the top 75 in baseball history, and it is the fifth highest in franchise history.

400 On August 23, 1998, Barry Bonds launched his (400th) career homer in a 10-5 victory vs. the Florida Marlins. Kirt Ojala was on the mound for Florida. It was an historic blast for Bonds, who with 438 career steals at the time became the first player in history to join the 400/400 club.

Barry Bonds—the first player in club history with two batting titles. (Courtesy National Baseball Hall of Fame Library, Cooperstown, NY)

"I was born to hit a baseball. I can hit a baseball."

— *Barry Bonds*

Chapter Five

The Batting Champions

IT HAS BEEN said many times that hitting a baseball is the hardest thing to do in all of sports. This very well may be true, but in reality there is no real way to compare the difficulty of the skill involved in one sport against that of another. And that's okay. The argument can be left unresolved for the next batch of enthusiasts, and us baseball fans of today will always know that if it isn't the most difficult, it's pretty darn close.

If we take it a step further though and say that getting a hit in a big league game is the hardest thing to do in all of sports, *then* we might really be on to something. After all, putting the bat on the ball against a major league pitcher would be challenging enough, but actually hitting it hard enough and in the right place so big league fielders can't get you out . . . now those are some pretty long odds for your average adult.

Then there are guys like Ted Williams.

The Boston Red Sox Hall of Famer made hitting major league pitchers look about as hard as teeing up a beach ball and taking a mighty whack with a tennis racket, with the only goal being to make contact. Williams was the last player to eclipse the .400 mark. He did so in 1941 when he collected 185 hits in 456 at bats. Teddy Ballgame was great no doubt, but there have been some great hitters in the National League too, and many of them were Giants.

The last player to bat .400 in the National League was Bill Terry, who batted .401 in 1930 by collecting a ridiculous 254 hits in 633 at bats.

It was a remarkable year for the lefty Memphis Bill, and with it came his only career batting title. He was actually the fourth Giant to lead the league in batting. Roger Conner was the first in 1885. Jack Glasscock did it in 1890, and then in 1915 Larry Doyle was tops in the N.L.

It wasn't until 1954 that a Giants player led the N.L. again. Willie Mays collected 195 hits in 565 at bats for a .345 average. Teammate Don Mueller finished just behind him with a .342 average and a league-leading 212 hits in 619 at bats.

In the first 71 years of franchise history, five players won batting titles. It took 48 years before a member of the Giants claimed another one.

Barry Bonds, who is the godson of Willie Mays, batted .370 in 2002 with 149 hits in 403 at bats to become the sixth player in franchise history to have a higher batting average than all other National Leaguers. In 2004, he did it again by batting .362, making him the only player in franchise history to win two batting titles.

Connor, Glasscock, Doyle, Terry, Mays, and Bonds—talk about an elite group! There are only six members of that club, and these guys, among others, make it hard for us fans to win the argument about the difficulty of hitting a baseball. Everyone sees them do it with a certain grace, and this apparent ease tricks fans of other sports into thinking it can't be all that hard.

Of course we always have the numbers.

Ted Williams is the only player since 1930 to bat higher than Bill Terry's .401 average—and he didn't beat it by much. When we consider that the greatest hitters in the game's history barely got 40 hits per 100 at bats in the *absolute best seasons on record*, we really don't need to argue the point.

Besides, baseball is not really meant to be compared with other sports. It has its own unique rhythm. One that the hitting greats are able to slip into in a way that we can only imagine, and this melding of rhythm and skill is just one of the many reasons we love this game.

401 Bill Terry batted (.401) in 1930. The legendary Hall of Famer set the franchise record and won the only batting title of his career, and it was the last time in the 20th century that a N.L. player hit .400 in a season. "To hit .400," Terry reflected, "you need a great start and you can't have a slump. The year I did it . . . I was really hitting the ball on the nose."

402 The on-base percentage (.402) for Roger Connor during parts of ten seasons with the club from 1883-94. He led the league once, in 1885 when he posted a .435 OBP. Connor was among the league's top ten leaders 12 times during his career, including eight times with the Giants, and his OBP with the club is the fourth highest in franchise history.

403 The on-base percentage (.403) for Roger Bresnahan from 1902-08. Six times during that stretch the Hall of Fame catcher was among the league's top ten leaders, and his career OBP with the Giants is the third highest in franchise history.

404 The on-base percentage (.404) for Ellis Burks during parts of three seasons with the Giants. The outfielder was traded to the Giants by Colorado on July 31, 1998, and from that point through the 2000 season, Burks reached base at a clip that was .041 higher than his career average. Burks batted .344 in 2000, tying his career high, and he set a career high with a .419 on-base percentage.

405 The earned run average (4.05) for Mike Caldwell during three seasons with the Giants. The lefty was 14-5 in 1974, giving him the third best winning percentage in the league (.737), and his 2.95 ERA was also among the league's top ten leaders. The next two seasons, however, his ERA skyrocketed (4.79, 4.86) and he was a combined 8-20. The Giants traded Caldwell to St. Louis in 1976. St. Louis traded him to Cincinnati in 1977. And Cincinnati traded him to Milwaukee three months later—where he was 22-9 and placed second in Cy Young balloting in 1978.

406 Dave Bergman batted (406) times during parts of three seasons with the Giants. He was one of the best utility guys in the game for a decade and a half, and he enjoyed three productive seasons in San Francisco: a .271 average, 13 homers, 54 runs, and 51 RBI in limited play—not bad at all. Bergman was traded in 1984. Good timing on his part, he landed in Detroit and won the 1984 World Series.

407 Red Murray scored (407) runs during parts of eight seasons with the Giants. His total is among the 60 highest in franchise history, and he scored seven more during three consecutive trips to the World Series from 1911-13.

408 The slugging percentage (.408) for Fred Lewis during 58 games in 2007. His best game was on Mother's Day, just four days after getting called up from Triple-A Fresno. Lewis was 5 for 6 with a double, triple, a three-run homer, and four RBI. Lewis was the first player to hit for the cycle on Mother's Day since Mark Grace did it for the Cubs in 1993, and he was also the first player in nearly 90 years to hit his first major league triple and his first major league homer during a game in which he hit for the cycle. Lewis said later, "I didn't wake up thinking I'd have a game like this. I never would have thought I'd have a day like today. I'm just glad to get into the lineup."

409 Dave Kingman played (409) games during parts of four seasons with San Francisco. The Giants drafted the powerful slugger out of USC in 1970, and by midseason 1971 he was in the starting lineup. Kong, as he was sometimes called, hit six homers in 41 games as a 22-year-old rookie. He hit 29, 24, and 18 homers from 1972-74 before he was sold to the New York Mets. Kingman hit 442 career home runs, but was only 37 when he played his final game.

410 The slugging percentage (.410) for Rich Aurilia in 2003. He hit only 13 homers, a far cry from the 37 he hit two years earlier. Aurilia, however, had no problems hitting the ball coming back from the All-Star break. He was 8 for 14 with two doubles, a triple, four runs, and seven RBI in four games that week. Aurilia's average went from .256 to .270 and his slugging percentage went from .402 to .421. And for his efforts he was named the Bank of America National League Player of the Week.

411 The number of total bases (411) for Barry Bonds in 2001. His total set a career high and a franchise record—but his total was only third best in the league, despite 73 home runs and 107 extra-base hits. Sammy Sosa led the league with 425 total bases for the Cubs, and Luis Gonzalez was second with 419 total bases for the Diamondbacks. It was Bonds, however, who won his fourth MVP Award—with Sosa and Gonzalez placing second and third respectively in the balloting.

412 Casey Stengel batted (.412) vs. the New York Yankees during World Series play. The legendary manager, who is in the Hall of Fame because of the ten pennants and seven world championships he won with the Yankees, played for the New York Giants in the 1922 World Series and the 1923 World Series against the Yankees. He was 7 for 17 with two homers, three runs, and four RBI—and his first world championship came *at the expense* of the Yankees.

413 Stan Javier got (413) hits during parts of four seasons with the Giants. His most productive season was 1997, when he got 126 hits, batted .286, and stole 25 bases. Javier was on the Oakland club that beat San Francisco in the 1989 World Series, and in 1997 he did his part to try and get a title for the Giants as well. He batted .417 in the Division Series vs. Florida, but the Giants got swept anyway.

414 The career on-base percentage (.414) for Mel Ott. The Hall of Famer was among the league's top ten leaders 16 times. His career OBP is among the top 30 in baseball history, and it is the second highest in franchise history.

415 The earned run average (4.15) for Noah Lowry during 17 starts for the Fresno Grizzlies in the Pacific Coast League in 2004. Lowry was 7-5 with 73 strikeouts in 89 innings, earning his way back to the big club in June where his numbers were even more impressive. Lowry was 6-0 with a 3.82 ERA as a rookie, striking out 72 batters in 92 innings. On August 3, Lowry pitched his first big league shutout, a three-hitter with nine strikeouts vs. Cincinnati. Five days later he beat the Cubs, and for the week he was 2-0 with a 1.10 ERA, 15 strikeouts, and only two earned runs. Lowry earned Bank of America National League Player of the Week honors, which came with a Tourneau luxury Swiss timepiece from the Tourneau Safari collection.

416 Bobby Bonds got (416) extra-base hits during seven seasons with the Giants—one of the top 20 totals in franchise history. Bonds was among the league's top ten leaders seven times in his career—not bad for a guy who performed better batting leadoff—including five consecutive seasons from 1969-73.

417 Walter Johnson won (417) career games—the second most in baseball history. He was a 36-year-old veteran and the A.L. Most Valuable Player in 1924, having surpassed 20 wins that season for the 11th time in his career with the Washington Senators. None of that mattered a bit to 18-year-old rookie third baseman Fred Lindstrom, who became the youngest player in World Series history and figured, while he was at it, he ought to make the most of it. Lindstrom was 4 for 5 with two RBI vs. Johnson in Game 5 as the Giants moved to within one win of clinching the series. Lindstrom hit .333 for the series, but unfortunately, the Senators rallied and won the final two games, taking the clincher in extra-innings.

418 The number of RBI (418) for Chili Davis during six full seasons with the Giants. His best season total was 81, in 1984, the same year he made his first All-Star team. Davis' career total for the club is among the top 50 in franchise history.

419 Frankie Frisch stole (419) career bases. He stole 224 of those bases in eight seasons with New York, and was the team leader seven consecutive seasons from 1920-26 before being traded to St. Louis for fellow-Hall of Famer Rogers Hornsby.

420 The on-base percentage (.420) for Willie McCovey in 1973. He batted just .266 but he was fourth in the league with 105 walks, and third in OBP. It was the sixth and final time that his OBP was among the league's top five leaders.

421 The slugging percentage (.421) for Lance Niekro from 2003-07. The son of Joe Niekro and nephew of Hall of Famer Phil Niekro, the Giants selected him in the second round of the 2000 amateur draft. Niekro batted .246 with 17 homers, playing a total of 195 games.

Niekro batted .307 with 49 homers during 451 minor league games from 2000-08.

422 The slugging percentage (.422) for Chili Davis during 874 games with the Giants. He batted .267 with 101 homers and 418 RBI, and his slugging percentage is one of the top 50 in franchise history.

423 The on-base percentage (.423) for Mel Ott in 1944. He batted .288 and drew 90 walks, giving him the fourth highest OBP in the league. It was a big comeback year for the 35-year-old veteran. Ott batted just .234 the previous season—of course even then, he was so good at getting on base that his OBP was .391, sixth best in the league.

424 The on-base percentage (.424) for Jeff Kent in 2000. A career high and sixth best in the league, it is one of the top 50 season efforts in franchise history.

425 The on-base percentage (.425) for Willie Mays in 1971—his last complete season with the Giants. Mays batted .271 but led the league in OBP for the second time in his career because he also walked a league high 112 times. Mays played 19 games for the Giants in 1972 before he was traded to the Mets.

426 Amos Rusie pitched (426) games during eight seasons with the Giants from 1890-98 (he missed the 1896 season). Rusie completed an astounding 372 of 403 starts—the third highest total in franchise history. The *New York Herald* once said of the Hall of Famer known as The Hoosier Thunderbolt, "The Giants without Rusie would be like Hamlet without the Melancholy Dane." Translation: Rusie made the Giants a better team.

427 The length in hours and minutes (4:27) of the longest nine inning game in franchise history. On October 5, 2001, Barry Bonds hit his 71st and 72nd homers of the season, but the Giants lost to the Dodgers, 11-10. The teams combined to throw 361 pitches using 12 different pitchers.

428 Mike Tiernan stole (428) career bases. One of the top 75 totals in baseball history, it is also a franchise record.

429 The career winning percentage (.429) for journeyman pitcher Ed Crane. He was 72-96 during parts of eight seasons with seven different clubs, including two stints with the Giants. On September

27, 1888, however, it was Crane who tossed the first no-hitter in franchise history. The 3-0 victory vs. Washington was the highlight of his career, at least until he went 4-1 during the 1889 World Series vs. the Brooklyn Bridegrooms. One of two pre-modern era series won by the franchise, Crane also was 5 for 18 at the plate with a double, triple, and a home run.

430 Rube Marquard walked (430) batters during 239 games pitched for the Giants. His total is one of the 35 highest in franchise history, and while that might sound like a bad thing, he also pitched 1,546 innings—one of the 25 highest totals in franchise history. The math works out to a fairly tidy 2.50 walks per nine innings.

431 Carl Hubbell started (431) games for the Giants. It is the third highest total in franchise history and one of the top 100 in baseball history.

432 Chili Davis scored (432) runs for the Giants from 1981-87. A switch-hitting outfielder with power, Davis was a two-time All-Star in San Francisco, and he scored one of the top 50 runs totals in franchise history.

433 Christy Mathewson pitched a franchise record (433) complete games for the Giants. He led the league twice, in 1908 and 1910, and was among the league's top ten leaders 13 times. Six times he completed at least 30 games in a season.

434 Joe McGinnity pitched (434) innings in 1903. It was the third of four consecutive seasons that he led the league in innings—and he earned the nickname Iron Man for his exploits. It originally was given to him because of his offseason job working in an iron foundry, but he later earned it on the mound with a reputation for pitching both ends of doubleheaders—a feat he did three times during a single month in 1903, and he won all six games.

435 The number of RBI (435) for Jeffrey Leonard during eight seasons with the Giants. His best total was 1983 when he hit 21 homers with 87 RBI. He came right back in 1984 with 21 homers and 86 RBI. He was the team's leading RBI man both seasons.

436 The earned run average (4.36) for Noah Lowry after the southpaw beat Houston 5-2 on August 6, 2005. He came into that game with a 4.59 ERA, but tossed seven shutout innings, giving up one hit and striking out eight for the win. Lowry reeled off five straight victories in August, giving up only 22 hits and three earned runs in 39-plus innings, while striking out 33 and lowering his ERA to 3.68. He was the overwhelming choice for National League Pitcher of the Month honors. "It comes down to consistency and being able to do it inning after inning," Lowry said. "Things are coming together, and I hope to build off it."

437 The on-base percentage (.437) for Johnny Mize in 1946. The Hall of Fame first baseman hit .337 and his OBP was the highest of his five seasons with the Giants. Mize is among the top 75 in baseball history for career OBP. He reached base at a .389 clip during his time with the Giants—one of the ten highest marks in franchise history.

438 The slugging percentage (.438) for J.T. Snow during 1,183 games with the Giants. Snow collected 1,043 hits for San Francisco, and of those, 228 went for two bases, he legged out 15 triples, and he went yard 124 times. His slugging percentage ranks among the top 40 in franchise history.

439 Danny Richardson scored (439) runs during 696 games with the Giants. Richardson was a middle infielder for New York from 1884-91, and his runs total is among the 50 highest in franchise history. He scored a career high 102 runs in 1890. Richardson also scored 14 runs during two pre-modern World Series, winning both, in 1888 and 1889.

440 The winning percentage (.440) for the Giants vs. Brooklyn in 1951. The club was only 11-14 against the hated Dodgers, but after posting a 54-23 record in the second half of the season the Giants rallied from a 13-game deficit to force a three-game playoff against Brooklyn with the pennant on the line. New York took the first game 3-1, but the second game was all Brooklyn, 10-0. The third game made Bobby Thomson immortal, and his dramatic walk-off home run gave the Giants a 5-4 victory and the pennant.

441 Marvin Bernard scored (441) runs for the Giants. Bernard was selected by the Giants in the 50th round of the 1992 amateur draft. One of the last players chosen, nearly 1,400 guys were drafted ahead of him. Three years later he made his big league debut—and he went on to a nice career, scoring one of the top 50 runs totals in franchise history.

442 The on-base percentage (.442) for Mel Ott in 1938. Ott batted .311 with 36 homers and he led the league in OBP for the third time. He led the league again in 1939.

443 Mike Tiernan batted (443) times in 1888. He hit .293 with 33 extra-base hits, including eight triples, one of which came vs. Philadelphia on August 25, allowing Tiernan to become the first player in franchise history to hit for the cycle.

444 The winning percentage (.444) for the Giants in 2008. The club struggled to a 72-90 record, but no one could blame Tim Lincecum. The Cy Young hurler was 18-5, making him only the fourth pitcher in major league history to post a record at least 13 games above .500 for a club that was at least 13 games below .500.

445 The slugging percentage (.445) for catcher Bengie Molina in 2008. He led the club in slugging, homers (16), and RBI (95). Molina's last homer of the season was a bizarre one to say the least—it hit the green roof above the right field façade at AT&T Park and bounced back into play. Molina stopped at first, as the umpires ruled it was not a home run. Manager Bruce Bochy argued, and after using instant replay the umpires reversed their earlier call and signaled it was a home run—the only problem is that by that time Molina had already been lifted by pinch-runner Emmanuel Burriss. The rules are very clear on this—once you leave for a pinch-runner you cannot reenter the game. So . . . Molina hit the homer, but Burriss got to run the bases.

446 The slugging percentage (.446) for Hank Leiber during seven seasons with the Giants. One of the top 35 in franchise history, his best season in New York was 1935 when he belted 22 homers for a .512 slugging percentage. His career highs were 24 homers and a .556 slugging percentage for the Chicago Cubs in 1939.

447 Irish Meusel scored (447) runs during six seasons with the Giants. He hit the century mark in consecutive seasons in 1922-23, and he scored another ten runs in the World Series from 1921-23.

448 The on-base percentage (.448) for Hall of Famer Rogers Hornsby in 1927. He led the league in OBP and was second in batting with a .361 average. In his only season with the Giants, Hornsby recorded one of the top 20 on-base percentages in franchise history.

449 Roger Connor got (449) extra-base hits during parts of ten seasons with the Giants. Connor led the league three times: once with the Troy Trojans in 1882, once with the Giants in 1889, and once with the Philadelphia Phillies in 1892. Baseball's original home run champion powered his way to 812 extra-base hits during 18 seasons, and his total for the Giants ranks among the top 15 in franchise history.

450 The earned run average (4.50) for Charlie Faust in 1911. He claimed a fortuneteller predicted a pennant for the Giants . . . if only manager John McGraw would let him pitch. Faust, better known as Victory, was allowed by the superstitious McGraw to become the team mascot. The Giants won 40 of 53 games thereafter, moved from 3.5 down to first place, and won the pennant by 7.5 games. Faust got to pitch twice after the games were rendered meaningless: two innings, two hits, one earned run, and no decisions. The Giants lost the World Series—apparently Victory Faust and the fortuneteller had nothing to say about that—and he went back to being the team mascot. Faust died in an insane asylum two years later.

451 Matt Williams got (451) extra-base hits during ten seasons with the Giants. He won his first Silver Slugger Award in 1990 after collecting 62 extra-base hits, the eighth highest total in the league. Williams was among the league's top ten leaders four times in five seasons from 1990-94, and his overall total for the Giants ranks among the top 15 in franchise history.

452 The on-base percentage (.452) for Bill Terry in 1930. He drew only 57 walks, but hit .401 to achieve a career high OBP. The Hall of Fame first baseman posted a .393 OBP for the Giants from 1923-36, a mark that ranks among the top 100 in baseball history and the top ten in franchise history.

453 Rich Aurilia made (453) outs in 2001. Sound like a lot? Not really—the Giants All-Star shortstop was second in the league with 636 at bats, first with 206 hits, and sixth with 364 total bases. He also launched 37 big flies while reaching base at a healthy .369 clip. Not bad at all. Aurilia, Jeff Kent, and Barry Bonds gave the Giants three Silver Sluggers in 2001.

454 The on-base percentage (.454) for Barry Bonds in 2006. He led the league, despite reaching base at his lowest clip since 2000.

455 The career winning percentage (.455) for Ed Halicki. He was only 55-66 in seven seasons, all but four decisions coming with the Giants. Halicki was a towering presence on the mound, literally—he was 6' 7". His best year was 1977, when he led the club with a 16-12 record, a 3.32 earned run average, and logged nearly 260 innings.

456 John Montefusco gave up (456) earned runs during 185 games pitched for the Giants. The Count logged more than 1,180 innings for San Francisco for a 3.47 earned run average—one of the 50 best in franchise history. His best season in terms of allowing earned runs was his 1976 sophomore campaign. After winning top rookie honors in 1975, he made his only career All-Star team in 1976 with 16 wins and only 80 earned runs in 253-plus innings—good for a team best 2.84 ERA.

457 The slugging percentage (.457) for Hank Thompson during 906 games with the Giants. He batted .267 with 103 doubles, 33 triples, and 129 homers, giving him one of the top 30 slugging percentages in franchise history.

458 The on-base percentage (.458) for Mel Ott in 1930. Ott hit .349 and set a franchise record for OBP that stood for 20 years. It was also the first of four seasons that he led the league in OBP.

459 Larry Doyle got (459) extra-base hits during 13 seasons with the Giants. The second baseman won a batting title and an MVP, and placed among the league's top ten leaders for extra-base hits six times. His overall total for the Giants ranks among the top 15 in franchise history.

460 The on-base percentage (.460) for All-Star second baseman Eddie Stanky in 1950. It was the second time he led the league in OBP, and it set a franchise record that lasted nearly half a century. Stanky batted .300, led the league with 144 walks, and placed third in MVP balloting. It remains the highest non-Bonds OBP in franchise history.

461 The on-base percentage (.461) for Barry Bonds in 1996. It is the sixth highest OBP in franchise history—Bonds owns all of the top six—but at the time it was a new benchmark for the club. It also happens to be the only one of those top six that did not lead the league. Gary Sheffield led the league with a .465 OBP for the Florida Marlins in 1996.

462 The earned run average (4.62) for Brian Wilson in 2008. The Giants closer gave up 32 earned runs in 62-plus innings, a fairly high number—but he also saved 41 games, third best in the league. Wilson made his first All-Star team, as did Tim Lincecum, the Giants only representatives at Yankee Stadium for the mid-Summer Classic.

463 The winning percentage (.463) for the Giants in 2005. The number that hurts the most: seven games out of first, despite playing 12 games under .500. San Diego won the division with 82 victories—and the Giants record vs. San Diego was 6-12.

464 The slugging percentage (.464) for Bob Brenly in 1984. The catcher set career highs in numerous categories: average (.291), hits (147), doubles (28), homers (20), RBI (80), runs (74), on-base percentage (.352), and total bases (235). He also cracked the league's top ten for slugging—and for his efforts he made his only career All-Star team.

465 The slugging percentage (.465) for rookie catcher Eliezer Alfonzo in 2006. He hit 12 home runs in 87 games—including one on June 3, in his first big league game. The two-run shot against Orlando Hernandez put the Giants ahead to stay in a 6-4 win vs. the Mets. The last Giants player prior to Alfonzo to homer during his first big league game was Randy Kutcher on June 19, 1986. Other Giants to perform that memorable feat include: Will Clark, Bobby Bonds, Orlando Cepeda, and pitcher John Montefusco.

466 The slugging percentage (.466) for Felipe Alou during 719 games with the Giants. He batted .286 with 119 doubles, 19 triples, and 85 homers, good for one of the top 25 slugging percentages in franchise history. His best season effort for the Giants was 1962, when he belted 25 homers for a .513 slugging percentage. Alou's career high was in 1966, when he hit 31 homers for a .533 slugging percentage for the Atlanta Braves.

467 The slugging percentage (.467) for Bob Brenly in 1987. Three years after setting career highs in nearly everything else, Brenly capped off a four-year stretch that saw him blast 20, 19, 16 and 18 home runs by posting a career high slugging percentage.

468 The slugging percentage (.468) for Marquis Grissom in 2003. The veteran outfielder batted .300 with 20 homers as the Giants ran away with the N.L. West. Things were going so well for the Giants that Grissom batted .318 with four homers and 15 RBI in July and was nominated for the N.L. Player of the Month . . . but lost top honors to his teammate, Barry Bonds, who was in the midst of a 45-game stretch in which he batted .360 with 19 dingers.

469 Willie McCovey hit (469) home runs for the Giants—the fourth highest total in franchise history. Mac won three home run titles: 1963 (44), 1968 (36), and 1969 (45). He was among the league's top four leaders seven times from 1963-70.

470 The slugging percentage (.470) for Reggie Smith in 1982. It was the only season in San Francisco for the 37-year-old veteran. He did well, batting .284 with 18 homers in only 349 at bats. He parlayed that success into a huge contract with the Giants—the Yomiuri Giants, that is. Smith took his powerful bat to Japan in 1983 for a reported $1,000,000 and three cars.

471 Barry Bonds batted (.471) during the 2002 World Series. In nine postseason series' the only time Bonds batted above .300 was vs. Anaheim in the 2002 Fall Classic—and in that series he was a one-man wrecking crew. Bonds was 8 for 17 with two doubles, four home runs, six RBI, eight runs, and 13 walks. The Giants had a 5-0 lead in Game 6 and needed just nine outs to clinch the series, but it wasn't to be—and Bonds never got another shot to play for a ring.

472 The winning percentage (.472) for the Giants in 2006. Felipe Alou led the club to 76 wins, but lost 85—this after 87 losses the previous season. Alou took over for Dusty Baker in 2003 and claimed the division title with 100 wins, but a second place finish followed in 2004, and after back-to-back third place finishes in 2005-06, Alou was out, Bruce Bochy was in.

473 Johnny Mize scored (473) runs during five seasons with the Giants—including a career high 137 in 1947, best in the league. Mize was third in the league with 110 runs in 1948, and his overall total for the Giants is among the top 50 in franchise history.

474 Orlando Cepeda got (474) extra-base hits during parts of nine seasons with the Giants—one of the ten highest totals in franchise history. Cepeda was among the league's top ten leaders for extra-base hits nine times throughout his career, smashing 823 for one of the top 100 totals in baseball history.

475 The slugging percentage (.475) for Mark Carreon during four seasons with the Giants. Carreon was an outfielder originally drafted by the Mets, but he played a valuable role for the Giants during the epic battle vs. Atlanta for the 1993 division title. He batted .327 with seven homers and 33 RBI in a part-time role, only 150 at bats in 78 games. Two seasons later he was getting a lot of playing time, and he batted .301 with a career high 17 homers and 65 RBI in 396 at bats.

476 Barry Bonds batted (476) times in 2001. His stats: a .328 average, 73 homers, 137 RBI, .515 on-base percentage, and a .863 slugging percentage. Bonds won his first career Hank Aaron Award that season. The Hank Aaron Award was established in 1999 to honor the 25th anniversary of Hank Aaron surpassing Babe Ruth's all-time home run record, and it is given annually to the "best overall offensive performer" in both leagues.

477 The on-base percentage (.477) for Barry Bonds during 15 seasons with the Giants. He led the league in OBP eight times during that stretch and he also recorded eight of the top ten on-base percentages in franchise history. His career OBP with the club is, obviously, a franchise record.

478 The slugging percentage (.478) for Larry Herndon in 1983. The Detroit Tigers outfielder hit .302 with 20 homers and 92 RBI, proving his 1982 season (.292, 23 homers, 88 RBI, .480 slugging percentage) was no fluke. Prior to 1982, Herndon played six seasons with the Giants, during which time he batted .267 with 24 homers and 186 RBI—*in 682 games!*

479 Mark Davis struck out (479) batters during 230 games with the Giants. He was primarily a reliever, making just 61 starts in five seasons. Davis was only 25-45 with 11 saves for the Giants, thanks to back-to-back campaigns in which he was 5-17 and 5-12 in 1984-85. He did strike out a career high 131 batters in 1985, but by midseason 1987 he was traded to the San Diego Padres . . . and then two years later he was the N.L. Cy Young winner with 44 saves, a 1.85 earned run average, and 92 Ks in 92-plus innings. For what it's worth, the MVP that season was Kevin Mitchell—one of the guys the Giants got from the Padres in the Davis deal.

480 The on-base percentage (.480) for Barry Bonds in 2007. Bonds hit only .276, but he was still feared a great deal as evidenced by his 132 walks—including a league high 43 that were intentional. The result was a sixth consecutive season in which Bonds led the league in OBP.

481 The slugging percentage (.481) for 18-year-old rookie Whitey Lockman in 1945. He hit a home run in his first big league at bat on July 5, and batted .341 with three homers during 32 games overall. He missed all of 1946, however, serving in the military, and then he missed 1947 with a broken ankle. Lockman finally got on track with a full season in 1948, and he stayed in baseball in some capacity—player, manager, coach, front office executive—through 2001, spending nearly 60 years in the game.

482 Hank Thompson scored (482) runs during eight seasons with the Giants. He scored a career high 82 runs in 1950, but the highpoint of his career would have to be batting .364 with six runs during a four-game sweep of the Cleveland Indians in the 1954 World Series.

483 It was (483) feet to dead center field at the Polo Grounds, the Giants home field from 1911-57. The Giants won 13 pennants and four World Series titles during that stretch—including 1954, when Willie Mays made "The Catch."

484 The slugging percentage (.484) for Bobby Thomson during 1,135 games with the Giants. One of the top 15 in franchise history, Thomson batted .277 with 192 doubles, 56 triples, and 189 homers. His best season effort was 1951, when he belted 32 homers for a .562 slugging percentage that was fourth in the league.

485 The slugging percentage (.485) for Frankie Frisch in 1923. New York's second sacker was phenomenal: 223 hits, .348 average, 116 runs, 12 homers, and 111 RBI. He was the team leader in slugging, and contributed significantly to the Giants third consecutive pennant.

486 The winning percentage (.486) for Leo Durocher as manager of the Brooklyn Dodgers in 1948. Horace Stoneham, the Giants owner, did the unthinkable and in midseason hired Durocher away from the hated Dodgers and made him New York's new manager, replacing franchise icon Mel Ott. Durocher was 35-37 for Brooklyn, and a marginally better 41-38 for New York. He began rebuilding the team, however, and by 1951 the Giants were N.L. champs once again.

487 The winning percentage (.487) for the Giants during the second half of 1978. It was a disappointing season because the club was 52-34 at the break, a .605 winning percentage. After spending much of the season (80 days) in first place the club lost the lead for good on August 16, lost seven straight in September to fall out of contention, and was only 37-39 after the break. It wasn't as dramatic as Boston's collapse in the American League that same season, but it was still painful—especially since it was the Dodgers that overtook the club on August 16, and that went on to win the pennant.

488 Mel Ott hit (488) career doubles. This one is an oddity—the guy was perennially among the league leaders in home runs, but only once did he crack the top ten leaders for doubles: in 1933, when he was sixth in the league with 36. His career high was 37. Despite not showing up on the season leader boards, Ott ranks among the top 75 in baseball history for career doubles.

489 Wes Westrum walked (489) times during parts of 11 seasons with the Giants. His career high was 104 in 1951, which was impressive because he was a catcher and played fewer games than most of his teammates. His career total is one of the 20 highest in franchise history, and that's interesting because Barry Bonds, the franchise leader with 1,947 walks, drew *755 free passes* from 2001-04. In that four-year stretch alone, Bonds drew enough walks to rank fifth in the franchise record book.

490 Red Ames gave up (490) earned runs during 282 games pitched for the Giants. He was on the mound for more than 1,800 innings for an impressive 2.45 earned run average—one of the absolute best in franchise history. In a career that spanned 17 seasons and included stops in Cincinnati, St. Louis, and Philly, Ames posted a 2.63 ERA that remains one of the top 75 in baseball history.

491 The winning percentage (.491) for Bob Knepper during 161 games pitched for the Giants. He was only 53-55, but with a respectable 3.71 earned run average. He won 17 games in 1978, but after consecutive losing seasons in 1979-80 he was traded to the Astros. After struggling for a couple of seasons in Houston, Knepper found his game and won 15 or more three consecutive seasons from 1984-86. He later returned to the Giants for the final few games of his career in 1989-90.

492 Mickey Welch pitched (492) innings in 1885. The Hall of Famer completed all 55 starts, and for good measure he also made a relief appearance. Welch was 44-11 and set a franchise record for wins, one that also ties him with Bill Hutchison for the 15th best season effort in baseball history—all of which occurred before the modern era. Jack Chesbro won 41 games for the New York Highlanders (Yankees) in 1904, and he remains the only 40-game winner in the post-1900 modern era.

493 Dick Dietz batted (493) times in 1970. After four seasons as the club's second string catcher, Dietz played fulltime in 1970 and responded with career best numbers: a .300 average, 82 runs, 22 homers, 107 RBI, a .426 on-base percentage, and a .515 slugging percentage. And to cap things off, he hit a ninth inning home run against Catfish Hunter in the 1970 All-Star Game.

494 The slugging percentage (.494) for Ed Bailey in 1963. The catcher was an All-Star for the fifth and final time that year, belting 21 homers in only 308 at bats. Bailey was with the club for the 1962 World Series vs. the New York Yankees. He was only 1 for 14 in that series, but his lone hit was a homer at Yankee Stadium.

495 Lindy McDaniel faced (495) batters out of the bullpen in 1966. In 64 games he pitched 121-plus innings. A solid pitcher for two decades in the majors, McDaniel was 10-5 with six saves and a 2.66 earned run average in 1966, his first season with the Giants. His stellar work from the pen was a big reason the Giants won 93 games. He was 1-0 against LA, and he was 2-0 during the final week of the season as the Giants won six straight and made one last push for the pennant—but unfortunately the club came up 1.5 games back of the Dodgers.

496 Darren Lewis played (496) games during five seasons with the Giants. He was a speedster outfielder who batted only .249, but stole 138 bases. Lewis was the Giants starting center fielder for four seasons—including Barry Bonds' first three seasons in the Giants outfield—until he was traded to the Cincinnati Reds in 1995 in a deal that brought Deion Sanders to San Francisco.

497 Glenallen Hill batted (497) times in 1995. His first season with the Giants, Hill blasted 24 homers in only 132 games. He hit 19 homers in only 98 games in 1996, but his production fell to just 11 bombs in 128 games in 1997, his last year with the club. Hill was a powerful guy who hit 186 homers in 13 big league seasons—but his 132 games in 1995 was a career high, and he played more than 100 games in a season only five times.

498 The slugging percentage (.498) for Matt Williams during ten seasons with the Giants—one of the top 15 in franchise history. Williams hit 43 home runs for a career high in only 112 games during the strike-shortened 1994 season, and he hit 23 home runs in only 76 games in 1995 for a career best .647 slugging percentage. He was a three-time Silver Slugger recipient with the club.

499 The Giants averaged a league best (4.99) runs per game in 1961—and the offense was second in the league with 183 home runs, thanks to the 46 hit by Orlando Cepeda. Juan Marichal was a rising star in his second year, and those two powerful forces combined to punish the Cincinnati Reds on August 23 in a particularly brutal fashion. The Giants carried a 2-0 lead into the top of the ninth when the offense exploded for 12 runs on 11 hits and five homers, giving Marichal & Co. a 14-0 shutout. The Reds, however, did go on to win the pennant.

500 The Giants are the only franchise in baseball with three members of its very own (500) home run club. Willie Mays (646), Barry Bonds (586), and Mel Ott (511) all hit more than 500 home runs while playing for the Giants. Babe Ruth (659) and Mickey Mantle (536) belong to the same club for the New York Yankees, as do Sammy Sosa (515) and Ernie Banks (512) for the Chicago Cubs.

Will Clark—The Natural.
(Courtesy National Baseball Hall of Fame Library, Cooperstown, NY)

"It was almost like, just call the thing. A lot of things are happening here that are more important than baseball. We had inter-squad games and did what we could to keep ourselves going, but the earthquake obviously put a damper on the World Series."

— Robby Thompson

Chapter Six

The Bay Bridge Series

A MEMBER OF the Giants claimed Most Valuable Player honors 14 times from 1911-2008. Barry Bonds skewed this number significantly by first winning the award in 1993 and then taking it four straight seasons from 2001-04.

Carl Hubbell and Willie Mays are the only other Giants to be named MVP more than once. Hubbell received the honor in 1933 and 1936, Mays in 1954 and 1965. The franchise also boasts five one-time MVP recipients: Larry Doyle (1912), Bill Terry (1930), Willie McCovey (1969), Kevin Mitchell (1989), and Jeff Kent (2000).

The 1989 season was a franchise-first in the MVP department. Kevin Mitchell won the award, but his teammate Will Clark was the runner-up. Opposing pitchers surely had sleepless nights thinking about facing Clark and Mitchell back-to-back, and for good reason. Clark batted .333 with 23 homers, and Mitchell checked in at .291 with a league-leading 47 jacks. They got off to a fast start too. On April 3, opening day at San Diego, Clark was 2 for 4 with a triple, and Mitchell was 2 for 5 with a home run. The very next day Clark was 3 for 5 with a double and a home run, and Mitchell was 3 for 5 with a home run. The Giants won both games.

The fast start was a sign of things to come and the duo continued their dominance right into the League Championship Series vs. the Chicago Cubs. The Giants won the pennant for the first time in nearly three decades. Mitchell was 6 for 17 with two blasts and seven RBI. The series MVP was Clark, who was an obscene 13 for 20 with two doubles, a triple, and two home runs, one of which was a grand slam.

The victory for San Francisco set the stage for the Bay Bridge Series, a showdown with the American League champion Oakland A's. It was the first all-Bay Area World Series in history.

The Giants big bats made the trip to Oakland for Game 1, but Dave Stewart pitched brilliantly for Oakland. Stewart tossed a five-hit shutout against the Giants high-powered offense and the A's seized the early momentum. Mike Moore took the mound for Oakland in

Game 2, and he held the Giants offense in check as well, this time a 5-1 setback.

The year-long hitting prowess of Mitchell and Clark gave fans plenty of reason to be optimistic, however, as the series shifted to Candlestick for Game 3.

It was October 17, and the fans pouring into the stadium were primed for the Giants to turn the series around at home. The atmosphere was festive despite the two-game deficit, and then at 5:04 p.m. the ground shook for 15 seconds. Afterwards, there was recognition that it had been a big quake, but no one realized how severe it actually was. The fans cheered and many still wanted to play ball as a nervous excitement shot through the stadium, not fear and panic. Fans in the upper deck were asked to proceed to the nearest exit, while fans in the lower deck were asked to head to the field.

Inside the stadium it was impossible to tell how widespread the destruction was in the surrounding area. The magnitude 7.1 Loma Prieta quake took 63 lives and injured thousands more, and in an instant the World Series was relegated to what it really is, just a game.

The series resumed ten days later on October 27. Kevin Mitchell, Will Clark, and the G-men showed a little life at the plate, but unfortunately the A's showed more, taking Game 3 by a score of 13-7 and completing the sweep the following night, 9-6.

It was disheartening, but it was still a tremendous year for the club, and the earthquake, as nature often does, put things into perspective.

501 The earned run average (5.01) for lefty Jonathan Sanchez in 2008. Sanchez was 9-12 after giving up 88 earned runs in 158 innings. Not the greatest numbers, but Sanchez had moments of brilliance along the way. On June 24, he gave up just five hits and one run in seven-plus innings vs. Cleveland, striking out eight. Five days later he gave up just four hits in seven innings vs. Oakland, striking out six. Sanchez was 2-0 that week with a 1.23 ERA, and for his efforts he earned the Bank of America National League Player of the Week honors. Sanchez later said, "It feels good. This makes me feel better like I'm doing well and doing what I'm supposed to do."

502 The number of plate appearances (502) for Monte Irvin in 1953. In only 444 at bats, Irvin belted 21 homers and 97 RBI, and he led the club in OBP (.406), slugging (.541), and OPS (.947).

503 The ratio (5.03) of strikeouts per walk for Gaylord Perry in 1966. It is one of the top five ratios in franchise history. Perry struck out 201 batters but gave up just 40 walks, setting a career high with the second best ratio in the league.

504 Willie Mays hit (504) doubles during 21 seasons with the Giants. He never led the league in doubles, but he was among the league's top ten leaders nine times, and his career total for the Giants is a franchise record.

505 The number of RBI (505) for Johnny Mize during 655 games with the Giants. The Big Cat surpassed the century mark three times for the club: 1942 (110), 1947 (138), and 1948 (125). His RBI total ranks among the top 35 in franchise history, though he barely makes the top 100 for games.

506 The slugging percentage (.506) for Roger Connor in 1883. He hit exactly one home run during the inaugural season of the New York Gothams. Connor did hit 28 doubles and 15 triples, however, in only 98 games—and by the time he retired in 1897 he was baseball's all-time home run leader with 138. He held that distinction until Babe Ruth passed him on July 18, 1921.

507 The slugging percentage (.507) for Chili Davis in 1984. He led the club in batting (.315), on-base percentage (.368), slugging, and OPS (.875). Davis launched 21 homers, to go along with 21 doubles and six triples, and placed fourth among league leaders in slugging. It was his highest slugging percentage for the Giants.

508 The number of RBI (508) for Fred Merkle during parts of ten seasons with the Giants. He drove home a career high 84 runs twice, in 1911 and 1912, and his overall total with the club ranks among the top 35 in franchise history. Merkle also drove home at least one run in five different World Series'.

509 The ratio (5.09) of strikeouts per nine innings for Mike McCormick during 357 games pitched for the Giants. He struck out a career high 163 batters in 1961, but his best ratio was 6.02 per nine innings in 1959—fifth best in the league. His overall ratio with the club is among the top 40 in franchise history.

510 The winning percentage (.510) for Sheldon Jones during parts of six seasons pitching for the Giants. He was 53-51 with a 3.83 earned run average. His best season was 1948, when he was 16-8 with a 3.35 ERA. Sheldon was seventh in the league that season in ERA, sixth in wins, and fifth with a career best .667 winning percentage.

511 Mel Ott hit (511) career home runs. He never hit more than 42 in any one season, but he was a six-time home run champion and was among the league's top ten leaders every season from 1928-45. John McGraw praised him early in his career, "He is a standout with me. Ott is the best-looking young hitter in my time with the Giants."

512 Travis Jackson got (512) career extra-base hits. Jackson got 55 of them in 1928, the only season he ranked among the league's top ten leaders for extra-base hits. Only six players, however, have more extra-base hits for the Giants than Jackson: Willie Mays (1,289), Mel Ott (1,071), Barry Bonds (1,008), Willie McCovey (822), Bill Terry (639), and Mike Tiernan (524).

513 Vida Blue faced (513) batters during the strike-shortened 1981 season. The lefty won eight games and was sixth in the league with a 2.45 earned run average, and he was also the winning pitcher in the 1981 All-Star Game. Blue was previously the winning pitcher for the A.L. during the 1971 All-Star Game, making him the first player in history to win the contest for both leagues.

514 The slugging percentage (.514) for Hall of Famer Monte Irvin in 1951. Irvin led the club with a career high 24 homers and he led the league with a career high 121 RBI. He also batted .312 and placed third in MVP balloting.

515 The on-base percentage (.515) for Barry Bonds in 2001. He got on base 342 times and led the league with an OBP that ranks 11th highest in baseball history—and the fourth highest in franchise history.

516 The slugging percentage (.516) for Darrell Evans in 1983. The 36-year-old veteran led the club and was fifth in the league in slugging after blasting 30 homers and 29 doubles. It was the highest slugging percentage for Evans since 1973, when he hit 41 homers and posted a .556 mark for the Braves.

517 The number of plate appearances (517) for Benito Santiago in 2002. The veteran catcher and former Rookie of the Year recipient played 126 games and posted his best offensive numbers in more than five years: a .278 average, 16 homers, 74 RBI, and a .450 slugging percentage, which made him an All-Star for the fifth and final time. And more importantly he contributed significantly to the Giants pennant-winning effort.

518 The career earned run average (5.18) for Dennis Springer during eight seasons pitching for the Phillies, Angels, Devil Rays, Marlins, Mets, and Dodgers. He never had a winning record and was 24-48 in his career, which explains the carousel of teams he played for. Springer was with LA for the tail end of 2001. Just long enough to be on the mound when Barry Bonds launched his historic 73rd home run of the season.

519 Buck Herzog got (519) hits during seven seasons and three tours of duty with the New York Giants. His total still ranks among the top 100 in franchise history, despite surpassing the century mark for the Giants only once, with 127 in 1912. Herzog also won four pennants with the Giants and he got an additional 23 hits in the postseason, but he had the misfortune of losing the World Series four times.

520 The road winning percentage (.520) for New York in 1916. The club was a respectable 39-36 away from the Polo Grounds, but during the month of May the Giants ran off an incredible 17 consecutive wins on the road, setting a record that was matched by only one other team during the 20th century—the 1984 Detroit Tigers.

521 Willie McCovey hit (521) career home runs. The Hall of Fame legend hit 45 home runs to set a career high during his 1969 MVP season, and his career total is among the top 25 in baseball history.

522 The slugging percentage (.522) for Orlando Cepeda in 1959. Baby Bull followed up his successful rookie campaign by slugging 27 homers and making his first All-Star team. Cepeda was sixth in the league in slugging, and second on the club behind Willie Mays.

523 The earned run average (5.23) for Matt Herges in 2004. Despite that high number he was the Giants closer, notching a team high 23 saves. Of course he also blew eight saves and opponents batted .338 against him—making Herges a desperate pickup at best for fantasy owners. The Giants traded him to the Diamondbacks in 2005. Herges originally played for the Dodgers, where he was a teammate of his brother-in-law Todd Hollandsworth.

524 The number of RBI (524) for Frankie Frisch during eight seasons with the Giants. Frisch hit the century mark twice, 1921 and 1923, and his overall total with the club ranks among the top 35 in franchise history.

525 Art Devlin scored (525) runs during eight seasons with the Giants. Devlin scored 81 runs as a rookie in 1904, but after a decade of baseball his rookie total turned out to be a career high. Devlin was on the 1905 world championship club, batting .250 with an RBI in the World Series.

526 The number of RBI (526) for Jim Ray Hart during 11 seasons with the Giants—one of the top 30 totals in franchise history. Primarily a third baseman, Hart hit 31 homers with 81 RBI and was second in Rookie of the Year balloting in 1964. He drove home a career high 99 runs in 1967.

527 The winning percentage (.527) for Mike McCormick during parts of 11 seasons pitching for the Giants. The first Cy Young recipient in franchise history won a career high 22 games during his award-winning 1967 season, but he won as many as 15 games only one other time during 15-plus seasons in the majors. He was 107-96 for the Giants—placing him among the top 20 in franchise history for wins.

528 The winning percentage (.528) for Luther Taylor during 270 games pitched for the Giants. He completed 156 of 233 starts, made a few more trips to the mound out of the pen, and overall he was 115-103 with a 2.77 earned run average. Taylor was among the league's top ten leaders for winning percentage three times in four seasons from 1905-08.

529 The on-base percentage (.529) for Barry Bonds in 2003. Bonds got on base 291 times during 130 games, and he led the league with a percentage that is among the ten highest in baseball history—and the third highest in franchise history.

530 The New York Gothams scored (530) runs in 1883. John Clapp managed the franchise in its very first season. Buck Ewing led the club with 90 runs, but the offensive leader was Roger Connor, who led the team in just about everything else: average, OBP, slugging, OPS, hits, total bases, doubles, triples, extra-base hits, and times on base. The offensive unit as a whole was fifth best out of eight teams in the league, and with 46 wins the club placed sixth in the standings.

531 The slugging percentage (.531) for George Kelly in 1924. Sixth in the league, it was the best on the club as Kelly set a career high for slugging. He also led the club in doubles, homers, and RBI.

532 Pablo Sandoval got (532) minor league hits from 2004-08. The switch-hitting prospect was playing rookie ball for the Giants in the Arizona League when he was 17, and he progressed nicely, batting .303 with 35 homers and a .445 slugging percentage through 452 games. He was batting .357 with eight homers and a .549 slugging percentage at the Double-A level in 2008 when he got the call to join the big club. Only 21, he made his debut on August 14, 2008, and batted .345 with three homers and 24 RBI in only 145 at bats, and put himself in a position to battle for the Giants starting third base job in 2009.

533 The slugging percentage (.533) for Willie Mays during 24 All-Star Games. Twice he was the MVP of the mid-Summer Classic (1963, 1968) and his performances were such that he inspired Ted Williams to say, "They invented the All-Star Game for Willie Mays."

534 Darrell Evans scored (534) runs for the Giants. Evans hit 30 homers and scored 94 runs in 1983—his highest season totals with the club—and he made his only All-Star appearance during eight seasons playing for the Giants.

535 Carl Hubbell pitched (535) career games—fourth most in franchise history. King Carl made 431 starts, completed 260 games, won 253, and tossed 36 shutouts on his way to Cooperstown.

536 The slugging percentage (.536) for Will Clark in 1991. It was the fourth consecutive season that he was among the league's top ten leaders in slugging, but it was the first and only time in his career that he actually led the league. Clark had 68 extra-base hits, including 29 that left the yard.

537 The slugging percentage (.537) for Jack Clark in 1978. The powerful outfielder belted 25 home runs, which led to a slugging percentage that was the best on the club and fourth best in the league. Clark also set a career high with 318 total bases.

538 The slugging percentage (.538) for Ray Durham in 2006. The second baseman hit .293 with a career high 26 home runs and 93 RBI. He led the club in slugging, OPS, and extra-base hits, and he tied Barry Bonds for the team lead in homers. Durham hit only .260 during the first half of 2006, but then he caught fire, hitting six homers in ten games after the All-Star break, and collecting 50 hits and 32 RBI in a stretch of 37 games to begin the second half of the season. Skipper Felipe Alou said of Durham during that stretch, "He's become a monster of a hitter, long ball, RBIs, both sides of the plate homers—he wasn't like that when he came over here."

539 Barry Bonds batted (539) times in 1993. He was the league MVP during his first season by the Bay. Bonds reached base at a .458 clip, giving him the best OBP in the league for a third consecutive season—and tying him with Mel Ott for one of the ten highest marks in franchise history.

540 The Giants scored (540) runs in 1956—only 3.51 runs per game, the worst offensive output in the league. Two seasons earlier the Giants won 97 games and the pennant after scoring 732 runs. The previous season the Giants won 80 games and slipped to third in the pennant race after scoring 702 runs. In 1956, the Giants beleaguered offense sent the club spiraling downward even further: 67 wins, sixth place, 26 games behind the pennant-winning Dodgers.

541 The slugging percentage (.541) for Moises Alou during two seasons with the Giants. He batted .312 with 41 homers, playing 221 games during 2005-06. Alou's 41 homers is only the second highest total among his family members that played for the Giants. His father (and manager) Felipe leads the way with 85, while his uncles Jesus and Matty hit 18 and 12 respectively.

542 The winning percentage (.542) for Jim Hearn during 221 games pitched for the Giants. He was 78-66 with a 3.74 earned run average, primarily as a starter, and his winning percentage is among the top 50 in franchise history. Hearn's best season in terms of wins was 1951, when he was 17-9. The previous season, however, he was 11-3 in only 16 starts, including 11 complete games, five shutouts, and a 1.94 ERA, after the Giants claimed him off waivers from the Cardinals.

543 The number of RBI (543) for Whitey Lockman during parts of 13 seasons with the Giants. His career high was only 73, in 1951, but he was primarily a leadoff guy who still posted one of the top 30 overall totals in franchise history. Lockman also hit a home run during the 1951 World Series, and he was on the club that won the 1954 World Series.

544 Kevin Mitchell, Will Clark, Brett Butler, and Scott Garrelts accounted for (544) total points in the 1989 league MVP balloting. With four players among the top 20 in balloting it's easy to understand how the Giants won the pennant—and with a league best

47 home runs for Mitchell, it's also easy to understand how he came away with the MVP.

545 The slugging percentage (.545) for Willie McCovey in 1968. It was the first of three consecutive seasons that the original Big Mac led the league in slugging. He also led the league in home runs in back-to-back seasons—1968 and 1969—and he nearly won the 1969 Triple Crown.

546 The number of RBI (546) for John Ward during nine seasons with the Giants—one of the top 30 totals in franchise history. The Hall of Famer drove home a career high 81 runs in 1886, despite hitting just two homers. In his last season, 1894, Ward drove home 77 runs without hitting a single home run, and he only played 136 games.

547 The slugging percentage (.547) for Mike Ivie in 1979. He was the first player taken in the 1970 amateur draft, and he made his big league debut for the Padres in 1971 when he was only 18. The Giants traded Derrel Thomas to get Ivie from the Padres in 1978, and the next season Ivie put up his career best numbers: a .286 average with a team best 27 homers and 89 RBI.

548 The winning percentage (.548) for Mickey Welch in 1890. With a 17-14 record, Welch had the best winning percentage on the club—but nowhere near the highest number of wins. Amos Rusie earned that distinction with 29 victories, although his winning percentage was nowhere near Welch's. That's because Rusie also *lost 34 games*.

549 The slugging percentage (.549) for Johnny Mize during five years with the Giants. The third highest in franchise history, he trails only Barry Bonds and Willie Mays.

550 Christy Mathewson started (550) games during 17 seasons pitching for the Giants. He started a career high 46 games in 1904 and was among the league's top ten leaders for starts every season from 1901-14. His career total with the Giants is a franchise record.

551 The winning percentage (.551) for Gaylord Perry during 367 games pitched for the Giants. His best season effort was a .724 winning percentage (fourth in the league) in 1966, when he was 21-8. Perry was 134-109 overall for the Giants, placing him among the top 50 in franchise history for winning percentage. The only time he led the league was in 1978, when he was 21-6 for the San Diego Padres—good for a career best .778 winning percentage.

552 Jim Davenport scored (552) runs during 13 seasons with the Giants. The third baseman scored a career high 83 runs in 1962, and made his only All-Star team. Davenport spent four decades with the Giants organization as a player, coach, manager, and executive.

553 The winning percentage (.553) for the Giants in 1938. Bill Terry won a world championship in 1933 during his first year managing the club, and in 1936 and 1937 he led the Giants to back-to-back pennants. New York won only 83 games in 1938, however, and slipped to third in the standings, five games back of the pennant-winning Cubs. Terry was never able to right the ship afterwards. The club placed fifth, sixth, and fifth from 1939-41, and then another legend, Mel Ott, got his turn at the helm.

554 The winning percentage (.554) for Vida Blue during 179 games pitched for the Giants. He was 72-58, almost exclusively as a starter, with a very respectable 3.52 earned run average. His best season effort for the club was 18-10, a .643 winning percentage that was sixth best in the league in 1978.

555 The winning percentage (.555) for Rube Benton during 172 games pitched for the Giants. He was 66-53, placing him among the top 40 in franchise history for winning percentage. Benton was among the league's top ten leaders for winning percentage three times: 1916, 1917, and 1919.

556 The winning percentage (.556) for the Giants in 1997. San Francisco was 90-72 and won the N.L. West by two games over the Los Angeles Dodgers. Dusty Baker earned Manager of the Year honors for the second time.

557 Pedro Feliz batted (557) times in 2007. He used his at bats well enough to reach the 20-homer plateau for the fourth consecutive season. Feliz left the Giants via free agency after the season and signed with the Phillies. It worked out for him. Feliz batted .333 vs. Tampa in the 2008 World Series and in his third trip to the postseason he finally got a ring.

558 Willie Mays batted (558) times in 1965. To say he used them well is an understatement on par with saying, "That catch Mays made during the 1954 World Series was pretty good." He was the best player in the league—period. He hit .317 with 52 homers, 118 runs, and 112 RBI. The sportswriters recognized his accomplishments by awarding him the MVP for the second time. It was also the first MVP by a Giants player during the San Francisco era of franchise history.

559 The winning percentage (.559) for the Giants in 1942. After replacing Bill Terry as manager, Mel Ott guided the club to a much improved 85-67 record—a third place finish, and the best showing for the club since 1937. Unfortunately, 1943-47 went like this: eighth, fifth, fifth, eighth, and fourth. Leo Durocher was brought over from the hated Dodgers to replace Ott during the 1948 season.

560 Jeff Kent hit (560) career doubles—one of the top 25 totals in baseball history. Kent hit 247 doubles in six seasons with the Giants, which puts him among the top 15 in franchise history. He hit a career high 49 doubles in 2001, and won his second straight Silver Slugger Award.

561 J.T. Snow scored (561) runs during nine full seasons with the Giants—one of the top 35 totals in franchise history. Snow scored a career high 93 runs in 1999.

562 The earned run average (5.62) for Jason Schmidt during April, 2004. Yes, he got off to a slow start . . . but he caught fire in May. Schmidt beat Florida on May 1, pitching seven strong innings while allowing only three hits and two earned runs. And he didn't lose again until the second week of June. After going 5-0 in May, including a one-hit shutout vs. Chicago in which he struck out 13, his ERA was down to 2.57. It was 1.53 for the month of May, earning Schmidt National League Pepsi Pitcher of the Month honors.

563 The winning percentage (.563) for Mark Gardner during six seasons pitching for the Giants. He was 58-45 with a 4.71 earned run average. His best season was a 13-6 campaign in 1998. Gardner has maintained close ties to the Giants organization since his playing days ended in 2001. He was named the Giants bullpen coach in 2003.

564 The slugging percentage (.564) for Willie Mays during 21 seasons with the Giants. The baseball icon led the league in slugging five times, and his career number with the club is second only to Barry Bonds in franchise history.

565 The slugging percentage (.565) for Jeff Kent in 2002. Kent batted .313 with 37 homers and 108 RBI, and earned his third consecutive

Silver Slugger Award. He did not, however, make the All-Star team—despite a .320 average, 14 homers, and 55 RBI at the break. Jose Vidro, Luis Castillo, and Junior Spivey all made the N.L. squad as second basemen instead.

566 The winning percentage (.566) for Scott Garrelts during ten seasons pitching for the Giants. He was 69-53 from 1982-91, and posted an impressive 3.29 earned run average. Only 89 of his 352 games were starts—but during three seasons in which he started 18 or more games he won 13, 14, and 12 games respectively.

567 The winning percentage (.567) for Tim Worrell during 252 games pitched for the Giants. He was exclusively a reliever, and a darn good one. He was 17-13, with 44 saves and a 3.25 earned run average during parts of four seasons with the club. In 2002, after struggling in the Division Series vs. Atlanta, Worrell was lights out vs. St. Louis in the League Championship Series. He won two games in that series, including the one that clinched the pennant. The following year, in 2003, Worrell was fourth in the league with 38 saves.

568 The winning percentage (.568) for the 2001 Arizona Diamondbacks. The D-Backs won the West by two games over the Giants, and of course, went on to win the World Series in dramatic fashion over the New York Yankees. The only consolation for Giants fans was that former catcher, coach, and long-time fan-favorite Bob Brenly finally got a ring... even if it was as Arizona's manager.

569 The slugging percentage (.569) for Ellis Burks in 1999. Burks launched 31 homers in only 390 at bats—that's a homer every 12.6 at bats, one of the best ratios in the league that season.

570 Jeff Kent scored (570) runs from 1997-2002. He scored enough runs in six seasons to rank among the top 35 in franchise history. Kent hit the century mark twice in that span, including a career high 114 in 2000.

571 The number of RBI (571) for Irish Meusel during six seasons with the Giants. He put together a remarkable run from 1922-25, posting season totals of 132, 125, 102, and 111. His career high 125 led the league in 1923. Meusel drove home another 17 runs in four trips to the World Series, and his overall total with the club ranks among the top 25 in franchise history.

572 The slugging percentage (.572) for Rich Aurilia in 2001. It's hard to believe that he didn't make the league's top ten leaders, but then again, he trailed teammate Barry Bonds by .291 points for the highest on the club. Eight N.L. players posted a slugging percentage above .600 in 2001—nonetheless, it was a banner year for the shortstop, who set career highs for hits, homers, RBI, and slugging.

573 Hack Wilson batted (573) times for the Giants from 1923-25. The Hall of Fame legend made his big league debut with the Giants on September 29, 1923. In very limited play with the club, Wilson batted .276 with 16 homers and 87 RBI. The Giants traded him to Toledo in the American Association in 1925, and later that year Wilson was drafted from Toledo by the Chicago Cubs—and that's where he became a star, at Wrigley Field. In his first five seasons with the Cubs, Wilson drove home 708 runs—including a major league record 191 in 1930.

574 The winning percentage (.574) for Jack Scott during 189 games pitched for the Giants. He was 62-46 with a 3.80 earned run average during parts of six seasons, but by far his finest moments came shortly after he joined the club in August, 1922. The Giants and Cardinals were locked in a battle for the pennant when Scott signed, and all he did was go 8-2 in the Giants unbelievable stretch run that culminated with a trip to the World Series. And then in Game 3 of the World Series vs. the New York Yankees, all he did was toss a complete game four-hit shutout. The Giants won the series two days later.

575 The number of times (575) Barry Bonds was walked intentionally from 1993-2007. That total is easily a franchise record, well ahead of Willie McCovey (235) and Willie Mays (187). Bonds was walked intentionally a total of 688 times in his career, which is a major league record. The man second on that list is Hank Aaron, who was walked intentionally only 293 times.

576 Dusty Rhodes played (576) games during seven seasons with the Giants. He was an outfielder who never batted 300 times in any one season and he played 100 games in a season only once—but his career is defined not by how seldom he played, but by what he did on the field of play during three days in the fall of 1954. In Game 1 of the 1954 World Series he delivered a pinch-hit game-winning home run in the tenth inning against Indians Hall of Fame pitcher Bob Lemon. In Game 2, he delivered a pinch-hit RBI single to score Willie Mays and tie the game in the fifth inning, and then, having stayed in the game, he hit a solo home run in the seventh as the Giants went on to a

3-1 victory and a two-game advantage in the series. In Game 3 he added a two-run single, putting his numbers for the series at 4 for 6 with two homers and seven RBI. And when the Giants swept the Indians the next day, he became a world champion.

577 The winning percentage (.577) for Chan Ho Park in 2001. He was 15-11 for the Dodgers with a 3.50 earned run average, and made his only All-Star team. Park gave up only 23 homers in 234 innings—but the 22nd homer he gave up just happened to be on October 5, in San Francisco, and it was the record breaking 71st of the season for Barry Bonds. Park gave up his 23rd homer just two innings later—it was the 72nd of the season for Bonds.

578 The slugging percentage (.578) for Mel Ott in 1930. So far as sluggers go, Ott was one of the best. He placed among the league's top ten leaders for slugging 12 consecutive seasons from 1928-39. He was only tenth in the league in 1930, which was the lowest he ranked during that 12-year run. He was among the top five nine times during that same stretch.

579 Mickey Witek played (579) games for the Giants. He spent parts of six seasons with the club from 1940-47, but lost a lot of time like so many other players during the war. Witek batted .277 with 22 homers and 196 RBI for his career. Not exactly stats that grab your attention, but . . . fewer than 100 players have taken the field more times for the Giants than he did.

580 The slugging percentage (.580) for Will Clark in 1987. Will the Thrill blasted a career high 35 homers and was fifth in MVP balloting. He was among the league's top ten leaders that season for average, slugging, OPS, total bases, and homers.

581 The on-base percentage (.581) for Barry Bonds in July, 2003. The Giants were 19-8 including a nine-game winning streak as Bonds' big bat led the way. He batted .415 with 11 homers, 21 RBI, 25 runs, 26 walks, and a 1.000 slugging percentage. His OBP was best in the league, easily, and on July 12 he tied a record held by Jimmie Foxx since 1940 by hitting 30 homers for the 12th straight season. Bonds was named the National League Pepsi Player of the Month.

582 The on-base percentage (.582) for Barry Bonds in 2002. Bonds broke the major league record .553 on-base percentage set by Ted Williams in 1941, and he won his first career batting title.

583 The slugging percentage (.583) for Willie Mays in 1958 and 1959. He led the league with a .626 slugging percentage in 1957, and then was second in the league in extra-base hits in each of the next two seasons—producing the same slugging percentage each time, but placing second and fifth respectively among league leaders. He never placed lower than fifth in slugging from 1954-66.

584 The number of RBI (584) for Art Fletcher during parts of 12 seasons with the Giants—one of the top 25 totals in franchise history. His career high was 79, a number reached by the shortstop in 1914.

585 Derrel Thomas scored (585) career runs. A switch-hitting middle infielder, Thomas led the Giants in runs in the only two seasons in which he played a full schedule with the club. He scored a team high 99 runs in 1975 (fifth best in the league) and a team high 75 runs in 1977. Thomas was a versatile player who throughout his career eventually played every position on the field except for pitcher.

586 The slugging percentage (.586) for Irish Meusel vs. the Yankees during the 1921 World Series. Meusel was the midseason acquisition that got the Giants past the Pirates for the N.L. pennant—and then in October, all he did was pick up two doubles, a triple, a homer, and seven RBI as the Giants defeated the Bronx Bombers. Coincidentally, his brother, Bob Meusel, batted .200 with three RBI for the Yankees during the 1921 World Series. The Meusel brothers faced each other in October three years in a row, with Irish and the Giants taking home the title twice.

587 Marquis Grissom batted (587) times in 2003. Grissom batted .300 during his first season in San Francisco, and he led the club with 176 hits and 33 doubles. The two-time All-Star batted .390 while playing in three consecutive World Series' with Atlanta and Cleveland from 1995-97, but unfortunately his experience did little for the Giants in the 2003 Division Series as he batted only .143 vs. the eventual world champion Marlins.

588 The slugging percentage (.588) for Mel Ott in 1936. It was the only time in his career that he led the league in slugging. Ott batted .328 with 33 homers, 120 runs, 135 RBI, 111 walks, and only 41 strikeouts . . . and placed sixth in MVP balloting. If it's any consolation, his teammate Carl Hubbell won the award.

589 Matt Williams batted (589) times in 1991. He was second in the league with 34 homers, fourth with 294 total bases, seventh with a .499 slugging percentage, eighth with 63 extra-base hits, and tenth with 98 RBI. He had a pretty slick glove too. The third baseman also won his first Gold Glove in 1991.

590 The winning percentage (.590) for the Giants in 2002. Dusty Baker's final season as manager ended in heartache as a world championship was within grasp, but slipped away. The Giants took care of business to be in that position, however, going 95-66 in the regular season to win the Wild Card, stunning the Atlanta Braves—the team with the best record in the league—in a heart-pounding five-game Division Series, taking two straight in St. Louis to start the League Championship Series, and then finishing off the Cardinals in five games.

591 The winning percentage (.591) for John McGraw during 31 seasons leading the Giants. The Hall of Fame manager posted 2,583 victories with New York—which means McGraw won over 1,000 more games than any other Giants skipper has even coached, let alone won. Dusty Baker was the manager for 1,556 games—second only to McGraw, who was the manager for an unprecedented 4,424 games.

592 Jim O'Rourke scored (592) runs during eight seasons with the Giants. A 19th century player, O'Rourke was brought back by manager and former teammate John McGraw for one game in 1904—at the age of 53! O'Rourke was 1 for 4, making him the oldest player in baseball history to hit safely. He also scored one final run during that game, which coincidentally, was the same day the Giants clinched the 1904 pennant.

593 Randy Winn batted (593) times in 2007. He used them exceptionally well. Winn led the club in average (.300), OBP (.353), slugging (.445), OPS (.798), hits (178), total bases (264), doubles (42), extra-base hits (57), and he tied Barry Bonds for the team lead in times on base (229).

594 Matt Williams scored (594) runs during ten seasons with the Giants. The first round pick out of UNLV set career highs in 1993, smashing 75 extra-base hits and scoring 105 runs.

595 The number of RBI (595) for Jack Clark during parts of ten seasons with the Giants. He hit the century mark once, driving home

103 in 1982. Clark barely makes the top 40 in franchise history for career at bats—but fewer than 20 players have driven home more runs for the club.

596 The slugging percentage (.596) for Jeff Kent in 2000. He batted a career best .334, but he didn't sacrifice any power. Kent blasted 33 homers to go along with 41 doubles and seven triples, a career best 81 extra-base hits in all. His slugging led to MVP honors and the first of three consecutive Silver Slugger Awards.

597 Jack Clark scored (597) career runs for the Giants—one of the top 30 totals in franchise history. Jack the Ripper hit 340 career homers and was one of the most feared sluggers in the league for more than a decade, most of which he spent with the Giants.

598 Randy Winn batted (598) times in 2008. For the second year in a row he was the offensive leader of the club. Winn led the team in batting (.306), OBP (.363), runs (84), hits (183), total bases (255), doubles (38), walks (59), stolen bases (25), extra-base hits (50), and times on base (242).

599 The winning percentage (.599) for the Giants in 2000. The club was 97-65, and won the N.L. West by 11 games over the rival Dodgers—and in the process Dusty Baker earned Manager of the Year honors for the third time.

600 Barry Bonds batted (.600) during a seven-game home stand vs. the Expos and Mets in August 2004. Bonds was 12 for 20 with three doubles, a triple, four home runs, seven RBI, and 29 total bases as the Giants won five times and took both series. Bonds earned Bank of America National League Player of the Week honors for his monstrous numbers. And for that accomplishment, he also received a Tourneau luxury Swiss timepiece from the Tourneau Safari collection.

1967 National League Cy Young Balloting

Rank	Name	Team	1st Place	W-L	ERA	WHIP	SO
1	Mike McCormick	Giants	18	22-10	2.85	1.15	150
2(t)	Jim Bunning	Phillies	1	17-15	2.29	1.04	253
2(t)	Ferguson Jenkins	Cubs	1	20-13	2.80	1.08	236

2008 National League Cy Young Balloting

Rank	Name	Team	1st Place	W-L	ERA	WHIP	SO
1	Tim Lincecum	Giants	23	18-5	2.62	1.17	265
2	Brandon Webb	D-Backs	4	22-7	3.30	1.20	183
3	Johan Santana	Mets	4	16-7	2.53	1.15	206

"As I told Timmy earlier today, 'You'll always be remembered as the winner of the Cy Young.' That's the way I'm identified, that's the way I'm introduced."

— *Mike McCormick, on Tim Lincecum winning the 2008 Cy Young Award*

Chapter Seven

Cy Young Worthy

HE WAS BORN in March 1867, and given the name Denton True Young. He grew up helping his dad on the farm and credited farm work with prolonging his career. It wasn't until 1889 when he was given the name that most people recognize. He was at a tryout in Canton, Ohio when the catcher who warmed him up said he was, "as fast as a cyclone." The nickname stuck, and eventually reporters shortened it to Cy Young.

Cy Young made his big league debut the next year, 1890. He stayed for 22 seasons with his career almost split down the middle between the National and American Leagues, and compiled a 511-316 record. He set numerous records and is, obviously, considered one of the greatest pitchers of all time.

Young passed away in November of 1955.

In 1956 baseball commissioner Ford Frick introduced the Cy Young award, given annually to the best pitcher in baseball. The award stayed as such for 11 seasons until Frick retired in 1966. William Eckert took his place and expanded the award to include a pitcher from both leagues. And this is where the San Francisco Giants come in.

The very first recipient of the National League Cy Young Award ... the Giants own Mike McCormick.

McCormick struggled out of the gate with a 4-3 record in 1967, but over his next ten starts he was 8-0, and his final two starts of the season were complete game victories. He was 22-10 with a 2.85 earned run average, and became the first Cy Young recipient in franchise history.

And for the next 41 years ... nothing, no one for the Giants won the Cy Young.

Not until Tim Lincecum *dominated* the league in 2008. In his sophomore season, Lincecum was 18-5 with a 2.62 earned run average. As an added bonus he started and ended his season with wins over the Dodgers.

McCormick and Lincecum were definitely Cy Young worthy—but plenty of other pitchers deserve high accolades for their performances on the mound for the Giants, and bear in mind, the Cy Young was not awarded until 1956.

In 1888, Hall of Famer Tim Keefe was 35-12, leading the league in wins and winning percentage at .745. His 1.75 earned run average was also best in the league, as was his WHIP ratio, hits per nine innings ratio, strikeouts per nine innings ratio, total strikeouts, and eight shutouts—very impressive.

In 1894, Hall of Famer Amos Rusie was 36-13, leading the league in just about all the same categories as Keefe. He pitched 444 innings with a league-best 2.78 earned run average.

Christy Mathewson led the league in wins in 1905, 1907, 1908, and 1910, and he sported the best earned run average in five separate seasons. His best case for the award would have been in 1905 when he led both leagues with 31 wins and a 1.28 earned run average. His stiffest competition probably would have come from strikeout pitcher Rube Waddell of the Philadelphia Athletics. Then again, Mathewson would have probably won in 1909 as well, and it's easy to make a case for 1908, or 1910, or 1913. That Mathewson kid could really pitch!

Carl Hubbell no doubt would have claimed the award in 1933 and 1936—after all, in both of those seasons he was the league MVP. He might have won it in 1937 as well. He led the league with a 22-8 record and 159 strikeouts.

Larry Jansen was a 26-year-old rookie in 1947 when he had what very well could have been a Cy Young year. He was 21-5, and led the league in winning percentage at .808. Jansen didn't even win Rookie of the Year—but one can understand that, seeing as a guy named Jackie Robinson won top honors in that category.

Sal Maglie was a teammate of Jansen's in 1951. The 24-year-old Maglie was 23-6, leading the league in wins. His 2.93 earned run average was second in the league. Maglie finished fourth in MVP balloting, but he received most votes than any other pitcher in the league.

John Antonelli was 17-22 after four big league seasons, but he was 21-7 with a 2.30 earned run average in his fifth season, 1954, his first year with the Giants. Antonelli finished third in MVP balloting, well ahead of any other pitcher.

In both 1966 and 1968, Hall of Famer Juan Marichal was great. Of course he was great in numerous other years as well, but he never won the Cy Young. He was 25-6 with a 2.23 earned run average in 1966, and he was 26-9 with a 2.43 earned run average in 1968. In 1966 Sandy Koufax's numbers were better, but not by much, and in 1968 it was Bob Gibson who had slightly better numbers. Marichal is arguably one of the best pitchers in the Cy Young Award era to walk away empty-handed.

It takes a special year to join the elite club of Cy Young recipients.

And there have been many special years for Giants pitchers, though only Mike McCormick and Tim Lincecum are members . . . *so far.*

601 Rick Reuschel pitched (601) innings during four-plus seasons with the Giants. He was 44-30 with a 3.29 earned run average, but Big Daddy was already a 38-year-old veteran when he joined the club in 1987. He led the club with 19 wins and 245 innings in 1988, and he led the club again with 17 wins and 208-plus innings at the age of 40 in 1989. Reuschel spent two decades pitching in the majors. He was a three-time All-Star and he won 214 major league games.

602 Art Fletcher scored (602) runs during parts of 12 seasons with the Giants—one of the top 30 totals in franchise history. He also won four pennants and scored five runs in the postseason, but lost all four World Series he played in: 1911, 1912, 1913, and 1917. Fletcher later was on the New York Yankees coaching staff during nine world championship seasons.

603 The number of RBI (603) for Fred Lindstrom during nine seasons with the Giants. He hit the century mark twice (1928, 1930) in accumulating one of the top 25 totals in franchise history. Lindstrom also drove home four runs during the 1924 World Series, but the Giants lost to Washington in seven games.

604 The winning percentage (.604) for the Giants in 1922. The Giants won the second of four consecutive pennants after posting a 93-61 record. The club then took care of the Yankees for the second consecutive year, winning the 1922 World Series for the third title in franchise history.

605 Alvin Dark scored (605) runs during seven seasons with the Giants—one of the top 30 totals in franchise history. Dark, who lettered in four different sports at LSU, hit the century mark twice, and set a career high with 126 runs in 1953.

606 The slugging percentage (.606) for Ellis Burks in 2000—one of the 30 highest in franchise history. He batted .344 with 34 homers and 96 RBI, in only 393 at bats. The previous season Burks hit 31 homers with 96 RBI in only 390 at bats.

607 The slugging percentage (.607) for Matt Williams in 1994. The players' strike cut the season short or else his numbers could have been truly monstrous. He led the league with 43 home runs to go along with 96 RBI, 270 total bases, 62 extra-base hits, and 74 runs, in only 112 games. He placed second in Most Valuable Player balloting behind Jeff Bagwell of the Houston Astros. It was also the last season that a player other than Barry Bonds led the Giants in home runs for better than a decade.

608 The winning percentage (.608) for the Giants in 1924. John McGraw led the club to a 93-60 record, becoming the first team in National League history to win four consecutive pennants—a feat no other team in the league accomplished in the 20th century.

609 The on-base percentage (.609) for Barry Bonds in 2004. He won his second career batting title with a .362 average, but his unprecedented 232 walks gave him a major league record on-base percentage. Bonds reportedly said, when asked about his ability to hit a baseball, "It's called talent. I just have it. I can't explain it. You either have it or you don't."

610 The offensive winning percentage (.610) for Randy Winn in 2008. He was clearly the team's offensive leader, and statistical models predict that if Winn could have been inserted at all nine spots in the lineup then the Giants would have won games at a .610 clip in 2008—as opposed to the meager .444 winning percentage actually posted by the club.

611 The winning percentage (.611) for Kirk Rueter after improving his career record to 124-79 with an 8-4 victory vs. Colorado on July 7, 2004. Jayson Stark of ESPN observed at the time that not only did Rueter have the eighth highest winning percentage among active pitchers with at least 100 victories, but that no pitcher in the previous half century had won as many games as Rueter while posting a winning percentage above .600 without earning at least one All-Star appearance. Rueter retired after 2005 with a career 130-92 record. He never made an All-Star team.

612 The slugging percentage (.612) for Willie McCovey in 1970. Mac led the league in slugging for the third consecutive season after belting 80 extra-base hits, including 39 homers. Of the 20 highest slugging percentages in franchise history, 16 belong to one of three players: McCovey, Willie Mays, or Barry Bonds.

613 On September 28, 2002, Barry Bonds homered for the (613th) time. His last game of the season, Bonds closed out the year with a .370 average, .582 on-base percentage, .799 slugging percentage, 46 homers, and 110 RBI—and for those prodigious numbers he earned his second consecutive Hank Aaron Award as the best offensive performer in the league.

614 The winning percentage (.614) for the Giants in 1921. The club won the pennant with a 94-59 record and then beat the powerful New York Yankees in eight games to win the 1921 World Series for the second title in franchise history. That series was the last best-of-nine ever played.

615 The number of RBI (615) for J.T. Snow during nine full seasons with the Giants—one of the top 20 totals in franchise history. His best season was 1997, his first with the club, when he drove home 104.

616 The Giants gave up (616) runs in 2002. It was the second lowest total in the league, and with only 566 of those runs earned, the Giants 3.54 earned run average was also second best in the league. Add a powerful lineup (198 homers, 783 runs) to a solid rotation (five guys with 12 or more wins) and you get a very satisfying outcome—in this case, 95 wins and a Wild Card.

617 The ratio (6.17) of strikeouts per walk for Hall of Fame hurlers Christy Mathewson in 1908 and Juan Marichal in 1966. Mathewson set the franchise record by striking out 259 batters and walking just 42, and then Marichal tied that record by striking out 222 batters and walking just 36. That ratio led the league for both pitchers, but Marichal was second in the league in strikeouts.

618 Frankie Frisch batted (618) times in 1921. It was a season of firsts for the Fordham Flash: first time hitting the century mark in runs (121) and RBI (100), first time surpassing the magical 200 hits, 30 doubles, .300 average thresholds (211, 31, .341), and the first time playing in the World Series. And first time as a world champion.

619 The slugging percentage (.619) for Bill Terry in 1930. A career high, it came during his historic .401 season and ranks among the top 20 in franchise history.

620 The winning percentage (.620) for Mickey Welch during nine full seasons with the Giants—one of the top 15 in franchise history.

He was 238-146, completing 244 of 446 starts. Welch won 307 career games, but played only 12 full seasons.

621 Willie Mays batted (621) times in 1962. Plenty of chances for Mays to do serious damage to opposing pitchers—and he certainly did that. He set a career high with 141 RBI, second best in the league. Mays surpassed the century mark in RBI ten times and his career total is among the top 15 in baseball history, but he never led the league in any one season.

622 The career winning percentage (.622) for Carl Hubbell—one of the top 15 in franchise history. Hubbell was 252-154, a two-time MVP recipient, a nine-time All-Star, and he was inducted into the Hall of Fame in 1947.

623 Kid Gleason got (623) singles during five seasons with the Giants from 1896-1900. One of the top 50 totals in franchise history, this is the same Kid Gleason who previously spent eight years pitching for Philly, St. Louis, and Baltimore before taking over as the Giants second baseman in 1896. Gleason won 38 games for Philly in 1890, and he won 17 or more games in five consecutive seasons. If his name is familiar but you can't quite place it . . . Gleason was also the manager of the 1919 Chicago White Sox, the team that made its bed with gamblers and fixed the World Series.

624 The winning percentage (.624) for the Giants in 1962. Alvin Dark led the club to 103 wins and a trip to the World Series in his second year as manager. The former shortstop batted .415 during two trips to the World Series while playing for the Giants, winning one title. Dark got a second title as manager—but unfortunately, it wasn't in 1962 and it was on the wrong side of the Bay. The Giants lost the 1962 World Series to the Yankees. Dark won the 1974 World Series managing the Oakland Athletics *(but at least he beat the Dodgers)*.

625 Bengie Molina batted (.625) during a six-game road trip to Colorado and Florida in May, 2008. Molina was 15 for 25 with six doubles and nine RBI, earning Bank of America National League Player of the Week honors. He later said, "It's a very good personal achievement, but at the same time I think a lot about the team. I would trade it for ten wins."

626 The slugging percentage (.626) for Willie Mays in 1957. It was the third time in four seasons that Mays led the league in slugging. He batted .333 with 35 homers, and was among the top six leaders in the Triple Crown categories.

627 The ratio (6.27) of strikeouts per nine innings for Mark Gardner during 175 games pitched for the Giants. He struck out 663 batters in 951-plus innings for one of the top 20 ratios in franchise history. Gardner set career highs with 13 wins and 151 strikeouts in 1998.

628 Christy Mathewson gave up (6.28) hits per nine innings in 1909—a franchise record, and the best ratio in the league for the only time in his career. Mathewson was on the mound for 275-plus innings but gave up just 192 hits.

629 The offensive winning percentage (.629) for Bobby Thomson in 1952. He was the team leader in slugging (.482), OPS (.813), total bases (293), doubles (29), triples (14), homers (24), RBI (108), extra-base hits (67), and times on base (245) . . . which contributed to a team high estimate of how the Giants would have fared with an all-Thomson lineup that season (Giants actual 1952 winning percentage: .597).

630 The winning percentage (.630) for the Giants in 1954. Hall of Fame manager Leo Durocher guided the club to a 97-57 record to win the pennant—and then the Giants swept the Cleveland Indians to win the 1954 World Series for the fifth title in franchise history.

631 George Burns batted (631) times in 1920. A career high total, he used them to set career highs in hits (181), runs (115), and homers (six). He batted .287 that season, which is also his career average.

632 The winning percentage (.632) for Joe McGinnity during seven seasons with the Giants—one of the top ten in franchise history. He was 151-88, completing 186 of 237 starts. McGinnity was inducted into the Hall of Fame in 1946.

633 Bill Terry batted (633) times in 1930—his .401 season. It took 254 hits for Terry to bat .401, and he needed them all. One hit less and his average would have been .39968, and though he likely would have found the NY press a bit friendlier than Ted Williams did in 1941, that final hit secured his place in history. There have been 25 officially recorded instances of a player batting .400 for an entire season—but only three have done so while batting more than 600 times: Terry, Rogers Hornsby (.401, 250 for 623, 1922), and George Sisler (.407, 257 for 631, 1920).

634 Christy Mathewson pitched (634) games for the Giants—second most in franchise history. Big Six made 551 starts, completed 434 games, won 372, and tossed 79 shutouts on his way to Cooperstown.

635 The slugging percentage (.635) for Mel Ott in 1929 and Kevin Mitchell in 1989—one of the top 15 in franchise history, and the highest not belonging to someone named Bonds, Mays, or McCovey. Ott was a 20-year-old kid playing his fourth season when he hit 42 homers in 1929. Mitchell was a 27-year-old slugger and already a world champion when he belted 47 homers in 1989.

636 The winning percentage (.636) for the Giants in 1993. The club was 103-59, tying the third highest win total in franchise history and earning Dusty Baker his first Manager of the Year Award. The Giants held a ten-game lead on July 22, and spent 133 days in first throughout the course of the season, but an eight-game skid in September opened the door for a red hot Braves club to make up ground. The Giants also got hot, winning 14 of 17 to close out the schedule, but the two clubs were tied when play began on the final day of the season. The Giants lost to the Dodgers, the Braves beat the Rockies—and despite 103 wins the Giants sat home in October.

637 Leo Durocher won (637) games managing the Giants. The Hall of Famer won two world championships as a player, and he won a pennant as player-manager for the Brooklyn Dodgers in 1941, but he won his only World Series as a manager while leading the New York Giants in 1954. Durocher won two pennants in eight seasons with New York, and his victory total is the fourth highest in franchise history.

638 The Giants gave up (638) runs in 2003. It was the second consecutive season that the Giants gave up the second lowest runs total in the league, once again resulting in the second best earned run average in the league—which in turn led to 100 wins and back-to-back division titles.

639 Bill Terry got (639) career extra-base hits. His best stretch was 1927-32, when he was among the league's top seven leaders for extra-base hits five times in six seasons. His career total is the fifth highest in franchise history.

640 The Giants scored (640) runs in 2008. The second worst total in the league, it explains a lot when asking how the club could finish 12 games back in a division in which the first place team won a mere 84 games. Only Randy Winn (hits) and Fred Lewis (triples) could be found among the league's offensive leaders.

641 The winning percentage (.641) for Art Nehf during parts of eight seasons pitching for the Giants—seventh best in franchise history. He was 107-60, completing 95 of 181 starts. Nehf also won four games in the postseason—including the title-clinching games in the 1921 and 1922 World Series' vs. the New York Yankees.

642 Jack Sanford gave up (642) runs during 233 games pitched for the Giants. He toed the rubber more than 1,400 innings, good for a 3.61 earned run average. Sanford was 89-67, and ranks among the top 30 in franchise history for wins. The 1957 Rookie of the Year for Philly, he came to San Francisco in 1959, and his best season was 1962 when he won 16 consecutive starts, was 24-7, and placed second in Cy Young balloting behind Don Drysdale.

643 Buck Ewing scored (643) runs during parts of nine seasons with the Giants—one of the top 25 totals in franchise history. Ewing hit the century mark just once in his career, scoring 117 times in only 116 games in 1893 . . . for Cleveland, after scoring just 58 times during his last season with the Giants in 1892.

644 Dave Koslo faced (644) batters in 1951. He was 10-9, and started only 16 of 39 games in which he pitched, but he also tossed a pair of two-hit shutouts. Allie Reynolds tossed a pair of no-hitters that season for the Yankees, and when the Yankees and Giants met in the World Series it was Reynolds who got the Game 1 start. No surprise there. Big surprise, however, that Koslo got the pearl for the Giants. He got the job done, too—a complete game 5-1 victory.

645 The slugging percentage (.645) for Willie Mays in 1965. It was the fifth and final time that Mays led the league in slugging. His .557 career slugging percentage is among the top 25 in baseball history.

646 Willie Mays hit (646) home runs during parts of 21 seasons with the Giants. He was a four-time home run champion who hit 52 big flies in 1965 for a career high. One of baseball's all-time great home run hitters, the 646 he hit for the Giants are a franchise record.

647 Gary Lavelle pitched (647) games during parts of 11 seasons with the Giants. The lefty made only three starts, all of which came in 1981 (he was 0-2, 12.27 ERA), but he was twice an All-Star reliever and he pitched in more games for the Giants than any other player in franchise history.

648 Bobby Thomson scored (648) runs during parts of nine seasons with the Giants—one of the top 25 totals in franchise history. Thomson scored 105 runs as a rookie in 1947, but from 1948-60 he never hit the century mark again.

649 National League teams combined to hit (649) home runs in 1939—and though the Giants struggled to a 77-74 record (a distant fifth in the pennant race) New York's offense far and away led the league with 116 long balls. No other team hit the century mark. Twice that season the Giants hit seven homers in a single game. On June 6, in a 17-3 pounding of Cincinnati, New York hit five homers in the fourth inning and seven total for the contest—and then later in the season the Giants again hit seven homers, this time in a 11-2 thrashing of Philadelphia.

650 Will Clark batted (.650) vs. the Chicago Cubs during the 1989 League Championship Series. He was 13 for 20 with six extra-base hits, including a pair of homers against Greg Maddux (one of them a grand slam). The Giants won the pennant, and Clark won MVP honors for the series.

651 Dave Bancroft batted (651) times in 1922. The Giants shortstop batted a career best .321 and scored 117 runs. A .279 career hitter, Bancroft batted .310 during five seasons with the Giants.

652 Orlando Cepeda scored (652) runs during parts of nine seasons with the Giants. One of the top 25 totals in franchise history, Cepeda hit the century mark three consecutive seasons from 1961-63.

653 Monte Irvin played (653) games for the Giants. Irvin, who was inducted into the Hall of Fame in 1973, played a decade of baseball in the Negro Leagues and spent three years in the military during World War II before getting a chance to play major league baseball. He made his big league debut on July 8, 1949, at the age of 30. Irvin played parts of eight seasons in the majors, seven for the Giants and one for the Cubs.

654 The winning percentage (.654) for Jim Hearn in 1951. He was 17-9 for the seventh best winning percentage in the league, the second of three consecutive seasons he placed among the league's top ten in that category. The Giants won the pennant in 1951, and

Hearn got the start in Game 3 of the World Series vs. the New York Yankees. His line from that game is rather bizarre: seven-plus innings, five hits, one earned run, *eight walks*, and only one strikeout. He got two outs in the eighth before he was relieved, and despite the control issues he escaped with a 6-2 victory.

655 Felipe Alou got (655) hits during six seasons with the Giants. His total is among the top 100 in franchise history. In his best season with the Giants, Alou got 177 hits in 1962. He set a career high with 218 hits for the Atlanta Braves in 1966.

656 The slugging percentage (.656) for Willie McCovey in 1969. He led the league with a career best slugging percentage after hitting 45 bombs for his third career home run title.

657 The winning percentage (.657) for Carl Hubbell in 1933. He led the league in wins with a 23-12 record, and he also posted a 1.66 earned run average that led the league and remains among the ten best in franchise history. Hall of Famer Billy Herman once said of Hubbell's command, "He could throw strikes at midnight. I never saw another pitcher who could so fascinate the opposition the way Hubbell did."

658 Jim Mutrie won (658) games during nine seasons managing the New York Metropolitans and New York Giants. He won two pre-modern era pennants with the Giants and a third with the New York Metropolitans, posting an overall record of 658-419 for a .611 winning percentage. Mutrie's best team, however, was the 1885 Giants club that lost the pennant by two games despite posting a record of 85-27. His roster that season included six Hall of Famers: Roger Connor, Buck Ewing, Tim Keefe, Jim O'Rourke, John Montgomery Ward, and Mickey Welch.

659 Jason Schmidt gave up (6.59) hits per nine innings in 2003. His career best ratio led the club and was second best in the league. He held opposing batters to a .200 average, giving up just 152 hits in 759 at bats. Schmidt was 17-5 in 29 starts, but the Giants also won all seven of his no-decisions—giving the club a 24-5 record with Schmidt on the hill.

660 And in 2004 he gave up just (6.60) hits per nine innings—giving Schmidt two of the top ten ratios in franchise history in back-to-back seasons. He improved to 18-7 in 32 starts, but one negative is the Giants were only 1-6 during his seven no-decisions in 2004.

661 The ratio (6.61) of strikeouts per nine innings for John Montefusco during 185 games pitched for the Giants. He posted the best ratio in the league with 7.94 strikeouts per nine innings in 1975, and he was among the league's top ten leaders three times in four seasons from 1975-78. The Count's career ratio with the Giants is among the top 15 in franchise history.

662 The number of plate appearances (662) for Bill Terry in 1931. His average fell .052 points, he got 41 fewer hits, he scored 18 fewer runs, he had 17 fewer RBI, and he amassed 69 fewer total bases than he did in 1930, and yet . . . he was second (.349), second (213), first (121), third (112), and second (323) in the league for each of those categories. Lets you know exactly how good he was the year before.

663 Bobby Bonds batted (663) times in 1970. In addition to his 200 hits, 26 homers, and 48 stolen bases, Bonds set a major league record . . . for strikeouts. Actually, Bonds set the record the previous season when he struck out 187 times, eclipsing the record 175 strikeouts for Dave Nicholson back in 1963—but in 1970, Bonds broke *that* record when he struck out 189 times. A dubious feat at best, his record held until Adam Dunn fanned 195 times in 2004. Ryan Howard set a new standard with 199 Ks in 2007, but that lasted only a season as Mark Reynolds fanned 204 times in 2008.

664 The winning percentage (.664) for Christy Mathewson during 17 seasons pitching for the Giants—fourth best in franchise history. One of the game's greatest legends, Mathewson was 372-188 for New York.

665 Jeff Tesreau gave up (6.65) hits per nine innings in 1914—giving him the best ratio in the league for a third consecutive season, one of the ten best ratios in franchise history, and three of the top 30 ratios in franchise history. Not bad at all. Plus, he won a career high 26 games.

666 The slugging percentage (.666) for Barry Bonds during 15 seasons with the Giants. He hit 586 home runs during that span and led the league in slugging five times. Bonds' slugging percentage for the Giants is a franchise record.

667 The slugging percentage (.667) for Willie Mays in 1954. It was a career high and the first of five seasons that he led the league in slugging. His percentage came on the strength of 41 home runs and 87 extra-base hits, and his performance resulted in the sportswriters voting him the league MVP for the first time in his career. That made him the first player in franchise history to earn Rookie of the Year and Most Valuable Player honors. It was also the last MVP for a Giants player during the New York era of franchise history. In 1965, Mays won the first MVP for a Giants player during the San Francisco era of franchise history.

668 Juan Marichal gave up (6.68) hits per nine innings in 1966—a career best, the best in the league, and one of the ten best in franchise history. Marichal also led the league that season in fewest walks per nine innings: 1.05. It's pretty easy to see how he won 25 games.

669 The Giants gave up (669) runs in 1987. It was the lowest total in the league and only 601 were earned, producing a league best 3.68 earned run average. Mike LaCoss led the club with 13 wins. On the offensive side, the Giants scored 783 runs—the third highest total in the league, led by Will Clark, who crossed the plate 89 times and drove home 91. That combination of outstanding pitching and timely hitting led to 90 wins in the regular season, and a division title.

670 Christy Mathewson gave up (6.70) hits per nine innings in 1905—second best in the league, and one of the 15 best ratios in franchise history. It was the third time in five seasons from 1901-05 that Mathewson had the second best ratio in the league.

671 The number of career home runs (671) for the five players drafted ahead of Barry Bonds in 1985: B.J. Surhoff (188), Will Clark (284), Bobby Witt (1), Barry Larkin (198), and Kurt Brown (0). Witt was a pitcher, and Brown was a catcher who never made it to the big leagues. Bonds, the number six overall pick, hit 762.

672 Rosy Ryan pitched (672) innings for the Giants. He was 49-36 from 1919-24, starting 64 games and pitching 107 in relief. Among pitchers with 500 innings, his .576 winning percentage and 3.50 earned run average both rank among the top 50 in franchise history. Ryan also earned a win during Game 1 of the 1922 World Series vs. the New York Yankees, and he became the first N.L. pitcher to hit a World Series home run when he took Washington's Allen Russell yard during Game 3 of the 1924 World Series.

673 The Giants gave up (673) runs in 1955. It was only the fourth lowest total out of eight teams in the league, and it was significantly higher than the league best 550 runs given up by the pennant-winning 1954 team. That difference showed up in the standings. The offense was virtually unchanged from 1954, but the team won 17 fewer games and fell to third in the standings in 1955.

674 Ken Henderson played (674) games for the Giants. A switch-hitting outfielder known for his defense more than his ability to swing the lumber, Henderson made his big league debut as a 19-year-old kid in 1965. It wasn't until 1969 that he found a permanent home in the Giants outfield, and his best season with the club was 1970 when he batted .294 with 17 homers, 88 RBI, and 104 runs. The Giants traded Henderson and pitcher Steve Stone to the White Sox after the 1972 season. He later played for the Braves, Rangers, Mets, Reds, and Cubs before calling it a career.

675 Tim Keefe gave up (6.75) hits per nine innings in 1885—best in the league, and one of the top 15 ratios in franchise history. Keefe actually gave up 300 hits, but he spent 400 innings on the mound.

676 The winning percentage (.676) for Larry Jansen in 1951. He led the league with a career high 23 wins and was fifth in the league in winning percentage. It was his fifth consecutive season of at least 15 wins to begin his career, but he won just 26 games total the next four seasons before he called it a career. Jansen later became the Giants pitching coach where he mentored such greats as Gaylord Perry, Juan Marichal, and Mike McCormick.

677 The slugging percentage (.677) for Barry Bonds in 1993. In his first season by the Bay, Bonds hit 46 home runs with 123 RBI and won his third career MVP. Bonds had eight seasons of 40-plus home runs for the Giants.

678 The winning percentage (.678) for Jason Schmidt during six seasons pitching for the Giants—third best in franchise history. Schmidt was 78-37 from 2001-06, earning three All-Star appearances and a runner-up in Cy Young balloting.

679 The slugging percentage (.679) for Pedro Feliz during a six-game road trip to Houston and Oakland in May, 2006. Feliz earned Bank of America co-National League Player of the Week honors, along with Pittsburgh's Jason Bay, after he hit three homers—including a grand slam—with ten RBI and eight runs scored on the trip. The Giants were 5-1 that week, and manager Felipe Alou said of Feliz, "He's staying on the breaking ball more and still hitting the fastball he likes to hit. He's a tremendous athlete."

680 The winning percentage (.680) for Tim Keefe during six seasons pitching for New York—second best in franchise history. Keefe was 174-82 with a 2.53 earned run average during 272 games with the Giants. His victory totals from 1885-89 are fairly impressive: 32, 42, 35, 35, and 28.

681 Jo-Jo Moore batted (681) times in 1935. The outfielder was a six-time All-Star for the Giants from 1930-41, and his at bats total in 1935 set a franchise record. Willie Mays is the franchise leader for career at bats with 10,477.

682 The winning percentage (.682) for the Giants vs. St. Louis in 1911. New York was 15-7 against a much weaker Cardinals squad. In a game on May 13, it got so out of hand that the Giants scored 13 runs in *the first inning*, including seven before St. Louis recorded an out. First baseman Fred Merkle hit an inside-the-park homer and a double and drove home six runs... all in the first. The final score was 19-5.

683 Juan Marichal gave up (6.83) hits per nine innings in 1965—third best in the league, and one of the top 15 ratios in franchise history. Marichal won 22 games and was the starting pitcher in the mid-Summer Classic. He tossed three scoreless innings and gave up only one hit, earning MVP honors for the game.

684 Don Nattebart faced (684) batters for the Houston Astros in 1965. He was 4-15, with a 4.67 earned run average in 29 games. Not a good year, although Nattebart became an historical footnote when he delivered the pitch that Willie Mays ripped for his 500th career home run on September 13, 1965.

685 Amos Rusie gave up (6.85) hits per nine innings in 1892. The Hall of Famer was on the mound for an astounding 532 innings but gave up only 405 hits. Rusie completed 58 of 61 starts, made three relief appearances, and was 31-31. Imagine winning 31 games in a season, *yet having a .500 winning percentage!*

686 The winning percentage (.686) for the Giants in 1905. John McGraw led the club to a 105-48 record and a five-game victory vs. the Philadelphia Athletics in the 1905 World Series—the first title in franchise history. The skipper for the Athletics was the legendary Connie Mack, who demonstrated the respect people in the game had for John McGraw when he said, "There has been only one manager, and his name is John McGraw."

687 Will Clark scored (687) runs during eight seasons with the Giants—one of the top 25 totals in franchise history. He hit the century mark only twice, but he led the league with a career high 104 runs in 1989.

688 The number of times (688) Barry Bonds was walked intentionally—a major league record. He led the league 12 times, including 11 while playing for the Giants.

689 The number of RBI (689) for Jeff Kent during six seasons with the Giants. He hit the century mark six consecutive seasons from 1997-2002, and the future Hall of Famer led the club to the postseason three times.

690 Bobby Bolin gave up (6.90) hits per nine innings in 1965—fourth in the league, and one of the top 20 ratios in franchise history. Bolin had one of the league's top six ratios four times in five seasons from 1964-68, and his career 7.79 ratio is one of the top 75 in baseball history. He won a career high 14 games in 1965.

691 The Giants scored (691) runs in 1885. The second highest total out of eight teams in the league, it included an historic thrashing of the Buffalo Bisons. In franchise history, the most runs scored by the Giants in a shutout victory came vs. Buffalo in May, 1885, with a final score of 24-0.

692 The winning percentage (.692) for Sal Maglie in 1952. He was 18-8, after beginning the year in spectacular fashion. Maglie was 9-0 after nine starts, which is an exceptionally rare feat. Prior to Maglie, Atley Donald was the most recent to start in such fine form, having done so for the Yankees in 1939. After Maglie, the next to do so was Andy Hawkins, who began 10-0 in ten starts for the Padres in 1985—and more recently, Brandon Webb won his first nine starts for the Arizona Diamondbacks in 2008.

693 The winning percentage (.693) for Sal Maglie during 221 games with the Giants. He was 5-4 in 1945, but after playing in the Mexican Leagues he was suspended by Baseball Commissioner Happy Chandler and did not pitch for the Giants again until 1950. All total he was 95-42 during parts of seven seasons with the club from 1945-55, and that gives him the best winning percentage in franchise history.

694 Scott Garrelts gave up (6.94) hits per nine innings in 1989—fifth best in the league, and one of the top 25 ratios in franchise history.

Garrelts posted the best numbers of his career in 1989, placing sixth in Cy Young balloting after ranking among the league's top ten leaders in six different categories.

695 Atlee Hammaker faced (695) batters in 1983. Only 43 reached base and scored an earned run against him, giving Hammaker a 2.25 earned run average—the best in the league.

696 The on-base percentage (.696) for Barry Bonds in April, 2004—the best in the majors. Bonds also led the majors in batting (.472), homers (ten), slugging (1.132), and walks (39). He drove home 22 runs, scored 21, and reached base safely in all 23 games he played. Bonds was the overwhelming choice for National League Pepsi Player of the Month honors.

697 The number of plate appearances (697) for Barry Bonds in 1998. He got 552 official at bats, but it was the last time in his career he was free to swing the bat so many times. His 480 at bats in 2000 was his highest total from 1999-2007, mainly because opposing pitchers refused to give him anything to swing at, but also because of injuries. Bonds still hit 351 homers in that timeframe in only 3,226 official at bats: or, one homer every 9.19 at bats.

698 The number of plate appearances (698) for Dave Bancroft in 1921. He got on base 263 times and was third in the league with 121 runs. Bancroft only batted .152 during the 1921 World Series, but he also scored three runs—including the one that won the series.

699 The ratio (6.99) of strikeouts per nine innings for John D'Acquisto in 1974. The Giants first round pick in the 1970 amateur draft, D'Acquisto was clocked on the radar gun throwing nearly as hard as Nolan Ryan. His best season was 1974, when he was a 22-year-old rookie, his strikeouts ratio was fourth in the league, and he won 12 games. He played for six teams including the Giants from 1975-82, but won more than four games only once. He was once known as a first round pick that fizzled, but in 1996 he was sentenced to federal prison for fraud and money laundering. D'Acquisto admitted to using investor funds to buy part interest in a Mexican baseball team, among other things.

700 The slugging percentage (.700) for J.T. Snow during the 2000 Division Series vs. New York. Snow hit a pinch-hit three-run homer against Mets closer Armando Benitez in the bottom of the ninth in Game 2, tying the game 4-4 and sending it to extra-innings.

Unfortunately, the Mets won it in the tenth—and after winning the series opener, the Giants lost three straight... and the series.

Juan Marichal—Hall of Fame legend.
(Courtesy National Baseball Hall of Fame Library, Cooperstown, NY)

"The thing I hate about him is that it all looks so easy. With guys like Koufax and Drysdale, you can at least look out there and see cords standing out on their neck. They look like they're working, like they're worried. Marichal just stands there, laughing at you."

— Gus Triandos

Chapter Eight

Dominican Dandy

NO MATTER HOW great, sometimes players are remembered for one moment. A tremendous play, a huge error, a timely home run, or a terrible lapse in judgment can all lead to these snapshots in time—the ones that burn into our memories in a way that can't be forgotten.

Hall of Famer Juan Marichal's career is filled with a number of these moments, so many, in fact, that he was known as the Dominican Dandy. His first came during his debut, a one-hit shutout that was a no-hitter until the eighth. With so many great moments, his career can't be defined by just one. After all, he won 25-plus games three times, he was a nine-time All Star, and he collected 238 wins during his career . . . and that's just the tip of the iceberg.

By mentioning Juan Marichal and Johnny Roseboro in the same breath, however, all those wonderful moments fade. They don't go away, but the spotlight is shifted and Marichal is remembered for August 22, 1965.

Johnny Roseboro, the Dodgers catcher, returned the ball to Sandy Koufax as Marichal stood in the batter's box. And in the process he buzzed it by Marichal's chin. Then it happened—in the heat of the rivalry, Marichal's judgment lapsed for a split-second and he clobbered Roseboro with his bat. That instant and the ensuing brawl carved its way into both men's lives.

In 1975, almost a decade later, Marichal signed as a free agent with the hated Los Angeles Dodgers. In making this move, Marichal maybe inadvertently unlocked the door for reconciliation, and the retired Roseboro opened it. He made it clear that he held no ill will for the fight. Still, the 37-year-old Marichal struggled with the Dodgers in only two starts.

After his second tough outing he showed just how much character he had by going to owner Peter O'Malley and telling him he could not take his money if he couldn't pitch effectively. Fred Claire, a Dodgers executive, was with Marichal at the time and said, "It was remarkable. Most people would have stayed the rest of the year just for the money." Not Marichal, he called it a career.

A few years later Marichal and Roseboro met at an old-timers game. The wounds healed further as the two joked and talked of their playing days.

In 1982, Marichal missed the Hall of Fame on his second ballot.

And it was Roseboro who determined to help him in any way he could. He made it known that there were no hard feelings, he posed for pictures with Marichal, he put the spotlight back on the countless great moments Marichal had on the field of play, and away from the one moment that was a terrible lapse in judgment.

A year later, Juan Marichal deservedly became a member of the Hall of Fame.

Marichal and Roseboro were friends, close enough that Marichal invited Roseboro and his family to the Dominican Republic. Both families had a great time together and soon Roseboro became a manager of a winter-ball team in Santo Domingo. He and Marichal spoke frequently, further cementing their friendship built on a fight.

Marichal was a great baseball player and a very proud man. He still doesn't like talking of the fight and has said, "It's not who I am." The relationship between the two men signifies just how true this statement is. Marichal should be remembered for all those great games and seasons, not August 22, 1965.

In August 2002, some 37 years after the beginning of a friendship, it was Marichal who was doing the remembering. He spoke at his old friend's funeral and said, "I wish I could have had Johnny Roseboro as my catcher."

Later the man who opposed Marichal on the mound that fateful day, Sandy Koufax, turned to Marichal and said, "You would have loved pitching to John Roseboro."

It is hard to forget that day so long ago. And that's okay, as long as we recognize that it did not define either man—it was just a snapshot in time.

701 Rube Marquard faced (701) batters during 27 games with the Giants in 1915. He was only 9-8 and clearly on the decline after a string of highly successful seasons, but that same season, against the rival Brooklyn club, he found some of his former magic and tossed his only career no-hitter. Later that year, Marquard was traded to Brooklyn where he was 2-2 in six appearances.

702 Luther Taylor gave up (7.02) hits per nine innings in 1904—fifth best in the league. After losing 27 games in 1901, Taylor left the Giants for Cleveland as the 1902 season got underway. He was 1-3 in the A.L., and figured the smart move would be a return to the Giants. So that's what he did. He still lost 18 games that year, and was only

13-13 in 1903, but he finally got things figured out in 1904, when he was a career best 21-15.

703 The winning percentage (.703) for Hall of Famer Rube Marquard in 1912. He led the league in wins after posting a 26-11 record, but the truly astounding part? Marquard began the season 19-0, tying a major league record held by fellow Giants legend Tim Keefe.

704 The number of RBI (704) for Bobby Thomson during parts of nine seasons with the Giants. He hit the century mark four times in five seasons from 1949-53, and his overall total with the club ranks among the top 20 in franchise history.

705 Fred Lindstrom scored (705) runs during nine seasons with the Giants—one of the top 20 totals in franchise history. The Hall of Famer coached baseball at Northwestern University after his playing days, the same school his son Chuck Lindstrom attended. His son, a catcher, also made it to the majors, debuting on September 28, 1958. Chuck tripled and scored in his first at bat, but as it turned out, that was the only at bat of his career. Chuck Lindstrom is one of four players in baseball history to triple in his only career at bat—the other three were all pitchers.

706 The ratio (7.06) of strikeouts per nine innings for Gaylord Perry in 1967. Perry pitched 293 innings and led the club with 230 strikeouts. He also completed 18 of 37 starts, pitched three shutouts, gave up only 7.10 hits per nine innings (third best in the league), won 15 games, and yet... he had a losing record. Perry lost 17 times.

707 Ferdie Schupp gave up (7.07) hits per nine innings during parts of seven seasons pitching for the Giants. The lefty was primarily a reliever but in 1917 he made 32 starts and was 21-7. His other wins totals while with the Giants: 0, 0, 1, 9, 0, 1. Schupp does, however, own the franchise record for giving up the fewest hits per nine innings among all pitchers with at least 500 innings.

708 The offensive winning percentage (.708) for Bill Madlock in 1978. He was the team leader in average (.309), on-base percentage (.378), and OWP.

709 The number of RBI (709) for Will Clark during eight seasons with the Giants. He hit the century mark three times—including a career high 116 in 1991—and led the league once, with 109 in 1988. Clark possessed one of the purest swings in the game and he brought a powerful bat when he stepped up to the plate. In eight seasons he amassed one of the top 15 RBI totals in franchise history.

710 Gaylord Perry gave up (7.10) hits per nine innings in 1967—third best in the league. Perry won 15 games and made his first All-Star team.

711 The ratio (7.11) of strikeouts per nine innings for Russ Ortiz in 1999. He was 18-9, and struck out 164 batters in 207-plus innings for the best ratio on the club, and one of the top 30 in franchise history.

712 The offensive winning percentage (.712) for Fred Lindstrom in 1928. His .358 average, 231 hits, 14 homers, and 107 RBI placed him among the league's top ten leaders for OWP that season, but his OWP wasn't even the highest on the team.

713 That's because fellow-Hall of Famer Mel Ott was his teammate. Ott led the Giants with a (.713) offensive winning percentage in 1928, after batting .322 with 18 homers in only 435 at bats. Ott was still a teenager that season. He was only 19.

714 The winning percentage (.714) for Bill Swift in 1992. The Giants traded Kevin Mitchell and Mike Remlinger to the Mariners in exchange for Swift, Dave Burba, and Mike Jackson prior to the 1992 season. Swift paid immediate dividends, as he was 10-4 in 30 games with a 2.08 earned run average, and his winning percentage led the club and was the second best in the league.

715 Hank Aaron launched his (715th) career home run on April 8, 1974, to surpass Babe Ruth in the all-time record book. It took Aaron 2,967 games and 11,295 at bats to pass Ruth. On May 28, 2006, Barry Bonds launched his 715th career home run. It took Bonds 2,772 games and 9,252 at bats.

716 Rube Marquard gave up (7.16) hits per nine innings in 1911. He was 24-7, and gave up only 221 hits in 277-plus innings for the second best ratio in the league, and one of the top 35 in franchise history.

717 The ratio (7.17) of strikeouts per nine innings for Sam Jones during 633 innings pitched for the Giants. He was second in the league with 6.95 Ks per nine innings in 1959, the same season he led the league with 21 wins and a 2.83 earned run average. His ratio during three seasons with the Giants is among the top ten in franchise history among pitchers with at least 500 innings.

718 Ray Durham got (718) hits during 734 games with the Giants from 2003-08. His best season was 2006, when the switch-hitting second baseman collected 146 hits, a .293 average, 26 homers, and 93 RBI. When he was traded to Milwaukee in 2008, Durham left the club with one of the top 75 hits totals in franchise history.

719 Jason Schmidt gave up (7.19) hits per nine innings in 2002. Schmidt led the club with the sixth best ratio in the league, and it was obvious to anyone who was paying attention that getting out of Pittsburgh was turning his career around. He came over from the Pirates at the July trade deadline in 2001, and posted a 7-1 record the rest of the way. He was 13-8 his first full season with the club in 2002, and the next season he was an All-Star and the Cy Young runner-up.

720 The Giants gave up (720) runs in 2007. You can forget about the team's overall record—yeah, it was dismal—but the prospects for a turnaround in the very near future were looking pretty good when the club closed out the campaign having given up the third fewest runs in the league. Not bad, not bad at all. It always comes down to pitching—just ask Bobby Cox and the Braves, or ask the 2008 ~~Devil~~ Rays.

721 The winning percentage (.721) for the Cleveland Indians in 1954. Cleveland was so good that the New York Yankees posted a 103-51 record but came in second place, eight games back of the Indians. Cleveland won 111 games and boasted the best pitching staff and the second highest scoring offense in the A.L. That meant nothing to the Giants in the 1954 World Series. The New York club in the N.L. might have won "only" 97 games, but it outscored Cleveland 21-9 in a four-game sweep on the biggest stage of them all.

722 Tim Lincecum gave up (7.22) hits per nine innings in 2008. The Giants ace gave up only 182 hits in 227 innings for the best ratio in the league—but for what it's worth he also threw 17 wild pitches, a league high.

723 The length in hours and minutes (7:23) of the longest game in franchise history. On May 31, 1964, the Giants and the Mets played 23 innings in a game that lasted nearly seven-and-a-half hours. That game was also the backend of a doubleheader. Juan Marichal got the win in game one, but in game two it was Gaylord Perry who tossed ten scoreless innings *in relief* as the Giants prevailed by a score of 8-6. Total time of both games was 9:52.

724 The winning percentage (.724) for Gaylord Perry in 1966. He was 21-8, his first of five 20-plus win seasons. The Hall of Famer also made his first All-Star team, was third in the league in wins, and fourth in winning percentage. Baseball executive Gabe Paul once said, "Gaylord was fantastic, simply fantastic. Gaylord's contributions were even greater than the records show—and they show plenty."

725 The number of RBI (725) for Larry Doyle during 13 seasons with the Giants. The second sacker never hit the century mark—he set a career high in 1912 when he drove home 90—but during two stints with the club Doyle piled up one of the 15 highest totals in franchise history.

726 The on-base plus slugging percentage (.726) for the Giants in 2008 when leading off an inning. Conventional wisdom—and stats—tell us that the odds of scoring go up when the leadoff guy gets on base. So much the better if he gets on in scoring position. As a team the Giants batted .270 with 30 homers when leading off an inning, and reached base at a .323 clip. Randy Winn and Fred Lewis were the guys the Giants wanted leading off. Winn batted .339 with eight homers and a .910 OPS. Lewis batted .304 with 21 extra-base hits and a .880 OPS.

727 The winning percentage (.727) for Billy Pierce in 1962. The 35-year-old veteran lefty rejuvenated his career by moving from Chicago to San Francisco, posting a 16-6 record and placing third in Cy Young balloting. A seven-time All-Star in the A.L., Pierce is known for having thrown four one-hitters and for having lost a perfect game in the ninth inning. His resurgence in 1962 helped the Giants win the pennant, and then he tossed a three-hitter vs. New York in Game 6 of the World Series. The Yankees, unfortunately, won Game 7.

728 The Giants gave up (728) earned runs in 1970. Not good. The staff 4.50 earned run average was second worst in the league, and nobody allowed more runs: 826. On the other hand, the Giants scored 831 runs for the best offensive output in the league. You got to have pitching though, because without it, even though the Giants offense was tremendous the club won only 86 games—good for third in the division.

729 One reason the offense was so good in 1970 is because the Giants demonstrated a tremendous amount of patience at the plate and drew a league high (729) walks. Led by Willie McCovey (137) and Dick Dietz (109), that translated into a team .347 on-base percentage that was also first in the league. Again, on the flipside, the pitching staff issued 604 walks—the eighth highest total out of 12 teams in the league.

730 The offensive winning percentage (.730) for Fred Lindstrom in 1930. For the second time in three seasons his OWP was one of the ten highest in the league, but it wasn't the highest on the club. This time it wasn't even close. Despite batting .379 with 22 homers and 106 RBI, his teammate Bill Terry was a much better choice if you could pick one player and pencil that name into every spot in the lineup. Terry's OWP was .783 after batting .401 with 23 homers and 129 RBI.

731 The winning percentage (.731) for the Giants after posting a 19-7 record in the first month of play in 2003. The Giants lost the 2002 World Series, but began 2003 by winning seven straight and 12 of 13, becoming only the second team in baseball history to begin a season with at least a 12-1 record after having lost the World Series the previous year. The first team to do so was also the Giants—way back in 1918. John McGraw's 1918 club fell back to second in the pennant race, but Felipe Alou's 2003 club never trailed on its way to winning the N.L. West.

732 The number of RBI (732) for Matt Williams during ten seasons with the Giants. The third baseman was the league's top RBI man in 1990, driving home 122 runs—and his overall total for the club ranks among the top 15 in franchise history.

733 The winning percentage (.733) for Red Ames in 1905. The 22-year-old Ohio native was 22-8, placing third among league leaders for both wins and winning percentage. Ames won 183 career games, but he never won more than 15 after 1905, despite playing another 14 years. He did, however, lead the league with 23 losses in 1914.

734 Ray Durham played (734) games for the Giants from 2003-08. He was traded to the Brewers on July 20, 2008, after spending five-plus exceptionally productive seasons at second base for San Francisco. Durham batted .276 with 77 homers, 401 runs, and 356 RBI, and at the time of the trade he ranked among the top 25 active players in the game with more than 2,000 career hits in 14 big league seasons.

735 The winning percentage (.735) for Larry Benton in 1928. He was 25-9, and placed fourth in MVP balloting. It was the second year in a row that he led the league in winning percentage, so it's not like he came out of nowhere, exactly ... but he was only 17-7 in 1927, and in 13 seasons he never won more than 14 games except for 1927-28. And he was under .500 for his career.

736 Stu Miller gave up (736) hits during 804-plus innings pitched for the Giants. He was a reliever with a legendary repertoire of off-speed pitches that proved difficult to hit for even the best in the game—as evidenced by his ratio of 8.24 hits per nine innings for the Giants, one of the top 30 in franchise history. Miller's stuff was not overpowering. His pitches were often described as slow, slower, and even slower, but he could flat pitch. He made one All-Star team, in 1961, when the game was played at Candlestick Park. Miller was called for a balk in the ninth inning of that game when a strong gust of wind moved his shoulder. Miller, who lost the lead as a result, but ended up the winning pitcher, later said, "The next day, that's not what you read in the newspaper. The biggest headlines they could get read 'Miller Blown Off Mound.' Never mind that we won the game ... they made it sound like I was pinned against the center field fence, for crying out loud!"

737 The winning percentage (.737) for Scott Garrelts in 1989—best in the league, and one of the top 40 in franchise history. Garrelts also led the league with a 2.28 earned run average on his way to posting a 14-5 record. He was sixth in Cy Young balloting.

738 Monte Kennedy gave up (7.38) hits per nine innings in 1946—the best ratio in the league. Kennedy was a 24-year-old rookie just back from serving three years in the military during World War II. He played eight seasons with the Giants, only to leave the game after the 1953 season—one year too soon, as he missed out on the 1954 championship season. Kennedy returned to his native Virginia where he became a detective for the Richmond Police Department.

739 Arlie Latham stole (739) career bases. One of the speedsters of baseball's pre-modern era, Latham stole 738 bases prior to 1900—enough to rank him among baseball's all-time top ten leaders. Latham stole exactly one base for the Giants. The last steal of his career, it came after a ten-year hiatus from the game. The 49-year-old infielder got into four games for the Giants in 1909, batted twice, stole one base and scored one run—and in the process became the oldest player in baseball history to steal a base.

740 Ron Bryant gave up (7.40) hits per nine innings in 1972. He was 14-7, and gave up only 176 hits in 214 innings for the fifth best ratio in the league. Bryant was just gearing up for 1973, when he led the league in wins with a 24-12 record and was third in Cy Young balloting. The lefty was only 25 at the time, but his career was almost over. He fell hard in 1974, going 3-15. Bryant was traded to the Cardinals in 1975 for Larry Herndon. He was 0-1, and the Cardinals released him that July—and just like that, he was out of the game.

741 Matt Cain gave up (7.41) hits per nine innings in 2006—the third best ratio in the league. The 21-year-old rookie won 13 games. Add in his September call-up in 2005, and Cain won 15 games during his first 39 big league starts. He made 66 starts in 2007-08, but won only 15 more games.

742 The Giants scored (742) runs in 1936. Led by Mel Ott (120) and Jo-Jo Moore (110), the offensive unit was fourth in the league in scoring. The offense did just enough, and the pitching did the rest. The Giants gave up only 532 earned runs for a league best 3.46 earned run average. That combination of offense and pitching led to 92 wins—and the pennant.

743 The winning percentage (.743) for Juan Marichal in 1968. He was 26-9, fifth in MVP balloting, and made his seventh consecutive All-Star team. Fellow legend Carl Hubbell said of a young Marichal, "This guy is a natural... he amazes me."

744 The number of plate appearances (744) for Jo-Jo Moore in 1935. He got 201 hits, the first of back-to-back seasons he reached that plateau, and scored 108 runs. Moore was among the league's top ten leaders for hits, runs, and total bases three consecutive seasons from 1934-36.

745 The winning percentage (.745) for Tim Keefe in 1888—best in the league, and one of the top 35 in franchise history. He also won the pitching Triple Crown after posting a league best 32-12 record, 1.58 earned run average, and 335 strikeouts. Historian Lee Allen said, "Keefe was one of the first pitchers celebrated for his head work... he assured the Giants of a well-pitched game almost every day."

746 The number of RBI (746) for the Giants offense in 1997. Three players hit the century mark for the Giants: Jeff Kent (121), J.T. Snow (104), and Barry Bonds (101). The club was fourth in the league in scoring with 784 runs, led by 123 for Bonds. The pitching staff, unfortunately, was only ninth in the league for earned run average ... but despite that, the offense carried the club, and manager Dusty Baker won his first division title.

747 Mike Tiernan walked (747) times in his career. He walked 96 times in only 122 games in 1889 to set a career high (he was also third in the league with a .447 on-base percentage that year). His walks total is fifth highest in franchise history, trailing only four legends: Barry Bonds, Mel Ott, Willie Mays, and Willie McCovey.

748 The Giants gave up (748) runs in 2001. Led by Barry Bonds (73), Rich Aurilia (37), and Jeff Kent (22), the Giants clubbed a league high 235 homers and boasted one of the most productive lineups in the league. Too bad the pitching had such a hard time getting people out. Despite three guys with 13 or more wins (Livan Hernandez, Kirk Rueter, and Russ Ortiz), the staff gave up the ninth highest runs total in the league. The club won 90 games, but came in second two games back of the Diamondbacks.

749 The slugging percentage (.749) for Barry Bonds in 2003. It was the sixth time he led the league in slugging, and with 45 home runs he won his third consecutive MVP.

750 The winning percentage (.750) for Christy Mathewson in 1910. Mathewson led the league in wins after posting a 27-9 record, but was only fourth in winning percentage. One of the top 30 winning percentages in franchise history, five others players have matched it: Doc Crandall (15-5, 1911), Ferdie Schupp (21-7, 1917), Johnny Antonelli (21-7, 1954), Hoyt Wilhelm (12-4, 1954), and Joe Nathan (12-4, 2003). Schupp's was the only one to lead the league in winning percentage, and Mathewson was the only one to lead the league in wins.

751 Ed Halicki gave up (7.51) hits per nine innings in 1978—the best ratio on the club. He also led the club in hit batsmen, but hey, no biggie. Halicki was only 9-10, but he posted a 1.060 WHIP that was the best in the league. And on June 12, he pitched a one-hitter vs. Montreal. Steve Rogers pitched a three-hitter for the Expos, but Halicki and the Giants won the game, 1-0. The only hit for Montreal was a second inning single by Ellis Valentine.

752 The ratio (7.52) of strikeouts per nine innings for Bobby Bolin in 1964. One of the top 20 ratios in franchise history, Bolin was only 6-9, but he struck out 146 batters in 174-plus innings. His ratio led the club, and was also sixth best in the league.

753 The on-base plus slugging percentage (.753) for George Foster during 54 games with the Giants from 1969-71. The two-time world champion, 1977 Most Valuable Player, and 1977 home run champion for the Cincinnati Reds was a third round draft choice of the San Francisco Giants in 1968. Foster got a cup of coffee in 1969 and 1970, played 36 games in 1971, and then he became a star after being traded in 1971 to Cincinnati for Frank Duffy and Vern Geishert.

754 Bill Swift gave up (7.54) hits per nine innings in 1993. It was the second consecutive season that he posted the best ratio on the club, and in 1993 his ratio was also the second best in the league behind Pete Harnisch of the Houston Astros.

755 On August 4, 2007, Barry Bonds tied Hank Aaron in the all-time record book with his (755th) career home run. The blast came against Clay Hensley at San Diego's PETCO Park. "I'm really lost for words at this moment," Bonds said. "I think when I sit back and can grasp all of this I'll be able to say a little more a little later. But I'm still in a daze myself right now."

756 Three days later Bonds celebrated with the home fans at AT&T Park when he launched his (756th) home run. On August 7, 2007, Bonds surpassed Hank Aaron in the all-time record book against Mike Bacsik and the Washington Nationals. The ball traveled 435 feet and landed just right of center. Bacsik said afterwards, "I honestly didn't even watch it land. I watched Barry's reaction and by the sound of the bat, I knew it was gone."

757 The very next day Bonds launched his (757th) home run against Washington's Tim Redding. Bonds hit his final homer of the season, #762, on the road in Colorado. Willie Mays was on the road for his 500th and 600th career homers, and Willie McCovey was on the road for his 500th. Unlike those milestones for Mays and McCovey, Bonds hit most of his in front of the home fans—which was way cool, especially since Bonds was known to sit out a game or two on the road so he could get most of his at bats in San Francisco. Bonds launched number 70 in Houston in 2001, but numbers 71, 72 and 73 were at home. Bonds also launched career milestones 500, 600, 660, 661, 700, 715, and 756 at home.

758 The winning percentage (.758) for Juan Marichal in 1963. He was 25-8, beginning a stretch where he won 20-plus games six times in seven seasons. Marichal led the league in wins but was sixth in winning percentage.

759 The winning percentage (.759) for the New York Gothams in 1885. During a thrilling extra-inning game that season vs. the Philadelphia Quakers, manager Jim Mutrie is given credit for yelling in victory, "My big fellows! My Giants!" And ever since the club has been known as the Giants.

760 Lefty O'Doul batted (760) times during parts of three seasons with the Giants. He batted .314 with 26 homers for the Giants, but it's too bad he wasn't with the club in 1929. After batting .319 with eight homers in 1928, the club traded O'Doul *with cash* to Philly in exchange for Freddy Leach. Then in 1929, O'Doul batted .398 with 254 hits, 32 homers, and 122 RBI for the Phillies. That same season, Leach batted .290 with eight homers and 47 RBI for the Giants.

761 Tim Keefe gave up (7.61) hits per nine innings during six seasons pitching for the Giants—one of the top five ratios in franchise history. His career ratio was 7.91, one of the top 100 in baseball history.

762 The number of RBI (762) for George Kelly during parts of 11 seasons with the Giants—one of the top 15 totals in franchise history. The Hall of Famer led the league twice in five seasons from 1920-24, surpassing the century mark four times.

763 The offensive winning percentage (.763) for Johnny Mize in 1947. He led the club in on-base percentage (.384), slugging (.614), OPS (.998), runs (137), hits (177), total bases (360), doubles (26), homers (51), RBI (138), walks (74), extra-base hits (79), times on base (255), and ... just about everything, including offensive winning percentage. New York won just 81 games for a fourth place finish and a .526 winning percentage, and it sure could have used a couple more guys like Mize in the lineup.

764 Bobby Bolin gave up (7.64) hits per nine innings during nine seasons pitching for the Giants. Bolin, who pitched sidearm, tossed a pair of no-hitters in the minors, and he was pretty stingy for the big club as well, seeing as his ratio is one of the ten best in franchise history.

765 Bobby Bonds scored (765) runs during seven seasons with the Giants—one of the top 20 totals in franchise history. He led the league with 120 runs in 1969, and was second in the league with a career high 134 in 1970. Bonds was second in the league again in 1971 and 1972, and then he capped off a remarkable five-year stretch in 1973 by leading the league with 131 runs.

766 The on-base plus slugging percentage (.766) for Chief Meyers during seven seasons with the Giants. He set career highs in 1912 with a .358 average, a league leading .441 on-base percentage, a .477 slugging percentage, and a .918 OPS that was second in the league. The catcher batted .301 during 840 games with the Giants, and posted an OPS that ranks among the top 50 in franchise history.

767 The number of RBI (767) for Orlando Cepeda during parts of nine seasons with the Giants. His two-run triple in the first inning of a 3-1 victory vs. St. Louis on April 12, 1960, gave him the first two RBI in the history of Candlestick Park. Cepeda led the league with a career high 142 RBI in 1961, he ranks among the top 100 in baseball history for career RBI, and his total for the Giants ranks among the top 15 in franchise history.

768 The ratio (7.68) of strikeouts per nine innings for Rube Marquard in 1911. One of the 15 best ratios in franchise history, it was a franchise record at the time. After striking out a league high 237 batters in 277-plus innings, it was also the best ratio in the league. Marquard was among the league's top ten in this category eight times in his career.

769 The winning percentage (.769) for reliever Dave Burba in 1993. One of the big reasons San Francisco won 103 games that season was Burba's 10-3 record out of the pen.

770 Red Ames gave up (7.70) hits per nine innings during 11 seasons pitching for the Giants. *The Sporting Life* made it clear that Ames' curveball was largely responsible for his success, stating in 1906 that, "Ames is without question almost the hardest pitcher to catch of the professionals. Players say no man who holds a place in the pitcher's box is able to curve the ball so far as he can. It is a fact that he doesn't always know himself where his curves are going to land." Well, Ames did walk a lot of batters, too.

771 The winning percentage (.771) for Christy Mathewson in 1908. Mathewson owns three of the top 25 winning percentages in franchise history—including 1908. Always a hard worker, Mathewson was 37-11, and faced 1,499 batters in nearly 400 innings on the mound.

772 Moises Alou batted (772) times during two seasons with the Giants. His family name is well-represented and respected in both baseball history and Giants history, and during his short stay with the club during 2005-06 he was an important contributor to the club's offensive unit: a .312 average, 119 runs, 46 doubles, 41 homers, and 137 RBI in only 221 games.

773 The winning percentage (.773) for Jason Schmidt in 2003. He was fourth in the league with 17 victories, but after losing just five games (and posting a 5-0 record down the stretch) he closed out the season with the best winning percentage in the league.

774 The winning percentage (.774) for Rube Marquard in 1911. He was 24-7 for the best winning percentage in the league . . . after entering his fourth big league season with a career 9-18 record. Charlie Carr, a big leaguer himself, once told Marquard, "I've been in baseball a long time and I never saw anything like it. I never saw a kid like you, who can beat anybody and is so successful."

775 The winning percentage (.775) for Christy Mathewson in 1905—second best in the league, and one of the 20 best in franchise history. He won the pitching Triple Crown after posting a 31-9 record, 1.28 earned run average, and 206 strikeouts.

776 The offensive winning percentage (.776) for Ross Youngs in 1920. He led the league with 281 times on base, which explains why a lineup with the 1920 version of Youngs penciled in nine times would excel so well. He also set a career high with 204 hits, and with a .351 average he was the second leading hitter in the league behind Rogers Hornsby.

777 The ratio (7.77) of strikeouts per nine innings for Mark Davis during 555 innings pitched for the Giants. Davis started a career high 27 games for the club in 1984. His career high 131 strikeouts came in 1985, however, when he started only once but made 76 relief appearances. His career ratio with the Giants is among the top five in franchise history for pitchers with at least 500 innings.

778 The winning percentage (.778) for Art Nehf in 1924—third best in the league, and one of the 20 best in franchise history. Nehf enjoyed a nice career, winning 184 games over 15 seasons. He was 14-4 in 1924, helping the Giants to a fourth consecutive pennant. Nehf got the win vs. Washington during Game 1 of the World Series, but he was the hard luck loser in Game 6, 2-1, and the Senators won the series the next day.

779 Matt Cain gave up (7.79) hits per nine innings in 2007—the fifth best ratio in the league. The crazy part is he was 7-16. He was 4-1 in August, the only month all season during which he won more than one game. In seven wins his earned run average was 2.08, it was 2.73 in nine no-decisions, and it climbed to 5.03 in his 16 losses.

780 The 1905 New York Giants led the league with (780) runs scored—and as a result won 105 games and the pennant. A close look at the roster for the 1905 Giants reveals one of baseball's great stories—Archibald Wright Graham, better known as Moonlight, and popularized by the novel *Shoeless Joe*, which in turn became the movie *Field of Dreams*. Graham played one game in the majors, and it was for the 1905 New York Giants. He did not score a run, and in fact, he never even got to bat. He later became a doctor in Minnesota, and one of the storylines in *Field of Dreams* centered on Ray Kinsella (played by Kevin Costner) "easing the pain" of Graham for never getting to bat in the big leagues.

781 The earned run average (7.81) for Brad Hennessey in 2008. Hennessey, one of four guys not in the rotation who toed the rubber at least once in a starting role during 2008, pitched in 17 games, made four starts, and was 1-2. A former first round pick, he struggled, as did every starter once you got past Tim Lincecum and Matt Cain. After Lincecum (2.62) and Cain (3.76) it was brutal: Barry Zito (5.15), Jonathan Sanchez (5.01), and Kevin Correia (6.05) all made at least 25 starts but their combined record was 22-37, proving exactly how much the staff missed Noah Lowry. The team leader in wins in 2005 and 2007, Lowry endured two surgeries after being diagnosed with exertional compartment syndrome in March, 2008, and he missed the entire season.

782 The ratio (7.82) of strikeouts per nine innings for Gaylord Perry in 1965. One of the top 15 in franchise history, it was sixth best in the league that season. Perry struck out 170 batters in 195-plus innings, with nearly half his games coming in relief. He was in the rotation fulltime beginning in 1966.

783 The winning percentage (.783) for Tim Lincecum in 2008. He was 18-5 while playing for a club that won only 72 games all season.

His winning percentage was second best in the league, trailing only Adam Wainwright of the St. Louis Cardinals who was 11-3 after returning from injury to start 20 games.

784 Larry Jansen gave up (784) runs during 283 games pitched for the Giants. Only 683 were earned and he pitched 1,731 innings, which works out to an impressive 3.55 earned run average that ranks as one of the best in franchise history. Jansen won 120 games for the Giants during a career that lasted eight seasons, despite winning only four times during his final two years. His wins total is among the top 15 in franchise history.

785 Carl Hubbell gave up (7.85) hits per nine innings in 1936—the best ratio in the league. It was the third time he led the league in this category, and he was so good that beginning in July 1936 and continuing through May 1937, Hubbell set a major league record by winning 24 consecutive decisions. His dominance was so complete that he gave up two or fewer runs in 20 of the 24 wins.

786 The number of RBI (786) for Roger Connor during parts of ten seasons with the Giants. Connor surpassed the century mark four times, including a career high and league leading 130 in 1889. His total with the club ranks among the top ten in franchise history.

787 Joe McGinnity struck out (787) batters during 300 games pitched for the Giants. His highest season total was only 171, and he needed 434 innings to get that many—but over the course of seven seasons and more than 2,150 innings he racked up one of the top 25 totals in franchise history.

788 Hoyt Wilhelm gave up (7.88) hits per nine innings during five seasons pitching for the Giants—one of the ten best ratios in franchise history. The first relief pitcher inducted into Baseball's Hall of Fame, Wilhelm was also a World War II veteran who won a Purple Heart during the Battle of the Bulge. And he was tough to hit. Wilhelm once said, "I don't even try to fool anybody. I just throw the knuckleball 85 to 90 percent of the time. You don't need variations because the ball jumps around so crazily, it's like having a hundred pitches."

789 Jeffrey Leonard played (789) games during eight seasons with the Giants. He batted .275 and hit 99 homers from 1981-88. He was an All-Star outfielder once, in 1987 when he hit .280 with 19 homers, but he was a fan-favorite for the better part of a decade.

790 The offensive winning percentage (.790) for Barry Bonds in 1997. He played in a career high 159 games for the third time, and posted his usual monstrous numbers: a .291 average, 40 homers, 123 runs, and 101 RBI. His OWP estimate was third highest in the league.

791 The on-base plus slugging percentage (.791) for Fred Lewis in 2008. Lewis, an outfielder who saw limited duty in 2006-07, saw a lot of action in 2008 and made good use of it. He led the club in OPS, after hitting 25 doubles and a team high 11 triples. He batted .282 with nine homers and he also stole 21 bases. The one area he struggled in was strikeouts—he went down 124 times in only 468 at bats.

792 The winning percentage (.792) for Shawn Estes in 1997—one of the top 15 season efforts in franchise history. He was 19-5, was second among league leaders for wins, and third for winning percentage.

793 The winning percentage (.793) for Sal Maglie in 1951. His winning percentage was second best in the league, but with a 23-6 record he led the league in wins. Maglie made his first All-Star team that season and placed fourth in Most Valuable Player balloting.

794 Christy Mathewson gave up (7.94) hits per nine innings during his Hall of Fame career. The only season he led the league was 1909, but his career ratio is one of the top 100 in baseball history. Mathewson really excelled when it came to control. Seven times he led the league in fewest walks per nine innings—and combined with his reluctance to give up hits, he posted the best WHIP ratio in the league on four occasions.

795 The on-base plus slugging percentage (.795) for Dave Bancroft during four-plus seasons with the Giants. His career high .830 OPS came in 1921, when he batted .318 with a career high six homers. The Hall of Fame shortstop was never a power guy at the plate, but he held his own, thank you very much—and his OPS for the Giants ranks among the top 40 in franchise history.

796 Bill Swift gave up (7.96) hits per nine innings during three seasons pitching for the Giants—one of the 15 best ratios among players with at least 500 innings for the club. The former Olympian and #2 overall pick of the 1984 amateur draft was 31-12 for the Giants in 1992-93, and he gave up only 339 hits in 396-plus innings.

Swift was only 8-7 in 1994, his last season with the club, but even then he averaged just one hit per inning.

797 The on-base plus slugging percentage (.797) for Ray Durham during six seasons with the Giants. He batted .276 with 77 homers, not bad at all for a switch-hitting infielder. His best year for OPS was 2006. Durham reached base at a .360 clip while posting a career high .538 slugging percentage, good for a team best and career high .898 OPS. Durham's career OPS with the Giants ranks among the top 40 in franchise history.

798 The New York Yankees scored (798) runs in 1951. It was the second highest total in the American League behind New York's biggest rival, the Boston Red Sox. In the National League the Giants were second in scoring with 781 runs, trailing its biggest rival the Brooklyn Dodgers. It was the Giants and Yankees, however, that won the pennants and met in the 1951 World Series. Unfortunately, the Yankees offense carried the day and won the series, outscoring the Giants 29-18 in six games.

799 The slugging percentage (.799) for Barry Bonds in 2002. In his second of four consecutive MVP seasons, Bonds hit 46 homers and led the league in slugging for the fifth time.

800 The winning percentage (.800) for Mickey Welch in 1885—the highest in franchise history during baseball's pre-modern era. The Hall of Famer was 44-11, leading the league in winning percentage, but placing second in wins behind the 53 for John Clarkson of the Chicago White Stockings.

San Francisco Giants Splash Hits (2000-10)

#	Player	Date
1	Barry Bonds	5/1/00
2	Barry Bonds	5/10/00
3	Barry Bonds	5/10/00
4	Barry Bonds	5/24/00
5	Barry Bonds	7/19/00
6	Barry Bonds	9/20/00
7	Barry Bonds	4/17/01
8	Barry Bonds	4/18/01
9	Barry Bonds	5/24/01
10	Felipe Crespo	5/28/01
11	Barry Bonds	5/30/01
12	Barry Bonds	6/12/01
13	Felipe Crespo	7/8/01
14	Barry Bonds	8/4/01
15	Barry Bonds	8/14/01
16	Barry Bonds	8/31/01
17	Barry Bonds	9/29/01
18	Barry Bonds	5/13/02
19	Barry Bonds	5/18/02
20	Barry Bonds	5/18/02
21	Barry Bonds	9/8/02
22	Barry Bonds	9/28/02
23	Barry Bonds	10/12/02
24	Barry Bonds	4/14/03
25	Barry Bonds	4/30/03
26	J.T. Snow	6/5/03
27	Barry Bonds	6/27/03
28	Jose Cruz, Jr.	7/8/03
29	Barry Bonds	8/8/03
30	Barry Bonds	8/19/03
31	Barry Bonds	9/13/03
32	Barry Bonds	4/12/04
33	Barry Bonds	4/13/04
34	Michael Tucker	5/30/04
35	A.J. Pierzynski	7/6/04
36	Barry Bonds	7/30/04
37	Barry Bonds	8/3/04
38	Michael Tucker	4/9/05
39	Randy Winn	9/14/05
40	Barry Bonds	9/18/05
41	Barry Bonds	8/21/06
42	Barry Bonds	4/18/07
43	Ryan Klesko	5/21/07
44	Ryan Klesko	6/29/07
45	Barry Bonds	8/8/07
46	Fred Lewis	4/26/08
47	John Bowker	7/2/08
48	Andres Torres	6/15/09
49	Pablo Sandoval	7/30/09
50	Pablo Sandoval	8/29/09
51	Aubrey Huff	5/1/10
52	Aubrey Huff	6/16/10
53	Andres Torres	7/28/10
54	Pablo Sandoval	8/12/10
55	Pablo Sandoval	9/30/10

> "Until I played at Candlestick, I never realized how great Willie Mays must have been. My God, what would he have done in a real ballpark?"
>
> — *Ozzie Smith*
>
> "Dynamite."
>
> — *Jack Clark, on what would improve Candlestick Park*

Chapter Nine

Splash Hits

IT WAS 1996, Giants executives Larry Baer and Peter Magowan were seeking voter approval for a new ballpark, and they had an ace up their sleeves. The stadium would sit on the southeastern edge of downtown with the right field wall and China Basin right up against each other.

As executive vice president Baer explains, "We had a model, and we took it from place to place around the city and we showed balls landing in the water. It was great. People said, 'this is magical.'"

The Chicago Cubs and Wrigley have Waveland and Sheffield Avenues, both unique and exciting, but it is hard for anything to compare with the image of baseballs splashing into the Bay. Baer and Magowan knew this, and they used the image, along with a recording of Bob Costas calling a home run, to sway the voters.

It worked!

Approval was granted and the privately financed $357 million stadium would soon become a reality. Construction began on December 11, 1997, and there was an air of excitement in the city. The stadium went up and anticipation grew. Finally, on April 11, 2000, after starting the season on the road, the 3-4 Giants played in their new home.

At 1:05 on a Tuesday afternoon, 40,930 fans watched the beginning of a new era in San Francisco baseball. Lefty Kirk Rueter threw the first pitch, a ball, to Dodgers outfielder Devon White, and all was right in the City by the Bay.

All was not right over the next five days though. San Francisco dropped five straight in the new park and limped onto the road at 3-9. The club returned on April 28 and dropped its sixth straight at home when Montreal hammered out a 9-3 victory.

Finally, on April 29, Kirk Rueter took the mound once again, and heading into the eighth the score was tied 1-1. After John Johnstone, in relief of Rueter, retired the Expos in order in the top of the eighth, Barry Bonds led off the bottom half with his ninth blast on the year, and the Giants hung on for the 2-1 victory.

The club finally grabbed its first win at home, but the image of which Baer and Magowan had pushed some four years earlier—a splash hit home run into McCovey Cove—had yet to happen.

The Giants suffered another home loss on April 30, and then the Mets came to town on May 1. The Giants jumped all over them. The score was 6-0 in the bottom of the sixth when Barry Bonds came to the plate. New York's Rich Rodriguez delivered and Bonds turned on it. The ball sailed over the right field wall and splashed into McCovey Cove.

In that instant a vision became reality and the San Francisco Giants got real tough to beat. The club went on a seven-game winning streak, and after the 2-7 home start marched to a 53-19 record at home. At season's end, the Giants had the best record in the National League at 97-65 and claimed the West by 11 games.

Bonds went on to hit five more home runs into McCovey Cove in 2000. Two opposing players, Todd Hundley of Los Angeles and Luis Gonzalez of Arizona, did so as well.

The picturesque ballpark, with its 68 luxury suites, great sightlines, extra-wide concourse which allows fans to still see the action while at the concession stand, and tremendous setting, was and is a success.

The Giants launched 55 splash hits from 2000-10, with Barry Bonds the owner of 35 of them—opposing players hit 23 into McCovey Cove during that timeframe—but get ready for the home run-hitting prowess of Barry Bonds, here in Chapter Nine.

801 Jeff Kent walked only (801) times during his big league career. He struck out 1,522 times, but no big deal. He might have been a second baseman, but he was still a run producer. After all, Kent did bat *behind* Barry Bonds in San Francisco. His job was to swing the stick and drive home runs. And he did that well: six consecutive 100-RBI seasons for the Giants and 1,518 career RBI.

802 Kirk Rueter faced (802) batters in 1997. His first full season with the club, Rueter was 13-6 for a .684 winning percentage that was sixth best in the league. Rueter was released by the club in August, 2005, but a year later the Giants honored the lefty with "Kirk Rueter Day" at AT&T Park.

803 Hugh McQuillan pitched (803) innings during parts of six seasons with the Giants. He was 53-44 with a respectable 3.67 earned run average from 1922-27, and he was 14-8 in only 23 starts in 1924. The Giants traded Larry Benton, Fred Toney, Harry Hulihan, and

$100,000 in cash to get McQuillan from the Boston Braves in July, 1922, just in time for the man known as Handsome Hugh to win a world championship with the club. McQuillan was the starter and winner in Game 4 of the World Series, pitching nine innings but allowing only eight hits and three runs in a 4-3 decision vs. the New York Yankees.

804 The earned run average (8.04) for righty Greg Minton in 1978. The Royals third round pick in 1970 was ineffective during 11 games with the Giants in 1978, allowing 14 earned runs in 15-plus innings. It was the fourth consecutive season that he spent a few games with the big club, and none of his work suggested he'd get too many more chances. Then came 1979, when Minton was 4-3 out of the pen with a *1.81 ERA* in 46 games. And that began a stretch of four seasons when he was a dominant reliever. Minton's ERA was 2.46 and 2.88 the next two seasons, and then came his finest season, 1981. He was 10-4 with a 1.83 ERA, he made his only career All-Star team, and he placed sixth in Cy Young balloting.

805 Sam Jones gave up (8.05) hits per nine innings during three seasons pitching for the Giants—one of the top 15 ratios in franchise history. Jones won a league best 21 games in 1959, but there was only one Cy Young Award for both leagues at the time, and he placed second in balloting behind Early Wynn of the Chicago White Sox. A former Negro Leagues player, Toothpick Sam also led the league in strikeouts three times.

806 The winning percentage (.806) for Juan Marichal in 1966—one of the ten best in franchise history. Marichal was 25-6, and placed second in the league for both wins and winning percentage.

807 The Giants gave up (807) runs in 1984. Pitching, pitching, pitching . . . you got to have it if you want to compete. Just ask the 1984 squad that boasted the fifth highest scoring offense in the league, yet managed to win only 66 games. The Giants pitching staff gave up the most runs in baseball—*both leagues*—and finished with the league's worst record as a result. Three years later the pitching staff gave up only 669 runs, the lowest total in the league, and won 90 games and a division title. Pitching, pitching, pitching . . .

808 The winning percentage (.808) for 26-year-old rookie Larry Jansen in 1947. Jansen was 21-5 and led the league in winning percentage, earning him a second place finish in Rookie of the Year balloting and a seventh place finish in MVP balloting.

809 Jo-Jo Moore scored (809) runs during parts of 12 seasons with the Giants—one of the top 20 totals in franchise history. He hit the century mark three consecutive seasons from 1934-36, ranking among the league's top ten each season and scoring a career best 110 runs in 1936.

810 The winning percentage (.810) for Doc Crandall in 1910. He was 17-4, giving him the third best winning percentage in the league and one of the ten best in franchise history. Crandall won 102 games in parts of ten big league seasons—but he won over 200 additional games playing in the Pacific Coast League.

811 The on-base plus slugging percentage (.811) for Matty Alou in 1961. The two-time All-Star batted .310 during his rookie campaign with the Giants, but it was in Pittsburgh that Alou put up his best numbers. After three successive subpar seasons from 1963-65, the Giants traded him to the Pittsburgh Pirates. So of course, in 1966 he batted .342 and won the batting title. Alou batted .331 or better four consecutive seasons from 1966-69, and was among the league's top four leading hitters all four seasons.

812 The slugging percentage (.812) for Barry Bonds in 2004. He hit 45 home runs—the fifth consecutive season he reached that plateau—and it was the seventh time he led the league in slugging. All that power led to a fourth consecutive MVP Award for Bonds, the seventh and final of his career.

813 The winning percentage (.813) for Hooks Wiltse in 1904. The rookie lefty set a record by winning his first 12 decisions as a starter, and he had the second best winning percentage in the league after posting a 13-3 record. Wiltse later notched a pair of 20-win seasons for the Giants.

814 The winning percentage (.814) for Joe McGinnity in 1904. The Hall of Famer was 35-8, setting a franchise record winning percentage that lasted nearly five decades. It remains one of the five best in franchise history.

815 The offensive winning percentage (.815) for Barry Bonds from 1986-2007. Bonds' OWP is the highest among every player from his era. His estimated OWP was the highest in the league ten times, seven of which were for San Francisco.

816 The Giants scored (816) runs in 1887. That total was only fourth highest out of eight teams in the league, but the offensive unit was in high gear for at least two games in June. In a span of four days, New York beat Washington 26-2 and Philadelphia 29-1.

817 The number of RBI (817) for shortstop Edgar Renteria from 1996-2008. In 13 seasons with Florida, St. Louis, Boston, Atlanta, and Detroit, Renteria won a world championship, multiple Gold Gloves, multiple Silver Slugger Awards, and proved himself as one of the premiere shortstops in the game. The 33-year-old veteran signed a two-year deal with the Giants worth an estimated $18.5 million for 2009-10.

818 The winning percentage (.818) for Sal Maglie in 1950. He led the league in winning percentage after posting an 18-4 record—thanks to his 2.71 earned run average, which also led the league. At one point he tossed four consecutive shutouts and 45 consecutive scoreless innings, just falling short of the franchise record 46 1/3 consecutive scoreless innings for Carl Hubbell in 1933.

819 Vida Blue gave up (8.19) hits per nine innings during six seasons pitching for the Giants—one of the top 25 ratios in franchise history. Blue was so good, the Giants traded six players, a player to be named later, and $300,000 to get him from Oakland.

820 The on-base plus slugging percentage (.820) for George Burns in 1914. He was second in the league in on-base percentage (.403), ninth in slugging (.417), and sixth in OPS . . . but led the team in all three stats. He was also the team leader in average (.303), runs (100), hits (170), doubles (35), triples (ten), steals (62), extra-base hits (48), and times on base (264). Burns was fourth in MVP balloting.

821 The on-base plus slugging percentage (.821) for Barry Bonds in 1987. It was the second season for the Pirates outfielder, and Bonds was still trying to figure out how to get on base consistently. He worked it out. Bonds led the league in OPS nine times and was above a 1.000 OPS 14 times in 15 full seasons of play from 1992-2007. It would have been 15 for 15, but his OPS was .999 in 2006.

822 Willie McCovey got (822) extra-base hits during 19 seasons with the Giants. The Hall of Famer ranks among the top 60 in baseball history with 920 career extra-base hits, and his total with the Giants is fourth best in franchise history.

823 Bill Terry won (823) games managing the Giants. He was the skipper for ten seasons from 1932-41, posting a .555 winning percentage while claiming three pennants and the 1933 World Series. Terry, who was a player-manager for five seasons, is third in franchise history for managerial wins.

824 The on-base plus slugging percentage (.824) for Bengie Molina in 2008 when he worked the count to 2-0 or 3-0. Like all good hitters, Molina's numbers improved the deeper he went into the count. His overall OPS was .767.

825 The on-base plus slugging percentage (.825) for Santo Domingo native Eugenio Velez during September and October, 2008. The second-year player started the season with a .653 OPS during March and April. It was a miserable .341 in May, which put him back in the minors. He was up again in July, and so was his OPS: .579. It kept climbing in August: .792. And then in the season's final month he batted .341 with 12 RBI and eight extra-base hits in 85 at bats.

826 The Giants gave up (826) runs in 1970. It was the highest total in baseball, either league. The Giants scored 831 runs that season, which was also the highest total in baseball, either league. With no pitching the offense carried the club to 86 wins, but with no pitching, it was still 16 games behind the Reds.

827 The offensive winning percentage (.827) for Barry Bonds in 1996. His stats: a .308 average, 42 homers, 122 runs, 129 RBI, .461 on-base percentage, and a .615 slugging percentage. He was so good, his numbers became almost routine, such that his 1996 performance earned a rather "ho-hum" fifth place finish in MVP balloting. It would have been a career year for almost anybody else.

828 The ratio (.828) of walks plus hits per innings pitched (WHIP) for Christy Mathewson in 1909. It was the third time he led the league in WHIP, and he did so with a ratio that is among the top ten in baseball history and that is the best all-time for the Giants. Mathewson's career 1.057 ratio for the Giants is also a franchise record.

829 Shawn Estes faced (829) batters in 2000. He was 15-6, and led the club with a .714 winning percentage that was third best in the league.

830 Rich Robertson faced (830) batters in 1970. It was the fifth year in a row that Robertson got some PT with the Giants, but the previous four seasons he pitched fewer than 60 innings total, compared to 1970 when he started 26 games and pitched 183-plus innings. Robertson also got his name on the leader board that season . . . unfortunately, that wasn't a good thing. His only stat to top the charts was his 18 wild pitches. He was 8-9 on the mound, and after going 2-2 in 1971 his playing days were done.

831 The Giants gave up (831) runs in 1999. The team earned run average was 4.71, tenth worst in the league. Kirk Rueter won 15 games despite a 5.41 ERA because the club could flat produce on offense. The Giants scored 872 runs, third highest in the league, but without any pitching the best it could do was second place, 14 games behind the D-Backs.

832 Gaylord Perry faced (832) batters in 1964. He was already 25 years old when the 1964 season began, and yet he'd won only four career games. Perry was extremely effective that season, allowing only 63 of those batters to reach base and score an earned run—good for a 2.75 earned run average and 12 wins. He won only eight games in 1965, however, and he was 27 years old at the start of 1967, his sixth season, with only 24 career wins to his credit. And somehow he still managed to win 314 games before his Hall of Fame career came to an end.

833 The winning percentage (.833) for Hall of Fame knuckleball artist Hoyt Wilhelm in 1952. He was a 29-year-old rookie who went 15-3 and placed second in Rookie of the Year balloting behind Joe Black of the Brooklyn Dodgers. Wilhelm's record came completely out of the bullpen—he pitched in 71 games, but none of them were starts—and his winning percentage set a franchise record.

834 The on-base plus slugging percentage (.834) for the Giants in 2000. San Francisco won the division with a 97-65 record, thanks to solid pitching and an offense that scored the third highest runs total in the league, and was second in the league in OPS. Unfortunately, the Mets pitching staff limited the Giants offense to a .210 average and a .639 OPS in the Division Series. New York only outscored the Giants 13-11, but won the best-of-five series in four games.

835 Gary Lavelle gave up (8.35) hits per nine innings during parts of 11 seasons with the Giants—one of the top 35 ratios in franchise history. Lavelle was stingy in the runs department as well, posting a

2.82 earned run average with the club. He also won ten games in 1976, 13 games in 1978, and ten games in 1982—without making a single start in any of those seasons.

836 Bill Rigney managed the Giants for (836) games. He was at the helm for the final game in New York on September 29, 1957, and for the first game in San Francisco on April 15, 1958. Rigney, unfortunately, never placed higher than third during six seasons and two tours of duty with the club. His best season was 83-71 in 1959, but he was 406-430 overall.

837 The ratio (.837) of walks plus hits per innings pitched for Christy Mathewson in 1908—the second best in franchise history. Mathewson owns four of the top ten all-time ratios for the Giants.

838 George Davis scored (838) runs during parts of ten seasons with the Giants—one of the top 15 totals in franchise history. Davis never led the league in runs, and in fact, he was among the league's top ten leaders only twice, yet his 1,539 total runs ranks among the top 60 in baseball history.

839 Juan Marichal faced (839) batters in 1967. He was 14-9 and led the league with 162 strikeouts after a 3-1 complete game victory vs. Pittsburgh on August 1. Injuries limited Marichal to only one start the rest of the season, however, denying him his best chance at leading the league in Ks. Marichal's 2,303 career strikeouts is one of the top 50 totals in baseball history, but he never led the league in any one season.

840 Dusty Baker won (840) games managing the Giants. Baker led the club for ten seasons from 1993-2002, winning two division titles, one wild card, and one pennant. He was a three-time Manager of the Year recipient in San Francisco, and when he left the club he trailed only John McGraw in games (1,556), victories, and losses (715) in franchise history.

841 The slugging percentage (.841) for Willie Mays during August, 1965. In one of the most prolific displays of power on record, Mays hit 17 home runs, drove home 29 runs, scored 32 times, batted .363, and reached base at a .446 clip that month. The club scored 143 runs in August—after scoring just 172 in June and July combined.

842 The Dodgers scored (842) runs in 1962. It was the second highest total in the league behind the Giants, which is exactly where the Dodgers finished ... in second, behind the Giants. The Dodgers spent 95 days in first but hit the skids in the season's final month, going 13-14 in September after posting a winning record every month from April through August. The Giants caught the Dodgers and forced a three-game playoff, and in the first game Billy Pierce and Willie Mays came up huge. Pierce tossed a three-hit shutout and Mays hit a pair of homers, knocking Sandy Koufax out of the game in the first inning, and the Giants won 8-0. LA won the second game 8-7, but the Giants won the pennant 6-4 in the deciding game.

843 The on-base plus slugging percentage (.843) for Irish Meusel during the 1921 and 1922 World Series'. After batting .345 with a homer and seven RBI during the Giants 1921 World Series victory vs. the Yankees, Meusel led the club during the 1922 regular season with a .878 OPS. The Giants secured another pennant with 93 victories, and then Meusel kept the offense rolling in a rematch vs. the Yankees in the 1922 World Series with a two-run single in Game 1, a three-run homer in Game 2, an RBI single in Game 3, and yet another RBI in Game 4. The Giants won the series in five games—and Meusel got seven RBI in the World Series for the second consecutive season.

844 The number of times (844) the Giants struck out in 1965. It was the lowest total among all ten teams in the league—and because San Francisco put the ball in play better than any other team, it also boasted a .312 on-base percentage that was third best in the league. The Giants won 95 games but came up two games short of the Dodgers for the pennant.

845 Kip Wells faced (845) batters in 2002. Wells posted pretty good numbers for the Pirates. He won 12 games with a 3.58 earned run average and 134 strikeouts. Still, he would have preferred not to have faced Barry Bonds on August 9. It was Wells who served up Bonds' 600th career home run.

846 Kirk Rueter faced (846) batters in 2002. The lefty gave up 204 hits but allowed only 73 of those batters to reach base and score an earned run, good for a 3.61 earned run average. Rueter was 14-8 with the Giants high-powered offense backing him up, which gave him a .636 winning percentage that was best on the club.

847 The earned run average (8.47) for Padres pitcher Mike Corkins in 1969. Originally signed by the Giants in 1965, Corkins was selected by the Padres in the 1968 expansion draft and made his big league debut a year later. Two weeks into his career he faced the team that originally signed him, and on September 22, 1969, Corkins delivered the pitch that Willie Mays launched for his 600th career home run.

848 The offensive winning percentage (.848) for Barry Bonds in 1993. He was the league MVP in his first season by the Bay, blasting 46 homers and 123 RBI, batting .336, and scoring 129 runs.

849 Shawn Estes faced (849) batters in 1997. The 24-year-old lefty began his third big league season with a 3-8 record and a 4.23 earned run average in 14 career starts. A first round draft pick of the Mariners in 1991, people expected him to be good. Estes exploded onto the scene in 1997, exceeding everyone's expectations with a 19-5 record, and allowing only 71 of those batters to reach base and score an earned run—good for a 3.18 ERA.

850 The winning percentage (.850) for phenom Tim Lincecum after improving his record to 17-3 with a complete game shutout vs. the San Diego Padres on September 13, 2008. The Elias Sports Bureau reported that Lincecum became just the seventh player in franchise history to win at least 17 of his first 20 decisions to start a season. The others: Mickey Welch (17-3, 1885), Joe McGinnity (18-2, 1904), Christy Mathewson (17-3, 1909), Rube Marquard (19-1, 1912), Johnny Antonelli (17-3, 1954), and Gaylord Perry (18-2, 1966).

851 The number of career RBI (851) for Mike Tiernan. His season high was 102 in 1893, and his overall total ranks among the top ten in franchise history.

852 The on-base plus slugging percentage (.852) for switch-hitting infielder Emmanuel Burriss when batting with the bases empty in 2008. A first round selection in 2006, Burriss got a taste of big league action for the first time in 2008, batting .283 in 240 at bats. His OPS fell to .496 with runners on base, however, and fell again to just .433 with runners in scoring position—but don't assume his inexperience made him completely unable to deliver in the clutch. With the bases loaded his OPS was back up to .708, and he was 3 for 8 with a sacrifice fly and seven RBI.

853 The on-base plus slugging percentage (.853) for four-time All-Star Jack Clark in 1982. Clark led the club with 271 total bases, 30 doubles, 27 homers, 103 RBI, 60 extra-base hits, and 245 times on base. His OPS was among the league's top ten leaders, and his name was all over the offensive leader boards, but 1982 was *not* one of his All-Star seasons.

854 The number of strikeouts (854) for the Giants pitching staff in 1984. Mike Krukow, a Cal Poly product, led the team with 141 Ks. Unfortunately, as a whole the staff struck out the third fewest batters among 12 teams in the league . . . but gave up the most hits and the most runs, and as a result won the fewest number of games.

855 The career on-base plus slugging percentage (.855) for Mike Tiernan. The lefty batted .311 with 106 homers. With a .392 on-base percentage and a .463 slugging percentage, Tiernan ranks among the top 20 in franchise history for career OPS.

856 The on-base plus slugging percentage (.856) for Travis Jackson in 1926. The team leader in average (.327), on-base percentage (.362), slugging (.494), and OPS, the Hall of Fame shortstop was only 22, but he was in his fourth season starting for the Giants.

857 The Giants scored (857) runs in 1924. It was the highest total in the league as the Giants got the most hits, hit the most homers, hit for the highest average, and posted the highest on-base percentage and slugging percentage in the league. All of which led to 93 victories and a fourth consecutive pennant.

858 The on-base plus slugging percentage (.858) for Mike Aldrete in 1987. The Stanford product set several career highs during his sophomore season: average (.325), hits (116), runs (50), doubles (18), RBI (51), OBP (.396), slugging (.462), plus . . . OPS. Aldrete was only 1 for 10, however, during the League Championship Series vs. St. Louis, as the Giants lost in seven games. He got one more shot at a ring in 1996, his final season, and he got exactly one at bat in the 1996 World Series. Aldrete was 0 for 1, but he was playing with the Yankees—and he went out a world champion.

859 The ratio (.859) of walks plus hits per innings pitched for Juan Marichal in 1966—best in the league, and third best in franchise history. Marichal pitched 307-plus innings, but gave up only 228 hits and 36 walks. He also struck out 222 batters.

860 The on-base plus slugging percentage (.860) for Will Clark in 1992. He led the club in average (.300), OBP (.384), and slugging (.476), so naturally he led the club in OPS as well. His home run and RBI numbers were actually down that season, but Will the Thrill still made his fifth consecutive All-Star team, and he was among the league's top ten leaders for OPS.

861 Slim Sallee faced (861) batters in 1917. In his first full season with the Giants, Sallee was 18-7 with a 2.17 earned run average. The Giants won the pennant, but unfortunately, Sallee was 0-2 with a 5.28 ERA vs. the Chicago White Sox during the 1917 World Series. Chicago won that series in six games.

862 The Giants gave up (862) runs in 1996. It was the second highest total out of 14 teams in the league. The staff earned run average was 4.72, also the second highest in the league. The 1927 Yankees would find it difficult to overcome that hurdle ... and there was no chance for the Giants offense, which was the ninth worst in the league. It was a disastrous season, just plain ugly, but one year later the Giants were celebrating "worst-to-first." Dead last out West in 1996, the Giants completed a 22-game turnaround in one season and held off the Dodgers by two games to claim the division crown in 1997.

863 The slugging percentage (.863) for Barry Bonds in 2001. He broke the previous major league record .849 slugging percentage set by Babe Ruth in 1920. Bonds, of course, hit 73 home runs that season—but it was just the first of three campaigns where he produced a slugging percentage that ranks among baseball's all-time top ten.

864 The winning percentage (.864) for the Giants vs. Philadelphia in 1923. New York was 19-3 against the last place Phillies, which was a big reason why the Giants won the pennant by 4.5 games over Cincinnati (and 45.5 games over Philly...), but what the Giants did to the Phillies on June 1 was not only unprecedented, it was like something from a schoolyard playground. New York beat Philly 22-8, and in doing so, became the first team in the 20th century to score at least one run in every inning of a game.

865 The winning percentage (.865) for Sal Maglie from July 1950 through May 1952. During that timeframe the man known as the Barber, for his tendency to come in "high and tight" on opposing hitters, posted an astounding 45-7 record for the Giants.

866 The on-base plus slugging percentage (.866) for Monte Irvin during 653 games with the Giants. One of the top 15 in franchise history, Irvin batted .296 with 84 homers, a .389 on-base percentage, and a .477 slugging percentage.

867 The on-base plus slugging percentage (.867) for Bobby Bonds in 1971. He was eighth in the league after batting .288 with 33 homers, but he was only second on the club behind Willie Mays, who was fourth in the league with a .907 OPS.

868 The Giants on-base plus slugging percentage (.868) vs. left-handed pitching in 2001. The club batted .291 and hit 55 bombs against lefties, led by 17 for Barry Bonds and 12 for Rich Aurilia. The club batted .266 with a .802 OPS overall that season.

869 The on-base plus slugging percentage (.869) for Felipe Alou in 1962. It was his OBP that meant the most when he came to bat on October 3, trailing the Dodgers 4-2 in the top of the ninth with two men on, and his club down to its final two outs. At stake was a trip to the World Series when Alou coaxed a walk out of Dodgers pitcher Ed Roebuck. After an RBI single by Willie Mays and a sacrifice fly by Orlando Cepeda tied the game 4-4, Alou was on third, the bases loaded, and he was the potential winning run with Jim Davenport at the plate. Davenport worked a bases loaded walk, Alou scored the go-ahead run, and the good guys won the pennant.

870 Ron Bryant gave up (870) hits during 195 games pitched for the Giants. He was 57-55, and pitched more than 900 innings in those games. Bryant's best season was 1973 when he was 24-12 and earned *The Sporting News* Pitcher of the Year honors. Two other players won top honors for the Giants that season: Bobby Bonds, who was one home run shy of becoming baseball's first member of the 40/40 club, was *The Sporting News* Player of the Year, and Gary Matthews won Rookie of the Year. All that talent, the team still placed 11 games out of first.

871 Bob Brenly played (871) games for the Giants. He spent 705 of those games behind the dish, plus a few games at first or third, and some in the outfield. Brenly did not make his big league debut until he was 27, however, and he was 29 before he played a full season, which tends to skew his career offensive numbers. In his prime years, between the ages of 30 and 33, he hit 73 of his 91 career home runs and was a legitimate threat at the plate.

872 The Giants scored (872) runs in 1999. Third best in the league, the offense was built on power. Five guys belted 20-plus homers: Barry Bonds (34), Ellis Burks (31), J.T. Snow (24), Jeff Kent (23), and Rich Aurilia (22). All that power and yet the pitching staff served up more long balls than the Giants launched: 194-188. And pitching did the club in. The club won 86 games despite a staff ranked tenth worst in the league, but finished 14 games behind the D-Backs.

873 Robby Thompson turned (873) double plays for the Giants. The second baseman and 1983 first round draft pick earned one Gold Glove, in 1993, but he was a solid, consistent player during 11 seasons from 1986-96. His DP total is among the top ten in franchise history—but it is the highest on record for second basemen.

874 Chili Davis played (874) games for the Giants. Davis is labeled a winner in baseball circles for good reason. He made the postseason four times, won three world championships, and his teams won eight of nine postseason series' he played in. Unfortunately, the only postseason series Davis lost was his first—in 1989, his only playoff appearance with the Giants.

875 Noah Lowry faced (875) batters in 2005. That total led the club, as did his 13 wins, 3.78 ERA, 1.31 WHIP, 204-plus innings, 172 strikeouts, and 33 starts. Some will look at his 13-13 record and say his season was not especially noteworthy—but Lowry was only 6-11 with a 4.59 ERA when August began. He posted a 7-2 record down the stretch, however, and the Giants were 8-3 overall in his final 11 starts.

876 Jeff Tesreau, Christy Mathewson, and Rube Marquard combined to pitch (876) innings in 1913. The trio started 106 games, completed 62, and won 70. With three 20-game winners on the staff, the Giants cruised to 101 victories and another pennant.

877 George Burns scored (877) runs during parts of 11 seasons with the Giants—tenth best in franchise history. Burns led the league in runs five times, including a career high 115 in 1920.

878 The Giants scored (878) runs in 1962. Alvin Dark's team led the league in average (.278), on-base percentage (.340), slugging percentage (.441), hits (1,552), and home runs (204), and it easily scored the highest runs total in baseball. And yet with seven games left on the schedule the Giants trailed the Dodgers by four games. The Giants won 5 of 7, the Dodgers lost 6 of 7, and the two clubs finished the season with identical records, 101-61, setting the stage for another dramatic three-game playoff between the two rivals with a pennant hanging in the balance. Billy Pierce pitched a gem to win the first game, and after losing the second game 8-7, it took a four-run ninth inning rally in the third game to give the Giants a 6-4 victory and the pennant. On the mound to close out that game in the bottom of the ninth—Billy Pierce, who after opening the series with his 16th win, closed it out with his only save of the season. That's how it works when there is no tomorrow.

879 Phil Douglas gave up (8.79) hits per nine innings in 1922—the best ratio in the league. He also led the league in WHIP (1.199) and earned run average (2.63), all of which must have grated on opposing hitters, because the Giants offense made swinging the stick look so darn easy that year. Irish Meusel, Frank Snyder, George Kelly, Frankie Frisch, Dave Bancroft, Ross Youngs, and Casey Stengel all batted .321 or better, and the offense was going so good that Youngs hit for the cycle and Kelly hit a pair of inside-the-park homers . . . in the same game!

880 The on-base plus slugging percentage (.880) for Frankie Frisch in 1923. Ross Youngs led the club in on-base percentage (.412), but Frisch led the club in batting (.348), slugging (.485), OPS, hits (223), and total bases (311). Frisch also batted .400 with ten hits in six games during the 1923 World Series vs. the Yankees, but the Giants lost the series.

881 Red Murray played (881) games for the Giants. The outfielder was an integral part of John McGraw's teams that won three consecutive pennants from 1911-13, but he never won a world championship.

882 Gus Mancuso played (882) games for the Giants—one of the 50 highest totals in franchise history. The catcher spent time with the Cardinals, Giants, Cubs, Dodgers, and Phillies during his 17-year career, but his best days were in New York where he was a two-time All-Star and won the 1933 World Series.

883 The career on-base plus slugging percentage (.883) for Hall of Famer Roger Connor. One of the top 100 in baseball history, Connor was among the top five leaders 11 times from 1880-92, and he did most of his damage playing for the Giants.

884 Ruben Gomez faced (884) batters in 1958. Gomez and the first batter he faced in 1958 made history. Gino Cimoli batted leadoff for the Dodgers on April 15, 1958, at Seals Stadium in San Francisco for the first game in major league history to be played on the West Coast. Gomez was on the mound for the Giants, and he struck Cimoli out—

just one of six Ks on the day as he tossed a complete game 8-0 victory.

885 The on-base plus slugging percentage (.885) for Moises Alou from 1990-2008. One of the top 100 in baseball history, in two seasons with the Giants he did slightly better than his career average. Alou posted a .918 OPS in 2005 and a .923 OPS in 2006.

886 Dave LaPoint faced (886) batters in 1985. The Giants hit the century mark that season . . . in losses. Not a good year all around, and pitching was the root of the problem. LaPoint led the club in starts, innings, batters faced, and posted a respectable 3.57 earned run average but he only won seven games. Worse, he led the club and was second in the league with *17 losses*. The lefty was traded to Detroit in the offseason.

887 The on-base plus slugging percentage (.887) for Orlando Cepeda during nine seasons with the Giants—one of the top 15 in franchise history. Cepeda made his big league debut on April 15, 1958, the same date as the first game the Giants played in San Francisco. He got off to a great start, hitting a home run against Don Bessent as the Giants beat the Dodgers 8-0.

888 Juan Marichal faced (888) batters in 1973, his final season pitching for the Giants. He was a 35-year-old veteran and already a lock for the Hall of Fame. He was only 11-15, however, and just 17-31 during his final two seasons with the club. Marichal faced 13,958 batters during 3,444 innings pitched for the Giants—the third highest total in franchise history behind Christy Mathewson, who faced 19,093 batters, and Carl Hubbell, who faced 14,805 batters.

889 The career on-base plus slugging percentage (.889) for Willie McCovey. One of the top 100 in baseball history, he led the league three consecutive seasons from 1968-70.

890 Harry Danning played (890) career games—all of them for the Giants. He batted .285 for his career, but the catcher hit .300 or better three consecutive seasons and was a four-time All-Star during the 1930s and early 1940s.

891 Marvin Bernard played (891) games for the Giants—one of the 50 highest totals in franchise history. Not bad for a guy drafted in the 50th round.

892 The on-base plus slugging percentage (.892) for Kevin Mitchell during 624 games with the Giants. He batted .278 with 143 homers, 411 RBI, and a .536 slugging percentage. Mitchell's OPS ranks among the top ten in franchise history.

893 The slugging percentage (.893) for Barry Bonds at San Diego's Qualcomm Stadium in 2001. In his historic home run binge in 2001, Bonds punished San Diego's pitchers in their home ballpark to the tune of a .321 average and five homers in only seven games. Think that was bad? At Chase Field in Arizona Bonds batted .469 in ten games with five homers and a 1.063 slugging percentage. He did even more damage at Turner Field in Atlanta, where Braves pitchers were pummeled, a .700 average with six homers and a 2.600 slugging percentage, *in only three games!*

894 Jason Schmidt faced (894) batters in 2006. Opponents batted .238 against Schmidt for the season, but not during the month of May. Schmidt was 4-0 with a 1.17 earned run average in May. He struck out 35 batters in 46 innings, walked only seven, and gave up just 29 hits—a .174 average. He allowed more than one run only twice in six starts, and for his dominating performance he earned National League Pitcher of the Month honors. "It's the same stuff," Schmidt said, when asked about having previously won that honor in May, 2004. "I've just got a nice little rhythm going."

895 The on-base plus slugging percentage (.895) for Jack Clark in 1978. Clark only reached base at a .358 clip, but his OPS led the club because he smashed 79 extra-base hits. Clark also ranked sixth among league leaders in OPS.

896 The ratio (8.96) of strikeouts per nine innings for Jason Schmidt during 162 games with the Giants from 2001-06. Schmidt was among the league's top five leaders every year from 2002-05, and his career ratio with the club is a franchise record—at the moment—for pitchers with at least 500 innings. That should change in 2009, assuming Tim Lincecum remains healthy and keeps his same pace from 2007-08. Lincecum struck out ten batters per nine innings through his first 58 games and 373-plus innings with the Giants.

897 The Giants scored (897) runs in 1929. Led by Mel Ott (138) and Bill Terry (103), the Giants offense was the third highest scoring in the league. The pitching staff boasted a 3.97 earned run average that was the best in the league, and that combination gave the club 84 wins—but that was a disappointment, because with the best pitching staff and a powerful offense the Giants were a popular pick to win the pennant. Instead, the club placed 13.5 games behind the Cubs.

898 The on-base plus slugging percentage (.898) for Ray Durham in 2006. Durham set career highs that season in homers (26), slugging percentage (.538), and OPS—and he was the team leader in all three stats (though he was tied for the team lead in homers with Barry Bonds).

899 The career on-base plus slugging percentage (.899) for Bill Terry. The Giants all-time leading hitter epitomized the rare combination of power and average. Six times he was among the league's top ten for OPS—and his career mark is among the top 75 in baseball history.

900 Jeff Kent played (900) games for the Giants—one of the 50 highest totals in franchise history. His numbers: a .297 average, 175 homers, 247 doubles, 570 runs, and 689 RBI.

1951 National League Pennant Race

Team	W	L	WL%	GB
New York Giants*	98	59	.624	–
Brooklyn Dodgers	97	60	.618	1.0
St. Louis Cardinals	81	73	.526	15.5
Boston Braves	76	78	.494	20.5
Philadelphia Phillies	73	81	.474	23.5
Cincinnati Reds	68	86	.442	28.5
Pittsburgh Pirates	64	90	.416	32.5
Chicago Cubs	62	92	.403	34.5

*The Giants beat the Dodgers in a three-game playoff to win the pennant, after the two clubs finished the season with identical 96-58 records.

Days in First: Giants 5, Dodgers 120
Biggest Lead: Giants 1 game, Dodgers 13 games
Largest Deficit: Giants 13 games, Dodgers 2 games
Longest Winning Streak: Giants 16 games, Dodgers 10 games
Longest Losing Streak: Giants 11 games, Dodgers 4 games
Head-to-Head Record: Giants 11 wins, 14 losses

1962 National League Pennant Race

Team	W	L	WL%	GB
San Francisco Giants*	103	62	.624	–
Los Angeles Dodgers	102	63	.618	1.0
Cincinnati Reds	98	64	.605	3.5
Pittsburgh Pirates	93	68	.578	8.0
Milwaukee Braves	86	76	.531	15.5
St. Louis Cardinals	84	78	.519	17.5
Philadelphia Phillies	81	80	.503	20.0
Houston Astros	64	96	.400	36.5
Chicago Cubs	59	103	.364	42.5
New York Mets	40	120	.250	60.5

*The Giants beat the Dodgers in a three-game playoff to win the pennant, after the two clubs finished the season with identical 101-61 records.

Days in First: Giants 53, Dodgers 95
Biggest Lead: Giants 4.5 games, Dodgers 5.5 games
Largest Deficit: Giants 5.5 games, Dodgers 5 games
Longest Winning Streak: Giants 10 games, Dodgers 13 games
Longest Losing Streak: Giants 6 games, Dodgers 5 games
Head-to-Head Record: Giants 11 wins, 10 losses

"It was a pretty fierce rivalry ... we didn't like them, and they didn't like us."

— Bobby Thomson, on the Dodgers

Chapter Ten

The Rivalry

UNOFFICIALLY IT BEGAN on October 18, 1889. The Brooklyn Bridegrooms, champs of the American Association, made its way to the Polo Grounds to play the N.L. best New York Giants. The exhibition World Series began with Brooklyn claiming a 12-10 victory in Game 1, but the Giants stormed back to win the series six games to three.

Less than a year later, on May 3, 1890, the first official game was played at Brooklyn's Washington Park. The Bridegrooms won 7-3 and, little did anybody know, it had just started a rivalry that would become one of the greatest in all of sports.

It didn't take long for the rivalry to really develop. On June 12, 1890, a reported crowd of 551 watched as the Bridegrooms beat the Giants 12-6. This game was emotionally charged thanks to Brooklyn's third base coach Darby O'Brien. He pretended to be a runner and drew a throw to third. The seeds of a rivalry had been sowed and the roots ran fast, strong, and deep.

On opening day, April 11, 1912, the Giants were back in Washington Park and hammered the Dodgers 18-3. It might have been worse, but the game was called after six innings because the crowd was so big. The police were brought in to control the raucous fans, and ended up calling the game.

The police-intervention game was not long before a rivalry within the rivalry began. Wilbert Robinson, long-time Giants pitching coach and friend of manager John McGraw, was let go. He hopped over to Brooklyn in 1914 and this caused an even deeper divide between the former friends. Their constant feud further fueled the already deep rivalry.

The teams went back and forth through the years with the most spectacular finish to a season occurring in 1951. The Giants stormed back to force a playoff for the pennant and Bobby Thomson's "shot heard 'round the world" won it.

Then in 1957 the unthinkable happened. Walter O'Malley wanted a new stadium for the Dodgers, but he didn't get it. He began talks with the mayor of Los Angeles and pushed to move the team west. Once San Francisco mayor George Christopher heard of the plans, he teamed up with O'Malley to convince Giants owner Horace Stoneham to move west as well. After all, the rivalry had to continue.

On May 28, Philadelphia hammered the Giants 16-6 at the Polo Grounds, Brooklyn lost at Pittsburgh 3-1, and New York lost two teams as the National League owners voted unanimously to allow both clubs to move west. There was a stipulation attached to the move, it was either all or none. If one team decided to stay, the other had to stay too. This proved a non-issue. In August the Giants franchise announced it would move to San Francisco, Brooklyn's announcement came in October.

The rivalry crossed the continent and resumed in California on April 15, 1958.

The Los Angeles Dodgers traveled north to battle the San Francisco Giants and took an 8-0 thumping. Unfortunately it hasn't been so good for the Giants since the move. The Dodgers have won a few more, but the overall record still favors the orange and black.

Through 2008, the Giants hold the all-time series lead, 1,154-1,130 with 17 ties. The Giants won 722 times in New York, while the Dodgers claimed 671 victories. Since moving west, the Dodgers have won 459 times and the Giants 422.

In 2008, the teams finished deadlocked at 9-9. This was the 18th season in which they tied. They also played eight one-run games with the Giants winning six of them. Overall, the clubs have played 679 one-run games with Los Angeles holding the lead by one game, 340-339.

No team in baseball has won more games than the Giants: 10,256 wins through 2008. The Dodgers are fourth with 9,550 wins.

No doubt this is a rivalry amongst rivalries. It is not manufactured. It is deep and rooted in both the East and West coasts. And that is good. Our heroes in orange and black need their villains . . . and those villains wear blue and white.

901 The on-base plus slugging percentage (.901) for Willie McCovey during 19 seasons with the Giants. He made his debut in spectacular fashion, going 4 for 4 with a pair of triples against Hall of Famer Robin Roberts on July 30, 1959. Only five players in franchise history have a higher OPS—fellow Hall of Famers Willie Mays, Mel Ott, and Johnny Mize, and contemporary stars Jeff Kent and Barry Bonds.

902 The number of batters (902) faced by Jim Hearn in 1951. Hearn let 85 of those batters reach base and score an earned run, good for a 3.62 earned run average that was third best in the Giants rotation. He was also third in wins with 17. Hearn beat Philly 5-1 on September 25. His 16th win, it brought the Giants within one game of the Dodgers. On October 1, Hearn took the mound for the first game of the best-of-three playoff vs. Brooklyn and he was masterful—a 3-1 victory for his career high 17th win.

903 The on-base plus slugging percentage (.903) for Jeff Kent during six seasons with the Giants. When Kent announced his retirement in early 2009, former teammate Rich Aurilia said, "I would guess the next stop for him somewhere down the road will be Cooperstown." We'd have to agree with that assessment.

904 The on-base plus slugging percentage (.904) for Ross Youngs in 1920. The Hall of Fame outfielder led the club and was among the league's top three leaders in batting (.351), on-base percentage (.427), slugging percentage (.477), OPS, hits (204), and total bases (277). The Giants offense was the highest scoring in the league, but the club fell just short of Brooklyn in the pennant race, or else it could have been *five* straight pennants instead of four.

905 Jesse Barnes faced (905) batters in 1922. He gave up 236 hits and 83 of those batters reached base and scored an earned run against him—but Barnes, who played a key role in the 1921-22 back-to-back world championships, was nothing short of spectacular in a May 7 game vs. Philadelphia. None of the batters he faced that day scored against him. In fact, none of them got a hit either, as Barnes got the no-no and a 6-0 victory.

906 Larry Doyle scored (906) runs during 13 seasons with the Giants—ninth best in franchise history. He hit the century mark just once, scoring 102 runs in 1911, but he was among the league's top seven leaders six times from 1909-15.

907 The on-base plus slugging percentage (.907) for Willie Mays in 1971. It was the best on the team, but Mays was a 40-year-old veteran who was nearing the end of his career. And despite a lifetime .302 average, Mays batted only .271 in 1971. In fact, the Giants leading hitter that season was Bobby Bonds, and he batted just .288. Juan Marichal was the leading pitcher with 18 wins. Without a .300 hitter or a 20-game winner, manager Charlie Fox's team still won the first division title in franchise history by a single game over the Los Angeles Dodgers.

908 The on-base plus slugging percentage (.908) for Mike Donlin in 1905. Third highest in the league, it was the best on the team, as was his .356 average, .413 on-base percentage, .495 slugging percentage, 216 hits, seven homers, 54 extra-base hits, 274 times on base, and

300 total bases. Donlin only batted .263 with one RBI vs. Philadelphia in the 1905 World Series, but the Giants won in five games anyway.

909 The slugging percentage (.909) for Bengie Molina vs. the Washington Nationals in 2008. Molina flat *tore up* the Nationals, batting 11 for 22 in six games with three doubles, two homers, eight RBI, and a 1.431 OPS—his highest mark against any team. Nationals pitcher Jason Bergman gave up both long balls to Molina on July 22, and said afterwards, "Molina had my number today . . . he just did a good job of hitting and he hit two balls out."

910 The slugging percentage (.910) for Barry Bonds vs. right handed pitching in 2001. Bonds was 112 for 335 against righties, with 56 of his 73 homers. His slugging percentage against lefties was still a very healthy .752.

911 The on-base plus slugging percentage (.911) for J.T. Snow vs. the San Diego Padres in 2001. Snow was 13 for 37 against the division rival Padres, the only team in the league he collected double-digit hits against that season. He also drew nine walks in 11 games against San Diego, good for a .478 on-base percentage. It was Arizona that Snow struggled against, and unfortunately it was Arizona that the Giants were chasing after for the division title.

912 The on-base plus slugging percentage (.912) for Bill Terry in 1928. Tenth in the league, he was only second on the team behind Mel Ott. Terry did lead the team with 64 extra-base hits and 100 runs.

913 The on-base plus slugging percentage (.913) for Willie McCovey in 1967. He led the team and was fifth highest in the league. Mac was third in the league with 31 homers, but he launched three of those bombs with the bases juiced.

914 The ratio (.914) of walks plus hits per innings pitched for Juan Marichal in 1965—second in the league, and the fourth best in franchise history. Marichal faced 1,153 major league batters, but gave up only 224 hits and 46 walks. He did make one huge mistake in 1965. Marichal intentionally hit Dodgers catcher Johnny Roseboro on the head—with a bat, no less. He was suspended and fined, substantially, but later in life the two rivals became good friends.

915 The slugging percentage (.915) for Barry Bonds at AT&T Park in 2001. In his quest to break the single season home run record, Bonds batted .335 with 37 of his 73 homers at the Giants home ballpark.

916 Carl Hubbell faced (916) batters in 1940. He let 87 of those runners reach base and score an earned run, which gave him an uncharacteristically high 3.65 earned run average, and . . . at 11-12, the only losing season of his career.

917 The slugging percentage (.917) for Jeffrey Leonard during the 1987 League Championship Series vs. St. Louis. Leonard was 10 for 24 with four home runs in the series—and he won series MVP honors despite the fact St. Louis won the series. Leonard, unfortunately, never won a pennant.

918 The on-base plus slugging percentage (.918) for Moises Alou in 2005. He was an All-Star during his first season in San Francisco, batting .316 with 12 homers and 41 RBI at the break, but he was slowed by injuries in the season's second half.

919 Wes Westrum played (919) games for the Giants—one of the 50 highest totals in franchise history. The catcher was a two-time All-Star and a member of the 1954 world championship club, but he hit only .217 for his career. In fact, he never hit above .236 for a season, and three times he hit under .200. Westrum is best known for being the catcher on the very first cover of *Sports Illustrated* in August, 1954, and later, for briefly managing the Giants from 1974-75.

920 The on-base plus slugging percentage (.920) for Pablo Sandoval vs. San Diego in 2008. The young prospect was 11 for 30 against the Giants division rival, with two doubles and a homer in seven games. If you want to play for the Giants it's important to step up your game against the instate rivals . . . and Sandoval did even better against the hated Dodgers during his first taste of big league action. He was 7 for 12, with three runs, three doubles, and six RBI in six games against LA.

921 The on-base plus slugging percentage (.921) for Mel Ott in 1928. He was a 19-year-old kid but it was already his third season with the club. Fred Lindstrom led the Giants in batting (.358), Shanty Hogan led the club in on-base percentage (.406), but Ott was the team leader in slugging (.524), OPS, and home runs (18).

922 Hal Schumacher faced (922) batters in 1936. He was only 11-13, but with a respectable 3.47 earned run average. The Giants won the pennant, and in Game 5 of the World Series against the Yankees, Schumacher achieved an extraordinary feat. With the bases loaded and nobody out in the third, he retired three consecutive Hall of

Famers without allowing any further runs to score: Joe DiMaggio struck out, Lou Gehrig struck out, and Bill Dickey flied out. Schumacher went the distance in a ten-inning 5-4 victory.

923 The on-base plus slugging percentage (.923) for Willie McCovey in 1968. Mac was the offensive leader in just about everything, belting 36 homers with 105 RBI, but with 88 wins it was a frustrating season to be a Giant. McCovey and his teammates, led by manager Herman Franks, placed second in the pennant race for the fourth consecutive season.

924 Chris Speier got (924) hits during ten seasons with the Giants. He came up with the Giants in 1971, and was the everyday shortstop until he was traded to the Expos after six games in 1977. Speier later signed with San Francisco as a free agent in 1987, returning to the Giants for the last three seasons of his career. He got a career high 151 hits in 1972, but batted a career high .271 in 1975.

925 The Giants scored (925) runs in 2000. That total is the highest on record since the club relocated from New York in 1958, led by Barry Bonds, who scored 129 times. Jeff Kent and Marvin Benard also surpassed the century mark, as the club posted the third highest total in the league—and claimed the division title.

926 Hal Schumacher gave up (926) career earned runs. He pitched 2,482-plus innings for the Giants from 1931-46, good for a 3.36 earned run average that ranks among the top 50 in franchise history. He also won 158 games—which puts him among the top ten for career wins.

927 The on-base plus slugging percentage (.927) for Aaron Rowand during day games in 2008. The Giants outfielder apparently prefers to play under the sun, as he batted .337 with seven homers and 32 RBI in only 193 at bats during the day—compared to .236 with six homers and 38 RBI in 356 at bats at night.

928 Bill Swift faced (928) batters in 1993. In his finest season as a professional, Swift was 21-8 with a team best 2.82 earned run average. Swift won his final four starts as the Giants battled the Braves down the stretch for the division title, including back-to-back games during which he tossed 17 consecutive scoreless innings.

929 The number of career RBI (929) for Travis Jackson. He hit the century mark just once, driving home 101 runs in 1934, but his career total is among the top ten in franchise history. Not bad for a guy Casey Stengel called, "The greatest bunter I ever saw." In all fairness, Stengel was actually praising Jackson, who was an excellent bunter and remains the franchise leader for sacrifices.

930 The on-base plus slugging percentage (.930) for Roger Connor in 1885. Baseball's original home run champion led the club in average (.371), on-base percentage (.435), slugging (.495), OPS, hits (169), total bases (225), and RBI (65), but he was *fifth* on the team in homers, with one ... and only *five* guys on the team even hit a homer that year. Buck Ewing led the way with six.

931 Irish Meusel got (931) hits during six seasons with the Giants. The outfielder was second on the club, and sixth in the league, with a career high 204 hits in 1922. Meusel batted .314 during his tenure with the club (and never batted below .292 in any one season), one of the ten highest averages in franchise history.

932 The on-base plus slugging percentage (.932) for Bengie Molina during 59 at bats in which he faced a 2-1 count in 2008. Molina posted a .457 on-base percentage and a .475 slugging percentage when he got ahead 2-1, compared to his .243 on-base percentage and .387 slugging percentage when he fell behind 1-2 ... which is why the most important pitch in baseball is strike one. You have to get ahead in the count if you want to be an effective pitcher.

933 Matt Cain faced (933) batters in 2008. That total led the club and was third in the league after Cain started a league best 34 games. Cain's record was only 8-14, but he was also among the league's top ten leaders for innings and strikeouts.

934 The slugging percentage (.934) for Barry Bonds after 62 games in 2001. Bonds was 3 for 3 with two homers vs. Oakland on June 15, his 62nd game, raising his average to .328, his on-base percentage to .491, and his slugging to its highest point of the season (not including opening day). Bonds, who hit 36 homers in those 62 games, set a major league record when he finished the season with a .863 slugging percentage.

935 The Giants scored (935) runs in 1889—*in only 131 games!* That works out to a franchise record 7.14 runs per game.

936 The on-base plus slugging percentage (.936) for Willie Mays in 1960. It was the first season at Candlestick Park, and for Mays it must have felt like his own personal sandlot. He led the club in average (.319), on-base percentage (.381), slugging (.555), OPS, runs (107), hits (190), total bases (330), triples (12), homers (29), RBI (103), steals (25), extra-base hits (70), and times on base (255). He placed third in MVP balloting behind a pair of Pittsburgh teammates: Dick Groat (.325, *two homers!*) and Don Hoak (*.282, 16 homers!*).

937 The ratio (.937) of walks plus hits per innings pitched for Tim Keefe in 1888. One of the ten best ratios in franchise history, it is the absolute best ratio for a Giants pitcher during baseball's pre-modern era.

938 The offensive winning percentage (.938) for Barry Bonds in 2002. The Giants won the pennant after capturing the Wild Card with a 95-66 record during the regular season. That equates to a .590 winning percentage. Not bad at all—but statistical models predict a lineup stacked top to bottom with the 2002 version of Barry Bonds could have won at a .938 clip. Now that's impressive. Bonds' estimated offensive impact using this model is among the highest in history—coming in just ahead of the 1920 version of Babe Ruth and the 1957 version of Ted Williams.

939 The on-base plus slugging percentage (.939) for Aaron Rowand at Turner Field in 2008. The Giants outfielder only batted .222 in Atlanta, but he powered the Giants to a 5-0 victory at Turner Field on August 18 with a homer and two RBI in a game that proved to be a significant win in an otherwise disappointing season. San Francisco won 3 of 4 games in the series, the first time since 1993 that the Giants won a road series against the Braves. Rowand said the Giants were just "trying to be consistent." Chipper Jones, however, said his Braves were playing "bad, bad baseball."

940 The on-base plus slugging percentage (.940) for Bengie Molina at Arizona's Chase Field in 2008. The Giants catcher did some of his best hitting on the road against division rivals. He batted .333 with 12 hits, two doubles, two homers, and seven RBI in nine road games vs. the D-Backs—his best road numbers against any team. He also got 11 more hits, two doubles, a homer, and four RBI in nine road games vs. the Dodgers.

941 The career on-base plus slugging percentage (.941) for Willie Mays. He led the league five times and his career OPS ranks among the top 35 in baseball history. Mays also posted a .899 OPS during 75 All-Star at bats, and on July 11, 1961, he scored the winning run in the tenth inning of a 5-4 N.L. victory in the first All-Star Game to be played at Candlestick Park.

942 John Burkett faced (942) batters in 1993. He led the league in victories with a 22-7 record after allowing only 94 of those batters to reach base and score an earned run against him. The Giants and Braves battled all season for the division title and the same was true for top honors among N.L. pitchers—unfortunately the Braves came out on top twice. Atlanta won the division title, and Greg Maddux won the Cy Young while his teammate Tom Glavine was third. John Burkett was fourth in Cy Young balloting while his teammate Bill Swift was second.

943 The number of career plate appearances (943) for Barry Bonds vs. the Philadelphia Phillies. He *only* hit 64 homers vs. Philly, the same number he hit against the Dodgers. Bonds hit more homers against the Padres than any other team: 87.

944 The slugging percentage (.944) for Willie Mays vs. Dick Drott in 58 career plate appearances. Drott won 15 games for the Cubs as a 20-year-old rookie in 1957, but he won only 11 games the rest of his career (1958-63). Willie Mays was part of Drott's problem. The Giants Hall of Fame slugger was 23 for 54 with seven doubles, seven homers, 19 RBI, a .426 average, .431 on-base percentage, and a 1.375 OPS against Drott.

945 The earned run average (94.5) for Atlee Hammaker during the 1983 All-Star Game. The Giants lefty got shelled in his only career All-Star appearance, allowing seven earned runs in only two-thirds of an inning. He gave up a grand slam to Fred Lynn—the first in All-Star Game history—and a solo homer to Jim Rice.

946 Roger Connor scored (946) runs during parts of ten seasons with the Giants—eighth best in franchise history. Connor hit the century mark six times for the Giants and eight times overall, and his 1,620 career runs is one of the top 40 totals in baseball history.

947 The on-base plus slugging percentage (.947) for Monte Irvin in 1953. After a broken leg during a preseason game limited the Hall of Famer to just 46 games in 1952, Irvin came back to hit a career high .329 in 1953. He also led the club in OPS after posting a .406 on-base percentage and a .541 slugging percentage.

948 The fielding percentage (.948) for Yankees shortstop Roger Peckinpaugh in 1921. He made 42 errors in the regular season, but the one he made during the first inning of Game 8 in the World Series is the one that impacted the Giants—in a good way. His two-out boot of a George Kelly ground ball allowed Dave Bancroft to score from second base. It was the only run of the game, as the Giants claimed the final game of the World Series by a score of 1-0.

949 The on-base plus slugging percentage (.949) for Willie Mays during 21 seasons with the Giants. The Hall of Fame legend led the league in OPS five times—and he held the franchise record until Barry Bonds (1.143) came along.

950 The slugging percentage (.950) for Barry Bonds vs. lefty reliever Mike Remlinger in 25 career plate appearances. Bonds was 6 for 20 with five walks . . . *but four of his six hits were bombs.* Nobody enjoyed coming out of the pen to face Bonds, but with numbers like that Remlinger *feared* such a confrontation.

951 The fielding percentage (.951) for all National League third basemen in 1994. Matt Williams fielded at a .963 rate for the Giants and won his third Gold Glove in four seasons. He was joined by outfielders Barry Bonds and Darren Lewis, who gave the Giants three of the league's nine Gold Glove recipients that season.

952 The ratio (9.52) of strikeouts per nine innings for Jason Schmidt in 2002. He struck out 196 batters during 185-plus innings for the third best ratio in the league. That same ratio, however, broke the franchise record held by Shawn Estes since 1997. Two years later, Schmidt set a new record when he struck out 10.04 batters per nine innings—but that ratio was also third best in the league (behind Oliver Perez and Randy Johnson). Tim Lincecum set a new standard in 2008, striking out 10.51 batters per nine innings.

953 The ratio (.953) of walks plus hits per innings pitched for Jason Schmidt in 2003. It was the best ratio in the league and one of the ten best in franchise history. Schmidt gave up only 152 hits and 46 walks in 207-plus innings, and he also led the league with three shutouts.

954 The number of career at bats (954) for Barry Bonds with two outs and runners in scoring position. His number of career *plate appearances* with two outs and runners in scoring position: *1,495.* Not exactly a big shock here, but in that situation he was intentionally walked 350 times . . . and walked 532 times overall.

955 The on-base plus slugging percentage (.955) for Barry Bonds vs. *the San Francisco Giants*. When he was a member of the Pittsburgh Pirates, Bonds batted .278 with 15 homers, 43 RBI, and 51 runs in 70 career games against the Giants.

956 The on-base plus slugging percentage (.956) for Will Clark during 904 career plate appearances in which he worked the pitcher to a full count. Opposing pitchers found out the hard way that it was nearly impossible to sneak one past Clark to get ahead in the count—40 of his 284 career homers came on the first pitch. And if you fell behind, well, his on-base percentage with a full count was a staggering .498. As for his power, he hit 24 homers with a 3-2 count, second only to his first pitch total.

957 The slugging percentage (.957) for Barry Bonds vs. Brian Lawrence in 34 career plate appearances. Lawrence was a starter for division rival San Diego from 2001-05, but it was Bonds who flat out *owned* him. The Giants slugger was 11 for 23 with two doubles, three homers, 11 walks, eight RBI, a .478 average, .647 on-base percentage, and a staggering 1.604 OPS. Lawrence could have had a longer career in a different division.

958 The on-base percentage (.958) for Will Clark during 313 career plate appearances in which he worked the pitcher to a 3-0 count. Clark worked 289 walks, and got out only 12 times. He was 11 for 23, batting .478 with a double, four homers, and a sacrifice fly.

959 The Giants scored (959) runs in 1930. The highest total for the franchise during the 20th century, the offense was led by Hall of Fame players Bill Terry (139), Fred Lindstrom (127), and Mel Ott (122). Each of those players surpassed the century mark in RBI as well.

960 Larry Doyle scored (960) runs in 14 big league seasons with the Giants and Cubs. Laughing Larry won an MVP, a batting title, led the league in hits twice, and he scored nine more runs during three trips to the World Series . . . but never won a championship.

961 The Giants outfield recorded (961) putouts in 1961 and made quite an impression on the rest of the league. Willie Mays and Orlando Cepeda made up two-thirds of the National League's starting outfield in the All-Star Game, and Mays won his fifth consecutive Gold Glove.

962 The ratio (.962) of walks plus hits per innings pitched for Christy Mathewson in 1907—second best in the league, and one of the ten best in franchise history. Mathewson was among the top three league leaders in WHIP for eight consecutive seasons from 1905-14.

963 The ratio (.963) of walks plus hits per innings pitched for Joe McGinnity in 1904—a career best ratio, and the best in the league that season. It also represents one of the top 15 ratios in franchise history. McGinnity, who ranks among the top 50 in baseball history for career victories, won at least 26 games six times in eight seasons from 1899-1906.

964 The fielding percentage (.964) for Matt Williams in 1991. The third baseman won his first of three Gold Gloves with the Giants. Williams, when asked about playing defense beneath the swirling winds at Candlestick Park, said, "If there's one thing I learned here, it's never take your eyes off the ball."

965 The career fielding percentage (.965) for Jim Davenport. He was the first Gold Glove infielder in franchise history, taking top fielding honors at third base in 1962.

966 Jim O'Rourke got (966) hits during 807 games with the Giants. One of the top 50 totals in franchise history, the Hall of Famer batted .299 with 21 homers and 446 RBI.

967 The on-base percentage (.967) for Barry Bonds during 1,081 career plate appearances in which he worked the pitcher to a full count. Bonds batted 22 for 56, a .393 average, with ten homers swinging 3-0. He walked 1,023 times, including 626 that were intentional.

968 The number of career RBI (968) for Jack Doyle. He spent most of his career in New York, some of it with the Giants, some of it with Brooklyn, but his finest season was 1894 when he hit the century mark in RBI dead on the nose ... and he did it in only 105 games, and with just three homers.

969 The fielding percentage (.969) for Rick Reuschel in 1987. Big Daddy pitched 34 games, 25 for Pittsburgh, and then nine more after joining San Francisco's playoff push in late August. It was a good season. He made the All-Star team, placed third in Cy Young balloting, and won his second career Gold Glove—becoming the first pitcher in franchise history to win top fielding honors. Well, sort of . . . so long as you don't mind he pitched 78% of his innings that season for the Pirates.

970 The fielding percentage (.970) for Matt Williams in 1993. He made only 12 errors in 144 games at the hot corner, and earned a well-deserved Gold Glove. The Giants could flat play defense that season—catcher Kirt Manwaring, second baseman Robby Thompson, and outfielder Barry Bonds also won Gold Gloves.

971 The number of plate appearances (971) for Jeff Kent at Candlestick Park. He batted only .259 at The Stick, with a .329 on-base percentage and a .484 slugging percentage. Kent apparently liked playing at AT&T Park a tad better, seeing as he batted .304, with a .384 on-base percentage and a .511 slugging percentage in 1,161 plate appearances at the Giants new home park.

972 The fielding percentage (.972) for Kevin Mitchell during 757 career games in left field. Mitchell was playing left field for the Giants on August 16, 1989, when he made a running bare-handed grab of an Ozzie Smith fly ball. Mitchell said, "I was running as hard as I could, and it just came back on me. All I could do was stick up my hand and there it was."

973 George Van Haltren scored (973) runs during parts of ten seasons with the Giants—one of the ten highest totals in franchise history. He scored 1,639 runs total. Van Haltren, Jimmy Ryan, and Pete Rose are the only players in history with 1,600 career runs who are not yet in the Hall of Fame.

974 Hal Schumacher faced (974) batters in 1940. It was the fourth consecutive season the 29-year-old veteran won exactly 13 games. Prince Hal won 19, 23, and 19 games from 1933-35, and then he won 11 or more seven consecutive seasons from 1936-42. After three years in the military from 1943-45, Schumacher returned for one last season in 1946 but won only four games, ending his streak of consecutive seasons with double-digit wins.

975 The fielding percentage (.975) for all National League left fielders in 1998. Barry Bonds won his eighth career Gold Glove, and third consecutively, after posting a .984 fielding percentage in 155 games in left field.

976 The number of career hits (976) for Jeff Kent during games in which his team lost. Kent batted .243 with 121 homers and 440 RBI during 1,051 losses in his career. His bat apparently decided a lot of games. Kent batted .332 with 255 homers and 1,076 RBI during 1,199 wins in his career. For what it's worth, he also went 1 for 4 with a homer vs. Atlanta on August 15, 2002, in a game that neither team won. It ended 3-3 due to rain.

977 The career fielding percentage (.977) for Bobby Bonds. The elder Bonds won three Gold Gloves in the Giants outfield from 1971-74, giving father and son 11 total—eight of which came for the Giants.

978 Sam Jones faced (978) batters in 1960. The first batter he faced was Cardinals right fielder Joe Cunningham, who on April 12 became the first player to bat in the Giants new home ballpark—Candlestick Park. Cunningham hit a pop foul caught by third baseman Jim Davenport for the first out. Jones struck out the next batter, Daryl Spencer, before yielding the first hit at The Stick to future N.L. president Bill White, who singled to right. Jones tossed a complete game three-hitter and the Giants prevailed 3-1.

979 The fielding percentage (.979) for Bobby Richardson during 1,339 career games at second base for the New York Yankees. In Game 7 of the 1962 World Series, with runners on second and third, two outs, and the Yankees leading the Giants 1-0 in the bottom of the ninth inning, Willie McCovey ripped a Ralph Terry pitch towards right field . . . but Richardson snared it. Giants third baseman Jim Davenport later said, "It happened so quick. It was over in such a split second. You always think back, 'If the ball had been that much further, we'd have had a championship ring on our fingers.'"

980 The on-base plus slugging percentage (.980) for Willie Mays during 168 career games at the Polo Grounds. His home field in New York, Mays batted .318 with 41 homers and 106 RBI. His on-base percentage was .385, and his slugging percentage was .595. After the club moved to San Francisco he played home games at Seals Stadium first, and later at Candlestick Park. Mays batted .307 with 32 homers and 108 RBI in 154 games at Seals Stadium. He batted .298 with 203 homers and 554 RBI in 889 games at The Stick.

981 The career fielding percentage (.981) for Willie Mays. He was a 12-time Gold Glove recipient. Roberto Clemente (Pirates), Curt Flood (Cardinals), and Mays made history when all three players won six consecutive Gold Gloves from 1963-68. It is the only time that the same Gold Glove "outfield" was selected in that many successive seasons.

982 The ratio (.982) of walks plus hits per innings pitched for Carl Hubbell in 1933—best in the league for the third consecutive season. Hubbell made it four straight in 1934, and he led the league two other times as well: 1936 and 1938.

983 The number of career RBI (983) for Reggie Sanders. The powerful outfielder with 305 career homers spent only one season with the Giants, but he proved that he either has a great sense of timing or that he brings something extra to a ball club. Sanders was a veteran with a reputation for driving in runs when he signed as a free agent with the Arizona Diamondbacks prior to 2001. Arizona, of course, won the pennant and the World Series. Sanders took his ring and moved to San Francisco where he signed as a free agent prior to 2002, and then the Giants won the pennant and came oh so close to winning the World Series. Sanders belted two homers and six RBI vs. Anaheim in the 2002 World Series, and he made it to the postseason six times in his career, including the World Series three times, but he only won the one ring.

984 Dave Bancroft set a major league record when he fielded (984) chances at shortstop in 1922. Bancroft was known for yelling "beauty" every time his team's pitcher threw a good pitch—hence "Beauty" became his nickname. The slick-fielding switch-hitter was a thing of beauty at the plate that year as well. He batted a career high .321 and led the Giants to a second consecutive world championship over the Yankees.

985 The ratio (.985) of walks plus hits per innings pitched for Bobby Bolin in 1968—fourth best in the league, and one of the top 15 in franchise history. Bolin was 10-5, starting 19 of 34 games in which he pitched. He certainly had his best stuff that season. Bolin posted a 1.99 earned run average while giving up just 6.52 hits per nine innings, both of which placed second among the league leaders.

986 Johnnie LeMaster played (986) games for the Giants—one of the 40 highest totals in franchise history. The shortstop was a first round selection in the 1973 amateur draft, and in his first big league at bat he hit an inside the park home run. Coincidentally, his last career home run was also an inside the park job. And while he had a strong arm at short, LeMaster batted only .222 for his career with 22 homers, which earned him the unfortunate moniker "Johnnie Disaster."

987 Mike Krukow faced (987) batters in 1986. In his finest season, Krukow was 20-9 and only 83 of those batters reached base and scored an earned run against him. That gave him a 3.05 earned run average that was eighth best in the league. He was second in wins, third in Cy Young balloting, and made his only career All-Star team.

988 The fielding percentage (.988) for Robby Thompson in 1993. He was the Giants opening day second baseman for 11 consecutive seasons from 1986-96, but by far his best campaign was 1993—offensively and defensively—and he was rewarded with an All-Star selection, a Silver Slugger Award, and a Gold Glove.

989 The fielding percentage (.989) in left field for Jackie Brandt in 1959. Brandt, Willie Mays, and Willie Kirkland were the Giants starting outfield that season—and Brandt and Mays both took home a Gold Glove. The next time the Giants had two Gold Glove outfielders in the same season was 1994, when Barry Bonds and Darren Lewis did the trick.

990 Eddie Grant played (990) major league games. Grant was an infielder for the Giants from 1913-15, playing 202 games and scoring one run during the 1913 World Series. A graduate of Harvard Law School, he was a practicing lawyer in the offseason. When the United States entered World War I, however, Grant was the first major league player to enlist in the military. On October 5, 1918, Grant died in Argonne Forest, France, the first major leaguer to be killed in action. Baseball Commissioner Kenesaw Mountain Landis said, "His memory will live as long as our game may last."

991 The on-base plus slugging percentage (.991) for Orlando Cepeda vs. Warren Spahn in 134 career plate appearances. In this matchup of Hall of Fame legends it was clearly the Giants slugger who came out on top. Cepeda abused Spahn throughout his career. He was 44 for 128, a .344 average, with six doubles, ten homers, 18 RBI, a .366 on-base percentage, and a .625 slugging percentage.

992 The fielding percentage (.992) for all National League first basemen in 2000. The Giants first baseman won the Gold Glove . . . again. J.T. Snow made it four straight from 1997-2000, after his .995 fielding percentage outshone the rest of the league. Snow also won two Gold Gloves in the American League and every season from 1993-2005 his fielding percentage was above the league average.

993 The fielding percentage (.993) for shortstop Omar Vizquel in 2006. He made only four errors in 152 games and earned his second consecutive Gold Glove for the Giants. It was his 11th Gold Glove overall.

994 The ratio (.994) of walks plus hits per innings pitched for Juan Marichal in 1969—best in the league, and one of the top 15 in franchise history. Marichal was 21-11, hitting the 20-win mark for the sixth and final time.

995 Eight different players spent at least one inning in right field for the Giants in 2003 and they combined for a (.995) fielding percentage. Only one of those players was the everyday guy, however, and in 2003 it was Jose Cruz, Jr. who started 157 games in right. Cruz scored 90 runs, hit 20 homers, and won his only career Gold Glove.

996 The ratio (.996) of walks plus hits per innings pitched for Juan Marichal in 1963—third best in the league, and one of the top 20 in franchise history. Marichal led the league in WHIP twice and his career 1.101 ratio is one of the top 20 in baseball history. He also owns four of the top 20 ratios in franchise history—two of which are among the top five.

997 The fielding percentage (.997) for Will Clark in 1991. In addition to winning a Silver Slugger Award at first base, he also picked up his only career Gold Glove.

998 The fielding percentage (.998) for catcher Kirt Manwaring in 1993. He played a career high 130 games and was nearly flawless behind the dish—and for his efforts he won his only career Gold Glove.

999 The fielding percentage (.999) for catcher Mike Matheny in 2005. Matheny, who previously won three Gold Gloves for the Cardinals, made only one error in 132 games during his first season in San Francisco. He won his fourth and final career Gold Glove.

1000 The winning percentage (1.000) for Carl Hubbell during the 1933 World Series. True legends make their presence felt when the stakes are the highest, and the Hall of Fame lefty did just that. Two complete games (the second went 11 innings), two wins, 20 innings, 13 hits, 15 strikeouts, no earned runs. King Carl, the Meal Ticket, 1933 world champion.

San Francisco Giants 2010 World Series Roster

- Aaron Rowand
- Andres Torres
- Aubrey Huff
- Brian Wilson
- Buster Posey
- Cody Ross
- Edgar Renteria (Series MVP)
- Eli Whiteside
- Freddy Sanchez
- Guillermo Mota
- Javier Lopez
- Jeremy Affeldt
- Jonathan Sanchez
- Juan Uribe
- Madison Bumgarner
- Matt Cain
- Mike Fontenot
- Nate Schierholtz
- Pablo Sandoval
- Pat Burrell
- Ramon Ramirez
- Santiago Casilla
- Sergio Romo
- Tim Lincecum
- Travis Ishikawa

"This buried a lot of bones – '62, '89, 2002. This group deserved it, faithful from the beginning. We're proud and humbled by the achievement."

— *General Manager Brian Sabean*

Epilogue

2010 World Champions

ON NOVEMBER 1, 2010, the San Francisco Giants won the World Series for the first time since 1954—making it the first title during the San Francisco era of franchise history.

MLB began divisional play in 1969 so it could expand the postseason. The last season the Giants won a pennant pre-divisional play was in 1962, when the club lost a hard-fought seven-game World Series to the New York Yankees. The first season the Giants made the playoffs during this new era of divisional play was 1971, but that club lost the best-of-five National League Championship Series in four games to the Pittsburgh Pirates. It was 1987 before the Giants made a return trip to the postseason and 1989 before the Giants made it back to the World Series—both seasons ended with disappointing losses.

There was more heartbreak in 1997 and 1999, and of course 2002—and again in 2003.

The 1969 Chicago Cubs wasted no time becoming the first team in baseball's expanded postseason era to blow a golden opportunity. The 1969 Cubs spent 156 days in first place in the N.L. East but failed to make the postseason ... despite holding a nine-game lead over the New York Mets on August 16. The Cubs lost eight straight games in early September, won only eight games that entire month, and could do nothing but watch as a nine-game lead turned into a nine-game deficit.

After the 1969 Cubs' epic fail, no team in baseball failed to make the postseason after spending at least 147 or more days in first place until the 2007 New York Mets (159 days in first).

And then it happened again in 2008, to the Arizona Diamondbacks (158 days in first) ... and then again in 2009, to the Detroit Tigers (165 days in first) ... and then, finally, in 2010, a major league team collapsed after leading its division for 147 days during the regular season for the fourth consecutive season, after nearly forty seasons in which it didn't happen a single time.

It was, of course, the San Diego Padres.

On August 25, the Giants trailed the Padres by 6.5 games.

On August 26, the Padres lost the first of ten consecutive games.

On September 25, the Padres fell out of first place for good.

On October 3, the Padres had a chance to conclude the regular season with a sweep at AT&T Park—which would have given the clubs identical records. The Giants prevailed, however, claiming the division after spending just 38 days in first all season.

And with that victory on the final day of the regular season, the 2010 Giants began an unlikely run that culminated with postseason glory. Here's a look back at how they did it, by the numbers.

2010 Schedule

92 First rule, they all count: the Giants won (92) regular season games—and it took every one of them to reach the postseason.

97 The Giants scored (97) runs during 19 extra-inning games in the regular season. The club was 11-8 when giving fans some free baseball—and it took every one of those 11 extra-inning victories to reach the postseason.

189 The Giants scored (189) runs during 52 regular season games that were decided by a single run: *52 one-run games*. The club won 28, lost 24—but you got it, it took all 28 of those one-run victories to reach the postseason.

224 It's true that one-run games are exciting, but blowouts can be fun, too—and the Giants scored (224) runs during 35 regular season games decided by five or more runs, otherwise known as blowouts. San Francisco won 22 of those blowouts and lost only 13.

467 In fact, when you break down the "splits" from 2010 the only subpar performance was interleague play—the Giants posted a (.467) winning percentage against the American League, winning seven games, but losing eight.

568 That first rule though, *they all count*: and when it was done, the Giants overall (.568) winning percentage was enough for a division title. The club was 92-70 overall, 49-32 at home, 43-38 on the road, and posted a .500 or better winning percentage in April, May, July, and September. The club's best months were July and September: 20-8 and 18-8. Worst month was August: 13-15. The Giants favorite opponent was the Arizona Diamondbacks: 13-5. Least favorite, no big surprise—the San Diego Padres: only 6-12. But hey, that sixth win against the Padres ... it was *huge*.

2010 Pitching Stats

4 Matt Cain led the pitching staff with (4) complete games—including a team best two shutouts. And here's a telling stat ... Cain led the club with 223-plus innings of work, but he *faced* fewer batters than did Tim Lincecum, who was second on the team with 212-plus innings of work.

13 Three members of the staff won (13) or more games: Matt Cain, Tim Lincecum, and Jonathan Sanchez.

16 The Freak led the club with (16) victories. Tim Lincecum was 16-10 and his 231 strikeouts gave him the league's highest total for the third consecutive season.

33 It takes a lot of things falling into place in order to win a division title, but when your starting rotation boasts four guys who each make exactly (33) starts ... then you're on to something. Matt Cain, Tim Lincecum, Barry Zito, and Jonathan Sanchez all made 33 starts, and they all pitched 190-plus innings.

48 It helps to have a solid closer to finish things off—and with (48) saves on the season, Brian Wilson is exactly that. Wilson appeared in 70 games, finished 59 of them, posted a 1.81 earned run average, and his 48 saves tied the franchise record set by Rod Beck in 1993.

178 The team posted a (1.78) earned run average in September—which was the best team effort in baseball for any given month since the Cleveland Indians had a 1.42 ERA in May 1968.

300 It also helps when you've got a rookie who makes 18 starts and posts a team best (3.00) earned run average. Enter Madison Bumgarner, who did just that.

336 And it really helps when your pitching staff is the best in the league—and the Giants did in fact lead the league with a team (3.36) earned run average. San Francisco was second in the league with 92 wins, first in ERA, fourth in complete games, fourth in shutouts, first in saves, first in fewest hits allowed, second in fewest runs (including unearned) allowed, third in fewest home runs allowed, and first in strikeouts.

2010 Offensive Stats

18 Pat Burrell hit (18) home runs in only 96 games for the Giants after being released by Tampa Bay earlier in the season. Burrell signed with the Giants on May 29, and his 18 home runs are the most in franchise history for any player who began the season with another team.

21 Buster Posey had a (21)-game hitting streak in July. He batted .417 for the month with 24 RBI and 43 hits—and he became the first rookie since Ryan Braun in 2007 to win National League Player of the Month honors.

24 Shortstop Juan Uribe was second on the club with (24) home runs and 85 RBI. Two of his homers and six of his RBI came in the second inning of a 13-0 Giants romp at Wrigley Field on September 23. Uribe became just the second visiting player to homer twice in the same inning against the Cubs.

100 Aubrey Huff led the team with (100) runs scored. He was also the offensive leader in hits (165), doubles (35), triples (5), home runs (26), and RBI (86).

121 It was the (121st) season that the Giants and Dodgers battled each other in some form—but the 2010 Giants managed to do something no other team in franchise history had ever done ... it rallied from four runs down to beat the Dodgers on the road not once, but twice in the same season. On July 20, the Dodgers trailed 5-1 but rallied for a 7-5 victory after scoring three ninth-inning runs against Jonathan Broxton. Then on September 4, the Giants trailed 4-0 in the seventh inning, but rallied with four home runs in the final three innings, including a two-run game-winning shot by Juan Uribe off Jonathan Broxton in the ninth. Broxton became just the second Dodgers reliever in 99 years to lose to the Giants three times in one season.

305 Buster Posey won Rookie of the Year honors after batting (.305) and pounding 43 extra base-hits in just 108 games—good for a .505 slugging percentage. The 2008 first-round draft pick out of FSU was called up in late May and quickly took over as the Giants starting catcher.

556 Buster Posey was a one-man wrecking crew during the final seven games leading up to the 2010 All-Star break. He batted (.556) and won Bank of America Player of the Week honors for the week of July 5 – 11. Posey was 15 for 27 and also led MLB with 14 RBI—plus, he hit five homers and had a pair of four-hit games.

2010 Postseason

2 Buster Posey attempted just (2) steals during the regular season and he was thrown out both times ... but in Game 1 of the Division Series vs. Atlanta, Posey was not only the first rookie catcher in history to bat clean-up in a postseason game, he also had two of the combined seven hits in the game, and he scored the only run of the game *after* stealing his first base of the year to get into scoring position.

3 Edgar Renteria hit only (3) home runs during 72 regular season games ... but he hit two during five World Series games. The World Series MVP was only 1 for 16 (.063) vs. Philadelphia during the League Championship Series ... but he was 7 for 17 (.412) vs. Texas during the World Series. Renteria's second homer of the series came in the seventh inning of the Giants title-clinching Game 5 win vs. Texas. It proved to be the game-winner, which makes Renteria the first player in MLB history to pick up the game-winning RBI in the seventh inning or later of the title-clinching game of the World Series ... *twice*. He also did it for the 1997 Florida Marlins.

4 Buster Posey picked up (4) hits during Game 4 of the National League Championship Series vs. Philly, making him only the second rookie catcher in MLB history to collect four hits in a single postseason game. Joe Garagiola did it for the Cardinals in 1946.

8 Cody Ross was the Giants (#8) hitter during Game 1 of the National League Championship Series vs. Philly. No worries ... all he did was go yard off Roy Halladay ... *twice*. Halladay had given up only two home runs all season to players batting eighth or ninth in the lineup.

10 And speaking of Cody Ross ... the late-season acquisition drove in (10) runs during the 2010 playoffs, including three vs. Atlanta and five vs. Philly to help the Giants clinch the pennant. In fact, when Ross broke a scoreless tie with a two-run fourth inning single vs. Philly during Game 3 of the NLCS, it was his fourth game-winning RBI of the postseason ... *in only seven games!* That's the fastest any player in history has accumulated four game-winning hits in the postseason.

14 Tim Lincecum tied a MLB record with (14) strikeouts in his postseason debut. He led the Giants to a 1-0 victory vs. Atlanta during Game 1 of the Division Series with a complete game two-hitter. Lincecum allowed only three base runners—which made him just the second player in MLB history to pitch a complete game shutout in the postseason while striking out at least 14 batters and allowing no more than three base runners. Roger Clemens did it for the Yankees vs. the Mariners in 2000.

18 Brian Wilson faced (18) batters vs. Philly in the National League Championship Series. Only four of those batters reached base—two hits and two walks—but none of them scored. Wilson earned three saves and a win vs. Philly, making him just the fourth pitcher in MLB history to win or save four games in a series.

22 The ability to win tight ballgames paid off big time for the Giants during the Division Series vs. the Braves—during the final (22) innings of that series, the biggest lead for either team was ... *one run.* All four of the games in that series were decided by a single run, which made it just the second series in MLB history to open with four consecutive one-run games.

30 Freddy Sanchez had only (30) extra-base hits during the 2010 regular season for the Giants—but during Game 1 of the World Series vs. Texas, he banged out three doubles vs. Cliff Lee, who had given up only three extra-base hits total during his previous three postseason starts. The Giants rolled to a surprising 11-7 victory—not surprising because the Giants won, but because the pitching matchup was Lincecum vs. Lee and the teams combined for 18 runs.

85 Matt Cain faced (85) batters during the 2010 postseason ... *and he didn't allow a single earned run.* He made three starts, pitched 21.1 innings, and gave up one unearned run vs. Atlanta, but that was it. He gave up just 13 hits, eight walks, and struck out 13. Cain became the first pitcher in two decades to not allow a single earned run in his first two career postseason starts—and he joined a very elite group when he didn't give up any earned runs in his third start: in MLB history only Christy Mathewson (1905), Waite Hoyt (1921), and Jon Matlack (1973) began their postseason careers with three consecutive starts without allowing an earned run.

218 Rookie Madison Bumgarner posted a cool (2.18) earned run average during three starts and four total appearances in the 2010 postseason. He was also the winning pitcher in the Division Series clincher at Turner Field. It was the first time since 1981 that a rookie starting pitcher clinched a postseason series on the road. Two guys did it in 1981: Fernando Valenzuela for the Dodgers and Giants pitching coach Dave Righetti, who did it for the Yankees.

276 The Texas Rangers were the best hitting team in MLB with a (.276) average during the 2010 regular season. The Giants pitching staff held the Rangers to a paltry .190 average during the World Series, while becoming the first team in 30 years to win three World Series games while surrendering one run or less. The Giants staff even held the Rangers scoreless for 18 consecutive innings from Game 3 through the seventh inning of Game 5.

419 The distance in feet (419) of Buster Posey's home run during Game 4 of the World Series. The bomb capped the Giants scoring, sealing a 4-0 victory and a commanding 3-1 lead in the series. Posey became just the fourth rookie catcher to homer in the World Series. Also in Game 4, Posey and Madison Bumgarner became the first all-rookie battery to start a World Series game since 1947—and Bumgarner tossed eight scoreless innings, becoming the first rookie starter to not allow an earned run in a World Series game since 1987, the first to do so while picking up a victory since 1969, and the first to do so while pitching at least eight innings since 1948.

About the Authors

TUCKER ELLIOT IS a Georgia native and a diehard baseball fan. A former high school athletic director and varsity baseball coach, he's now a fulltime writer and has authored or contributed to more than two dozen baseball books, to include the following Black Mesa titles:

- *Atlanta Braves IQ: The Ultimate Test of True Fandom*
- *New York Yankees IQ: The Ultimate Test of True Fandom*
- *Major League Baseball IQ: The Ultimate Test of True Fandom*
- *Tampa Bay Rays IQ: The Ultimate Test of True Fandom*
- *Boston Red Sox: An Interactive Guide to the World of Sports*

ZAC ROBINSON IS a teacher, coach and baseball fan. He is also passionate about Mixed Martial Arts and has written books on both subjects, to include the following titles:

- *Mixed Martial Arts: An Interactive Guide to the World of Sports*
- *Mixed Martial Arts IQ: The Ultimate Test of True Fandom (Volume I)*
- *Ranger Up Presents Mixed Martial Arts IQ: The Ultimate Test of True Fandom (Volume II)*
- *From the Fields to the Garden: The Life of Stitch Duran*

References

WE DO EXTENSIVE research for all of our titles, and because we know fans like us want to have access to as much material as possible we take great pride in making our own website interactive for our readers. In addition to that, we also want to make sure we provide a helpful list of all the sources that provide us with information as we write.

Our preferred method of research is actually to dig through piles and piles of old, dusty copies of *Sports Illustrated* and *Baseball Digest* magazines—and we did that, a lot—but technology being what it is today, we also made good use of LexisNexis to cull through decades of newspaper and Associated Press articles via the Internet.

We also made use of some other valuable websites. Major League Baseball at mlb.com has done an amazing job of making statistics available to fans. The individual team sites offer detailed franchise histories, and a virtual clearinghouse of player information from past and present. We also used espn.com and baseball-reference.com extensively, but we verified all statistics through the MLB site, and when discrepancies arose we always defaulted to the numbers put out by Major League Baseball. The SI Vault on cnnsi.com also proved to be a valuable research tool for this book.

Our personal libraries are filled with books on baseball. *The Team by Team Encyclopedia of Major League Baseball*, written by Dennis Purdy, is one of the best. It proved to be a valuable resource. We also used *The 2005 ESPN Baseball Encyclopedia*, edited by Pete Palmer and Gary Gillette; *100 Years of the World Series*, by Eric Enders; and *Baseball, an Illustrated History*, by Geoffrey C. Ward and Ken Burns.

Two additional books that proved to be valuable resources in our research are *101 Reasons to Love the Giants*, by David Green, and *Tales from the Giants Dugout*, by Nick Peters.

Of course, any mistakes found in these pages are our own.

We also recommend the following reading list for Giants fans: *San Francisco Giants: 50 Years*, by Brian Murphy and Danny Glover; *The Original San Francisco Giants: The Giants of '58*, by Steve Bitker; and *San Francisco Giants: Where have you gone?*, by Matt Johanson and Wylie Wong.

About Black Mesa

BLACK MESA IS a Florida-based publishing company that specializes in sports history and trivia books. Look for these popular titles in our trivia IQ series:

- *Mixed Martial Arts (Volumes I & II)*
- *Boston Red Sox (Volumes I & II)*
- *Tampa Bay Rays*
- *New York Yankees*
- *Atlanta Braves*
- *Major League Baseball*
- *Milwaukee Brewers*
- *St. Louis Cardinals*
- *Boston Celtics*
- *University of Florida Gators Football*
- *University of Georgia Bulldogs Football*
- *University of Texas Longhorns Football*
- *University of Oklahoma Sooners Football*
- *New England Patriots*

For information about special discounts for bulk purchases, please email:

black.mesa.publishing@gmail.com

www.blackmesabooks.com

Also in the Sports by the Numbers Series

- *Major League Baseball*
- *New York Yankees*
- *Boston Red Sox*
- *University of Oklahoma Football*
- *University of Georgia Football*
- *Penn State University Football*
- *NASCAR*
- *Sacramento Kings Basketball*
- *Mixed Martial Arts*

Available Soon

- *Texas Rangers*
- *Los Angeles Dodgers*
- *Boston Celtics*
- *Dallas Cowboys*

www.ingramcontent.com/pod-product-compliance
Lightning Source LLC
Chambersburg PA
CBHW061430040426
42450CB00007B/983